A RADICAL HEGELIAN

BY THE SAME AUTHORS

David Boucher

Texts in Context: Revisionist Methods for Studying the History of Ideas (Dordrecht, 1985).
The Social and Political Thought of R. G. Collingwood (Cambridge, 1989).
(ed.), R. G. Collingwood, *Essays in Political Philosophy* (Oxford, 1989).
(ed.), R. G. Collingwood, *The New Leviathan* (revised edition, Oxford, 1992).
(ed. with Paul Kelly), *The Social Contract from Hobbes to Rawls* (1994)

Andrew Vincent

(With Raymond Plant) *Philosophy, Politics and Citizenship* (Oxford, 1984).
Theories of the State (Oxford, 1987).
Modern Political Ideologies (Oxford, 1992).
(ed.), *The Philosophy of T. H. Green* (Aldershot, 1986).
(ed. with Michael George and tr. A. V. Miller), G. W. F. Hegel, *The Philosophical Propaedeutic* (Oxford, 1986).

A RADICAL HEGELIAN

THE POLITICAL AND SOCIAL PHILOSOPHY OF HENRY JONES

David Boucher and Andrew Vincent

CARDIFF
UNIVERSITY OF WALES PRESS
1993

British Library Cataloguing-in-Publication Data
A catalogue record for this book is available from the British Library.

ISBN 0-7083-1207-1

Published jointly with St Martin's Press, New York, USA

Jacket design by Stills Design Group, Newport
Typeset at Megaron, Cardiff
Printed in Wales by Dinefwr Press, Llandybïe

CONTENTS

PREFACE

In a book of this kind in which many of the sources have previously been unused, and in some cases which we have only recently brought to light, many debts have been incurred. We are indebted to J. Howard, Tomos Roberts, P. K. Escreet, Iain G. Brown, A. W. Goldsmith, Michael Bott, Colin Harris, Susan Woodburn, Cecily Close, Miss Sloggett, Jan Richards, K. S. Kerr, K. E. Smith, Sue Jones, and Rick Kuhn for the various services they have provided in identifying sources and readily providing copies when requested. Without the benefit of their professional expertise this book would not have been possible in the form it has taken.

We are especially grateful to Peter Nicholson for making our task much easier by generously providing us with an extensive bibliography of Jones's pubished works; to C. Lloyd Morgan of the National Library of Wales who did an extensive search of manuscript indices and provided us with many invaluable references; and, to John Williams, John Jones, and particularly Harding Rees, who provided much needed advice on Welsh sources. While we are appreciative of the help unselfishly given to us we, of course, accept full responsibility for all the faults that remain in the text.

We have been fortunate in obtaining the generous co-operation of Jean Hunt, the granddaughter of Sir Henry Jones, who has given us every encouragement and help throughout the gestation of this book. She has also been kind enough to provide us with a short reminiscence of her grandfather which we are pleased to include as an appendix. Most of the manuscript material is to be found in the Thomas Jones Collection in the National Library of Wales, Aberystwyth, and we are deeply appreciative of the co-operation of the Rt. Hon. Baroness White in granting permission to use her father's papers. We also had the good fortune to rediscover and consult Thomas Jones's lecture notes on Henry Jones's Ordinary and Honours Moral Philosophy lectures delivered in the University of Glasgow between 1897 and 1900. The notes are bound into three volumes and were presented to the trustees of 'Y Cwm', the memorial which was Henry Jones's childhood home, when it was opened to the public. The volumes are currently held by the trustees pending a decision about where they might best be deposited for general availability.

Work of this nature requires substantial funds and we are extremely thankful to La Trobe University, Melbourne and the Australian National University, Canberra, for awarding research grants to pursue our work. The Research School of Social Sciences (ANU) generously provided a three-month fellowship in 1989 for Dr Vincent, which allowed us to work together on the final stages of the typescript. We would like to thank Vibeke Wetselar and Wendy Hare for their more than generous assistance in preparing materials. We are grateful to Thelma Williams, and Judy Robson for typing a good deal of the book, and to Anne Gabbett for skilfully bringing all the pieces together and producing the final copy. In addition, we would like to thank the University of Wales College of Cardiff for providing assistance and encouragement. We are especially grateful to Neville Masterman for casting his eye over the proofs and alerting us to some inaccuracies.

It goes without saying that we would not have been able to have completed our studies without the indulgence and support of our respective long-suffering wives and families.

Dr David Boucher, University of Wales, Swansea
Dr Andrew Vincent, University of Wales, Cardiff

A NOTE ON REFERENCING

Quotations from, and references to, Henry Jones's published books will be cited in the following abbreviated form:

BPRT — *Browning as a Philosophical and Religious Teacher* (Glasgow, Maclehose, 1891).

DB — *Dinasyddiaeth Bur ac Areithiau Ereill (Pure Citizenship and Other Lectures),* (Carnarvon, Union of North Wales Quarrymen. No date: preface dated 16 September 1911).

ELE — *Essays on Literature and Education,* edited by H. J. W. Hetherington (London, Hodder & Stoughton, 1924).

FE — *A Faith That Enquires: The Gifford Lectures delivered in the University of Glasgow in the years 1920 and 1921* (London, Macmillan, 1922).

IPC — *Idealism as a Practical Creed* (Glasgow, Maclehose, 1909).

LPEC — *The Life and Philosophy of Edward Caird.* Co-authored with J. H. Muirhead (Glasgow, Maclehose, 1921).

OM — *Old Memories. Autobiography of Sir Henry Jones, CH, Late Professor of Moral Philosophy in the University of Glasgow,* edited by Thomas Jones (London, Hodder & Stoughton, 1922).

PC — *The Principles of Citizenship* (London, Macmillan, 1919).

PL — *A Critical Account of the Philosophy of Lotze: The Doctrine of Thought* (Glasgow, Maclehose, 1895).

SE — *Scottish Education Reform: A Scheme of District School Boards and a National Council.* Co-authored with Charles M. Douglas (Glasgow, Maclehose, 1903).

SP — *Social Powers: Three Popular Lectures on the Environment, the Press and the Pulpit* (Glasgow, Maclehose, 1913).

SR — *Social Responsibilities: Lectures to Businessmen* (Glasgow, Maclehose, 1905).

WFSR — *The Working Faith of the Social Reformer and other Essays* (London, Macmillan, 1910).

WP — *Wales and its Prospects* (Wrexham, North Wales Liberal Federation, no date). Preface dated 1889.

The unpublished writings of Henry Jones are deposited in many different collections and in a variety of locations. The less frequently cited references will appear in full in the endnotes. Those held in the National Library of Wales, Aberystwyth, will be followed by the letters NLW. The principal sources will be identified by the following abbreviations.

MA	Macmillan Archives Readers' Reports, British Museum, London.
TJC	Thomas Jones Collection, National Library of Wales, Aberystwyth.
TJN	Henry Jones, *Moral Philosophy Lectures*, Ordinary Class, session 1897–8, vol. 1 and vol. 2.
TJN(Hons)	Henry Jones, *Moral Philosophy Lectures*, Honours Class, session 1899–1900.

The dating and numbering of lectures is somewhat variable, and in consequence we identify the source of arguments and quotations in ways which the reader will find most helpful, that is, by lecture number, or date with the appropriate volume number.

Other manuscript items are to be found in the following libraries:

BLO	Bodleian Library, Oxford
EUL	Edinburgh University Library
NLS	National Library of Scotland
NLW	National Library of Wales
UCWB	University College of North Wales, Bangor
UGL	University of Glasgow Library
URL	University of Reading Library

CHAPTER ONE

'ON THE WAY'

In the last decade there has been a growing interest in Victorian and Edwardian philosophical and political thought and in the relation between Idealism and liberalism in the same period. The recent reaction against new right proposals for restructuring the welfare state and re-emphasizing individual in opposition to social responsibility has led many commentators to re-examine the initial response of social reformers, both philosophical and political, at the turn of the century to individualistic conceptions of society and the growth of the state. In particular the idea of an organic society and the ethical dimensions of citizenship have appeared especially apposite to contemporary concerns. It is not our intention to enter into the current controversies but rather to shed light upon certain philosophical, religious and social foundations. In this respect we explore the significant issues which preoccupied the best minds of the period: such as the controversy over evolution and its bearing upon religious faith; the relation between individualism and socialism; between the state and the citizen; and the place of ethics in international relations.

We have tried to adopt an approach in this work which uses Sir Henry Jones as an intellectual catalyst for introducing and discussing many of the major issues of late Victorian and Edwardian culture, and which at the same time allows us to articulate his specific and important contributions. Jones's immense reputation, at the time, as one of the leading philosophers concerned with applying philosophical principles to political and social problems, makes him an appropriate choice to act as our guide through the tortuous and intricate debates of this period. Jones's practical involvement in British politics, particularly through the Liberal Party, and his cultivation of personal friendships with its leading figures, like Lloyd George, H. H. Asquith, Lord Haldane, Munro Ferguson, H. A. L. Fisher and many others, made him, as the incumbent of the most prestigious philosophical chair in Britain, that of the University of Glasgow, well-placed to reflect upon and articulate the underlying principles at issue in the controversies.

Before discussing these controversies we must say something about Jones's remarkable personal circumstances which resonate even to the present day in Wales. The focus of this first chapter is therefore the immense struggles which took Jones from humble origins to respected philosopher and leading establishment figure. We will also give a brief introductory sketch of the religious and philosophical concerns which sustained him throughout his long career, and through many personal tragedies.

The Welsh university colleges, and particularly that of south Wales and Monmouthshire, located in Cardiff, had over a period of thirty years or so, more than their fair share of distinguished Idealist philosophers. Andrew Seth, W. R. Sorley, W. P. Ker, H. J. W. Hetherington and J. S. MacKenzie occupied positions at one time or another in Cardiff, and if J. H. Muirhead could have been persuaded to concentrate on classics it seems that he too would have joined their number.[1] In addition, Mungo W. MacCallum taught at Aberystwyth, and Henry Jones lectured in the same institution before becoming the foundation professor of Logic and Philosophy at the University College, Bangor. Seth ultimately became professor of Logic and Metaphysics in the University of Edinburgh,[2] while Hetherington, a representative of the following generation of Idealists, went on to become principal of the University of Glasgow in 1936.[3] MacCallum left Wales to become Professor of English in the University of Sydney, and subsequently its vice-chancellor.[4] Ker also left Wales to take up the chair of Poetry in the University of Oxford, while MacKenzie remained in Cardiff as professor of Logic and Philosophy until his death. Of these Idealists Jones was the only native Welshman, the others were Scottish, but his career was the most remarkable of them all.

It is not our intention in this chapter to rehearse in detail the facts of Jones's life, which are readily available elsewhere,[5] but instead to give an impression of his personality in order to illustrate the dynamic energy of the man. Through a gruelling process of public meetings, committee work, formal teaching, writing, and bringing personal influence to bear upon friends, demonstrating the need to reflect upon principles and to adopt them as guides to future conduct, Jones devoted his life to the enhancement of the condition of his fellow human beings.

Henry Jones was born at Llangernyw, Denbighshire (now Clwyd), north Wales to parents of less than modest means. His childhood home afforded spartan accommodation, and boasted a small lean-to workshop where his father practised the trade he was to impart to his son Henry.[6] He left school at the age of twelve-and-a-half to become apprenticed to his shoemaker father, and inspired by an irresistible desire to better himself, by the means the Welsh valued above all else, he resolved with the encouragement of his mother, and overcoming the inhibition of self-doubt, to return to school on a part-time basis. Jones continued to practise his pecuniary trade while managing to keep up with the school work by reducing his sleep to four or five hours a night. At the age of eighteen he won a scholarship to enter Bangor Normal College to train as a teacher. He obtained his teaching certificate two years later, and after a brief period as temporary tutor in the College, became Master of the Elementary School at Brynaman, south Wales.

After two years of enthusiastic service, during which time he more than doubled the number of children attending the school, his devotion to lay-preaching and aspirations to become a minister of the gospel instilled in him a dissatisfaction with school teaching. He resigned his position in order to apply himself to the full-time study necessary to compete for and win a Dr Williams Scholarship for aspirants whose calling inclined them towards entering the Nonconformist ministry. During the five months of intensive preparation, Jones preached nearly every Sunday around the towns of north Wales. After three months he was received as a preacher by the Calvinistic Methodists who entered his name in the diary of the Vale of Conway, where it remained for many years after he had chosen an academic vocation.[7]

The award of a Dr Williams Scholarship, tenable at Glasgow University, brought Jones into contact with the mainstream of European ideas, and provided him with welcome relief from the intellectual constraints and rivalries of Nonconformist religious sects who dominated Welsh society and education. At Glasgow he came under the influence of the philosophical Idealists, John Nichol and Edward Caird. Jones always claimed that it was being taught by the latter which occasioned his own rebirth.[8] Jones took first-class honours under Caird and won the prestigious Clark Fellowship in Philosophy that enabled him to spend four more years of study in Glasgow, with the exception of brief periods in Germany and Oxford. For most of the four years Jones assisted Caird, whom he so greatly admired, and with whom he remained a life-long friend.

Although Jones could have followed a ministerial calling, his mind had been liberated from narrow religious dogma, and it was the allure of a university career, and the encouragement of Nicol and Caird, that proved the stronger. Shortly after completing his honours degree, and during the tenure of his fellowship, Jones wrote of the struggle that had raised him from humble beginnings, and of the tremendous emotional and physical strain he endured. He was not unappreciative of the struggle, but swore that he would not like to see a dog try it again.[9]

Shortly after the expiry of his fellowship Jones was offered a lectureship in Philosophy at Aberystwyth. Wales did not have the strong university tradition that Scotland boasted, and Aberystwyth, at that time a remote coastal town in mid-Wales, housed its only, and recently established, university college. The remuneration was not very attractive, but a lack of alternative prospects forced him to accept, somewhat apprehensively, the lectureship which he was given to believe would become converted into a professorship in due course. Yet, the prospect of moving from the intellectually vibrant atmosphere of Glasgow to the stultifying parochialism of a remote Welsh country town filled him with trepidation. Jones wrote to Andrew Seth expressing his reservations:

> So I leave Scotland in January or perhaps December, and enter into the little squabbling, scandalmongering life of a country town. It is a trial to leave my Glasgow friends and Caird has been a father to me. Nor do I know that I have sufficient strength to live the higher life in my new surroundings: but I must try it, and hope that now and then I shall get a glimpse of the stronger race of philosophers and thinkers of the Scotch Universities.[10]

Unfortunately, Jones's reservations proved to be well-founded. His youthful impetuousness and independence of mind brought him into conflict with sections of the community over religious beliefs, but more seriously, from his point of view, relations with Principal Thomas Charles Edwards were less than cordial.[11] Jones's support for the establishment of a new university college to be situated in Bangor was, Principal Edwards believed, detrimental to the interests of Aberystwyth and Jones unceremoniously found himself without gainful employment at the end of the summer term of 1883. Jones busied himself with casual employment, including the drafting of the constitution of the new university college of north Wales, until a more divisive. Unable to resist entering into the fray, Jones soon found himself central to the forces that desired to rescue the merger and place both institutions upon a firm foundation in their formal relation. From the correspondence between Jones and Ronald Munro-Ferguson, who was a Scottish Liberal MP and a member of the University Court, and later Governor-General of Australia, it is clear that for the three years the former spent at St Andrews he was one of the principal organizers of the pro-merger forces which eventually won the day. Jones held the vacillation of Principal Donaldson, to whom he referred as 'King Muddle',[18] but whom he liked personally, largely responsible for the protracted struggle.[19]

Jones feared that his prominent role in the bitter feuding between the rival factions might prejudice his chances of being elected to the Glasgow chair of Moral Philosophy, which Caird vacated to become Master of Balliol in 1893. His fears in that respect, however, were unfounded.[20] It had been the publication of his book on Browning that had secured for him the St Andrews' professorship, and it was, at Caird's instigation, the writing of his book on Lotze that, in addition to his recently published articles in *Mind*, made Jones a serious candidate to succeed his mentor.[21] Jones was unsure about whether he could secure the support of Caird in view of the fact that Professor John Watson, a former student whom Caird taught and greatly admired, would be entering the competition. Caird believed that Jones was one of the best men to have studied under him, 'with a remarkable combination of Celtic fervour and lecturing power with capacity for philosophy',[22] but at the same time Caird thought that there was no one better than Watson at seeing 'clearly through any philosophical entanglement'. Caird inevitably felt 'braced by his conversation'.[23] As late as June 1894, a few weeks before the appointment was to be decided, Jones knew that Edward, and his brother Principal John Caird, had not yet made up their minds whom to support, and suspected that they would put their weight behind the candidate whom they thought most likely to be acceptable to the electors.[24] Edward Caird himself would not be involved in the formal selection process. Jones rallied as much support as he could from Bangor, St Andrews and Glasgow, and at the age of forty-two he succeeded to one of the most prestigious chairs of Philosophy in Great Britain. He wrote to Munro-Ferguson exclaiming, 'I have got the post which I would not exchange as long as my strength and vigour is my own, for any other post within our watery walls, if I can only play the man!'[25] The prospect of succeeding

Caird was somewhat over-awing, and he reconciled himself to the fact that it would be futile even to try to fill Caird's shoes, and resolved instead to make the best of himself. He wrote to Mrs Maclehose saying:

> If I can only fill my own place and put my heart's blood into my work for the young men I think I shall be happy. Nor will I be disappointed if I fail to fill Mr Caird's place because I do not expect to do so.[26]

Jones remained at Glasgow until his death in 1922. During his time there he exercised an immense influence on the students he taught, on the civic affairs of Glasgow, and Scottish and Welsh educational reform. He was awarded a knighthood in 1912, which he was reluctant to accept, and was made a Companion of Honour in December 1921.[27]

Although Jones had been dissuaded from continuing his vocation in the ministry of the Calvinistic Methodists by Nicol and Caird,[28] he never really abjured his religious calling. Idealism was, for him, as it was for Caird, an intensely religious philosophy. Such was the identity of religion and philosophy for Jones that he claimed Jesus of Nazareth for the school of philosophical Idealism, to whom he referred as 'the ancient Idealist' whose teachings anticipated the Hegelian doctrine that 'the Real is the Rational'.[29]

For Jones, Jesus is not set apart and differentiated from humanity by his divinity, and unity with God, but instead reveals to us the divine character of our own natures. Divine and human nature are unified in the love that God has for Jesus, and that both have for humanity.[30] The emphasis upon the exclusivity of Jesus irritated Jones who preferred to think of him as 'the firstborn of many brethren'.[31] All of humanity, Jones believed, is emotionally and intellectually united with the absolute. God's love and truth are no different in character from those of men and women, but whereas God is the ideal manifest in His children, human beings are always in the process, or 'on the way', to realizing this manifestation.[32] This process, although divine, is also human activity in that it is the free expression of spirit. The individual in expressing the will of God pursues his, or her, own highest will, and in conforming to the law which is his, or her, fundamental nature, obedience is offered to God. In this identity of the divine and the human Jones postulates the doctrine of unity in diversity, which is integral to the philosophy of modern Idealism.[33] He argues that: 'The unity of divine and human within the spiritual life of man is a real unity, just because man is free; the identity manifests itself through the difference, and the difference is possible through the unity.'[34] Jones's most heroic statement of the identity of philosophy and religion – heroic because it is testimony to the power of the religious spirit to triumph over human suffering – finds expression in his *Gifford Lectures*, whose title, *A Faith That Enquires*, is an apposite epitaph to the author.[35] Throughout his life Jones was unable to accept the teaching of any religious creed, but he always sympathized with the ideal each strove to express,[36] that is, the spiritual unity of the universe.

In spite of the fact that Jones put aside his ministerial vocation, he used the university lecture theatres, and public halls around the world to preach Idealism. Religious imagery abounds in the many descriptions offered of his powerful personality and charismatic lecturing performances. He is referred to by contemporaries as an 'apostle of ideas', a 'prophet', a compound of Isaiah and St Paul; a 'Pilgrim and Messenger'; and a preacher with missionary zeal.[37] Thomas Jones likens Henry Jones's moral philosophy lectures to 'the most refined of the great Welsh preachers in the architecture of a sermon',[38] and Agnes Saville, another ex-student, remarked that 'every young and generous spirit felt as if inspired with his contagious enthusiasm for the good'.[39] Metz probably best captures Jones's philosophy by describing it as 'Hegelianism become emotional'. For Metz: 'He is its prophet and apostle, and bore it like a missionary to the farthest frontier of the Empire.'[40]

Jones's originality of thought lay in the application of Hegelian principles, mediated by Caird, to the religious, social, political and philosophical problems of his day, and in the intensity with which he wished to disseminate the principles and conclusions in order, as he used to say, to moralize the institutions of the state. By the early years of the century his reputation as a public speaker was well established, and his services were always in great demand because he could be relied upon to excel in the company of any, even hostile, audiences from Glasgow businessmen to radical north Wales quarrymen and Merthyr socialists. During the First World War, for example, he was called upon by the Parliamentary Recruitment Committee to undertake a gruelling schedule of public meetings during October to December 1915 in north and south Wales to quell opposition and hostility to the Asquith Government, and to encourage recruitment into the armed services.[41]

If we take two examples of impressions of his character and public performance, those of his Martineau centenary lecture of 1905 and his visit to Australia in 1908, a more adequate appreciation may be gained of his quite remarkable personal qualities.

In his lecture on Martineau, to whom Jones was known to be antagonistic, he criticized Martineau for contending that Absolute Idealism was morally inimical because of its propensity to lose the person by merging him, or her, into the unity of God and Nature. Jones denies Martineau's charge that Absolute Idealism was pantheistic and a denial of human free will. He argued that the charge rests upon the unexamined hypothesis that to prove that there is a binding connection between the person and the broader world of reality is to deprive the individual of freedom. On the contrary, Jones contended, the relation between the self and not-self needs to be interpreted differently. The not-self only finds meaning in the self, and it is the self which unites and identifies the not-self with itself. On the principle of identity in difference, or unity in diversity, Jones argued that: '*Spirit comprises its differences without annulling them*: it possesses them and yet distinguishes them from itself.'[42]

Far from antagonizing the devotees assembled to honour Martineau, Jones ignited an electrifying excitement which transcended the differences of doctrine. One member of the audience at that talk given in the library of Manchester College, Oxford, has left a vivid account of the experience. He, or she, acknowledges that the faithful gathered to honour Martineau on the occasion of the centenary of his birth were apprehensive about being addressed by Jones and expected to be dismayed and deflated in being subjected to criticisms of their mentor. Instead the experience was

> of the wonder and admiration raised by the vivid personality of the lecturer as he stood before us, wrestling with his almost impossible task, flashing and scintillating with spiritual and intellectual energy, launching the rays of his own life and personality out into an intellectually unreceptive but spiritually sympathetic medium, maintaining by sheer personal radiance his hold upon an audience which his matter might have jaded and bewildered had not he himself kept them in hand and sustained an atmosphere of keenest life around them.[43]

When Jones was invited to Australia by Mungo MacCallum to give a series of lectures in Sydney in 1908, his reputation as a brilliant lecturer and philosopher preceded him. Walter Murdoch, for example, who was then a lecturer of English in Melbourne University, and subsequently after whom Murdoch University in Western Australia was named, wrote in his regular column in the Melbourne *Argus* of Jones's wonderful talent for popularizing, but not vulgarizing philosophical subjects.[44] Murdoch went as far as to suggest that 'no philosopher that ever lived had been more keenly intent' than Jones on applying philosophy to the problems of modern life.[45] The Australians were delighted with Jones's performance and his lectures were extensively reported in the local press. At the conclusion of his Sydney lectures, for instance, it was said that 'Professor Jones has confirmed and enlarged the opinion which a proportion of his hearers had formed by reading and hearsay'.[46] Wherever the venue in Australia, and upon whatever he lectured, from university education to poetry and socialism, Jones inspired waves of emotional cheering and spontaneous applause. Without doubt, the observer at Jones's 1905 Martineau lecture did not exaggerate the effect the Welshman had on an audience. Just one of many examples from the Australian tour will serve to confirm the general impression. Take for instance a report of one of Jones's Adelaide lectures where the sheer physical presence of the professor enraptured the journalist. Jones was a success before he uttered a word:

> A glance at the fine, intellectual face is enough. There are powers, unwavering earnestness, courage in it, commanding admiration for the profound thinker. It is one of those typically strong faces independent of oral evidence . . . The oratory has the euphony and vigour, the inspiriting fire of true Welsh emphasis.[47]

We will turn now to a brief sketch of Jones's philosophical principles and an outline of the chapters of the book. Jones's philosophical development took place at a time of great change in British society. He was representative of the concerns of the Victorian and Edwardian eras rather than of the post-1918 world. In fact, like some others in the Idealist school, he sounded ill at ease in the post-war era. There are a number of anxieties and preoccupations of the Victorian and Edwardian epoch which are worth briefly outlining.

The close of the Victorian age saw considerable anxiety about the character and future of religious thought. Jones, like most of his contemporaries, was aware of the pressures on religion. The 'higher criticism', emanating from German theologians, with its careful dissection of scriptures, often revealing inner contradictions, was deeply disturbing to many sensitive minds. Whilst he could not himself subscribe to any creed, he was convinced of the moral efficacy of religion, but took most of the general philosophical conclusions of such German thinkers for granted and consequently incurred the wrath of many of his own religious denomination in Wales. Oddly, he did not appear to feel this anxiety so intensely as many of his contemporaries.[48]

A second cultural preoccupation was the growth of the natural sciences, specifically Darwinian evolution. From a religious standpoint, evolution appeared to show, on one reading, firstly, that humans were animals, and thus not spiritual creatures; secondly, that they were determined by laws or forces beyond their control. For some, this undermined ideas of freedom and morality. As one contemporary of Jones remarked – the Victorian age was:

> deeply impressed by the contradiction between the views of the world's origin and prospects recommended to its notice by natural science and that traditionally associated with its religion, faith and hope. It was repelled on the one hand by a theology which seemed alien to and remote from much in the modern world that seemed splendid in performance and the richest in promise, and, on the other, by a naturalism which left man without a Father in heaven, without real freedom to will and to act.[49]

Jones entered into the fray with enormous relish as we will see in chapter four. He basically tried to overcome these problems through adopting Hegel's notion of emanation which essentially spiritualized evolution.

The anxiety about religion and science is linked to a third preoccupation, namely, the deeply earnest concern with practical conduct, moral character and active citizenship. This, along with the necessary role of education, is discussed in chapter five. Faith needed to be expressed in works. This theme connected with Jones's optimistic evolutionary meliorism. Samuel Smiles and Harriet Martineau had popularized the term 'character'. However thinkers like J. S. Mill and T. H. Green gave it a distinctively philosophical reading. Character and practical good conduct presupposed the predominance of a reasoning faculty, which enabled individuals to control and manage their lives. The person with character was the responsible active citizen, ideal father or mother, teacher or social worker. For thinkers like Mill, Green, Thomas Carlyle and Matthew Arnold, character was closely tied to the self-development and self-realization of the citizen. In the case of Carlyle this theme of the development of character was most likely derived from his admiration for Goethe's notion of *Bildung*, outlined in the novel (translated into English by Carlyle) *Wilhem Meisters Lehrejahre*. Such ethically developing earnest citizens were the heart of the maturity of a good state. Jones was an enthusiastic exponent of these ideas. Great stress was laid in all his writings not only on the evolution of practical moral conduct but also on its link with the essence of religion. Jones himself was deeply attracted to Carlyle's craggy moralism. As a student in Bangor Normal College his evident enthusiasm for the author earned him the nickname from his fellow students 'Carlyle Jones'.

Jones was an avowed Absolute Idealist and was confident that the Materialism and Subjectivism that had dominated so much of the nineteenth century in Britain was perceptibly on the wane. The power once exercised by Bentham and the Utilitarians had, Jones believed, now passed into the hands of the Idealists.[50] Hegelianism, as far as Jones was concerned, was the philosophy most in touch with modern life, and whose principles had penetrated most deeply into the theoretical and practical life of the times. Opponents of Idealism, Jones believed, were wholly preoccupied with criticism and had nothing positive to contribute to the furtherance of philosophical enquiry.[51] Jones's tenacious personality and resolution of will, which enabled him to overcome the impediments of his background, including the narrowness of religious dogma, had the effect, however, of making him less receptive to trends of thought that deviated from Hegelianism. This was a failing which Jones himself recognized, and much regretted. In a letter to Lord Haldane Jones laments that: 'It strikes me that you are a more sympathetic reader of rival schools than I am; and I often wish I could feel their power more. It always seems to me too easy to answer them, and therefore I don't learn from them, as you do and as I should.'[52] On the whole Jones tended to address only those critics who were Idealists opposed to Monism, like Lotze and Andrew Seth Pringle Pattison, or critics like Martineau and L. T. Hobhouse, who, although not overt Idealists, had sympathy with certain of its doctrines. The principal exception he made was a sustained attack on Herbert Spencer,[53] whose pervasive influence he deplored, and who, for Jones, represented more than any other thinker 'the stupidity of the English people'.[54]

Jones's Absolute Idealism provided the regulative ideals of his theoretical and practical life. It was Kant, Jones believed, who had brought about a Copernican revolution in philosophy by thinking differently about the relation between thought and its objects. Instead of assuming that thought must correspond to things, he enquired if things might not better be understood as corresponding to thought. Such a radical hypothesis implied that objects are related to mind, and that the principles by which thought is regulated enter into the constitution of reality. He assumed that reality is not a collection of mere fragments but a unity. However, he tried to account for this unity by reconciling differences. It was in this respect, as we shall see in chapter two, that Kant failed ultimately to reconcile thought to things and the noumenal to the phenomenal. The revolution was completed by Hegel who, instead of reconciling differences, assumed the universe to be a living spiritual unity. The task of philosophy, then, is not the reconciliation of differences, but the differentiation of unity.

Jones did not consider it necessary to offer a wholescale defence of Idealism itself. Such a defence was unnecessary given the inadequacy of other philosophical ideas to measure up to the fruitfulness of Idealism. Thus, much of Jones's writing was taken up with issues, events and ideas to which he *applied* the tenets of his philosophical beliefs. For this reason the systematic character of Jones's thought is implicit rather than explicit. In fact the term 'apply' gives a slightly false reading, in the sense that Jones saw the world as revealing an implicit order. Thus the philosophy was not so much applied, as revealed in a pre-existing reality – or to put it in Jones's own terms – reality imposes hypotheses on us.

Jones's Hegelianism was mediated through Edward Caird. Caird, however, relied more heavily than Jones upon revealing his philosophy in the course of a critical exegesis of past philosophers. Jones and Muirhead thus describe Caird's method to be that of the sympathetic exposition of the ideas of great philosophers who might be persuaded to be Kantians.[55] Caird delineates his own philosophical technique as follows:

> A philosophic temper is shown, above all things, in the power of entering into the views of another, and taking them for the moment almost as if they were your own, without prejudice to the subsequent critical reaction, which will be effective just in proportion to the degree of your previous sympathetic appreciation of the ideas criticised.[56]

Jones directly echoes this particular sentiment stating: 'the only true method of instruction is that which follows the path of discovery. To understand a philosophical system we must retrace the steps of its construction, and accompany the mind of the author on its quest for the truth.'[57] Jones suggests two points here: firstly, that to appreciate a philosophy or idea one must enter fully into its logic and articulate it from within. This is the basic method of Hegel's philosophy, most notably exercised in *The Phenomenology of Spirit*.[58] The only successful criticism is one which fully understands its subject from the inside.

Secondly, philosophical analysis must follow the contours of what is the case in the world. As Jones comments, philosophy 'is ruled by the facts which it explains'; it 'never can construct a world from an empty thought by means of deductive logic'.[59] This particular method characterizes many of his more serious pieces of philosophical criticism.

Jones's presumption of the principle of the unity of experience predisposes him to employ a formalized method of analysis. He characteristically portrays each problem in terms of a dualism, for example, those between Nature and Spirit; the cosmic and ethical processes; heredity versus environment; and Individualism versus Socialism. He then shows how each side of the dualism is ill-conceived, and proceeds to effect a unity which demonstrates that both sides of the purported opposition are in fact one, and that neither is independent of, nor possible, without the other.

Jones's metaphysics and religious views will be discussed at length in chapters two and three. It suffices to say that in taking Hegel as his starting-point Jones assumed that reality is a rational, evolving, spiritual unity, that is, God expressing Himself in and through every element in the living organism. As we shall see in chapter four, such an assumption entails understanding society as an evolving social organism whose parts are mutually inclusive. The person is therefore society-individuated, and the welfare of each is the responsibility of the whole, just as the welfare of the whole is the responsibility of each. It therefore behoves the individual and the state, which are not opposed, but mutually implicated, to develop institutions that encourage the process of individual moral development. Our own moral development, and by definition that of society as a whole, depends upon our active involvement in the moral development of others. In other words, each individual has social responsibilities that are fulfilled by ensuring that every place of work, every institution, and every home, is a school of virtue in which spirit is expressed, and expresses itself, in ever-increasing degrees of moral perfection. Within a society understood as an evolving spiritual unity, in the process of achieving moral perfection by degrees, all oppositions are false, and 'we can no longer speak of individual aims and individual welfare, apart from social aims and social welfare, any more than we can speak of social aims that are not also aims of individuals'.[60] Thus any attempt to promote the interests of one class at the expense of another is a denial of the common good and a perversion of the social ideal.

Jones never ceased to feel a strong affinity with the working classes from whose ranks he had risen, and felt his social responsibilities acutely in the dedication of his life to the betterment of their condition. As we shall see in chapter six, he regretted very much the rise of the Labour Party, not because he disagreed with the ideals at which it aimed, nor with most of its substantive policies, but rather with its class hatred and incitement of the workers to attain the instruments of power, not for the common good, but for class interest. The very name of the Party implied class interest, and therefore could not be condoned. He frequently made reference to this 'corruption of the working man', in private correspondence, public lectures and published articles.[61] In a letter to Munro-Ferguson, Jones expressed his attitude admirably: 'I stand out and out for the honesty and the rectitude and the intelligence of the working men of this country; they are the least prejudiced class I know; and *that* is why I am as angry with the Labour Leaders for prostituting them, as I am with Rosebery for his implicit distrust of them.'[62] There was nothing which Jones desired more than that the working class should gain its deserved share in the government of the country.[63] At the same time, however, he wanted to ensure that their minds were sufficiently developed, and their characters requisitely spiritualized, to take on, and admirably discharge, the obligations of citizenship. This is not to suggest that he thought the entrepreneurial class any less in need of education and spiritual development. 'Capital', he argued, 'must discover that it has duties',[64] and must be educated into realizing its social responsibilities to provide work-places conducive to the spiritual and moral development of the worker. If employers cannot be educated into converting their workshops into schools of virtue then they will be compelled because the employee is destined to inherit a greater degree of the power of the state, and to share more fully in the privileges and responsibilities of economic activity.

Jones was not blindly optimistic about the moral capacity of the leaders of industry to recognize and accept their social responsibilities. Indeed, he often had occasion to despair of their insensitivity to the human resources they exploited. In 1916, for example, while serving on Lord Haldane's Royal Commission on University Education in Wales,[65] Jones was clearly appalled by the evidence of the south Wales coal owners. He wrote despondently to a number of his friends about the experience. In a letter to Thomas Jones, he confessed that: 'The Philistinism of it all made me sick.'[66]

Philosophical Idealism, for Jones, was not an intellectual pursuit divorced from practice. The task of philosophy was to raise the practical person to the level of considering principles.[67] In particular, this meant providing the requisite education for developing the consciousness of the citizens of a nation. Through education, he believed, the economic, social and political institutions of the nation would gradually become moralized, that is, become expressions of the free wills which enter into them. The state, as the highest spiritual embodiment of the wills of the individuals who constitute it, is itself an educational institution charged with facilitating the moral development of its citizens,[68] and, in Jones's view, *'in the last resort it has to teach only one thing – the nature of the good'*.[69] Jones's pursuit of the educational ideal, through public meetings and participation in various government commissions, made him one of the most well-respected reformers of his day. There was no one, according to Harry Reichel, to whom Lloyd George attached more weight in 'matters of university education' than Henry Jones.[70]

Jones's theory of education and its relation to citizenship will be discussed in chapter five, but some mention should be made here of the extent of his practical involvement in educational reform. He was extremely active, for example, in the movement for the establishment of intermediate education in Wales;[71] he gave evidence to the Cross Commission;[72] he formulated proposals for a greater degree of parental control of elementary education in Scotland;[73] he argued vehemently, and turned the tide, against Sir Marchant William's scheme to centralize the authority of the University of Wales, and destroy the independence of the Colleges;[74] and, among his proudest achievements in Glasgow was to gain the recognition of the need, and actually get the funds, for a lectureship in Political Philosophy, the establishment of a class library and, in association with others, the vast expansion of the facilities for the natural sciences in the University.[75] In addition, Jones campaigned for university reform in Australia, and the establishment of a university in Brisbane;[76] he represented the Scottish and Welsh Universities on the British Education Mission to the United States of America, whose purpose was to promote greater educational exchanges between Great Britain and America;[77] and finally, he formulated a scheme for the co-operation of universities and churches to form an extensive network throughout Wales in order to make education more widely available to the adult population.[78]

The Australian example, because it was widely reported, and because little has been written on this episode in Jones's life, will serve to illustrate the passion and fervour with which he taunted his audiences into acknowledging the merits of the causes with which he associated himself.

Jones appears to have been well informed about Australian university matters and took every opportunity to express his views in the strongest terms. In an interview he gave on his arrival in Sydney he immediately betrayed the exalted view that he had of the place of the university in the nation. He told the Australian people, 'whatever you do, do what you can for your University . . . It is the soul of a nation'.[79] Prior to the Australian visit of 1908 Jones had devoted considerable energy to educational matters in both Wales and Scotland. In relation to university education three principal concerns emerge. Firstly, that professors should not be so overburdened with teaching that they could not adequately prosecute research. Secondly, that a university education should be for its own sake, and not subordinate to vocational demands. And thirdly, the study of social relations and political activity should be much more prominent than it was. In all of these respects Australia compared unfavourably with Britain, but what is more, Brisbane, a state capital, did not have a university at all.[80]

Jones was of the view that there is no distinction to be made in principle between the elementary schools and the universities. Both are equally vital for the health and welfare of a nation. The state, Jones believed, had slowly come to realize that its destiny depended upon the adequate provision of elementary and intermediate education, but continued to deny its responsibility in respect of universities, regarding them as places of culture for the privileged few, and treating them as private corporations undeserving of more than limited state support. 'The State', Jones complained, 'does not take Universities into its own hands and pour its own strength into them; it does not make them organs of its own body, and vehicles of its own life, precisely because, so far, it has not known the vital nature of its interest in their prosperity.'[81] In consequence, he was intolerant of the arguments put forward in Brisbane to delay the establishment of a university. Speaking on this issue in Melbourne, Jones told his audience that although Brisbane claimed to be civilized it was still without a university because it had been misled by metaphors into believing that the time was not right. There was no reform, he said, that had not been retarded by the metaphorical objection that it would be the thin end of the wedge. Similarly, the argument that other schools needed to be provided first and that the university was to be the coping-stone, was another example of the power of metaphors to mislead and inhibit reform. History shows, contended Jones, that universities, far from being the coping-stone, were the stimulus to the establishment of other schools.[82] Here, in fact, he was alluding to the fact that it was only after the establishment of the university colleges in north and south Wales that the momentum for intermediate education gained ground and eventually succeeded in a veritable explosion of schools supported by a penny rate levied upon the rate-payers by local authorities.

Jones wished to put his whole weight behind those striving for the establishment of the university and immediately went on the attack. He took particular delight in goading the dignitaries of Queensland, especially because of their incessant bragging about the extraordinary precociousness of their children. He accused the people of caring more for their minerals, land and animals than for developing the quality of humanity. Furthermore, he ridiculed the politicians for providing grand palaces for themselves and their public servants, while failing to provide a home for higher learning and the promotion of culture. Did they not realize, he argued, that a university promotes that development of character vital to the strength of a nation, and it enables the individual to fulfil his, or her, potential. He urged them to set up a university in Brisbane, like those in Scotland and Wales, which would be accessible to rich and poor alike. This could be done, he maintained, by private donations and the raising of a municipal rate.[83] Many years later Jones revived the idea of a municipal rate to support higher education in Wales,[84] forgetting that he had first advocated it in Brisbane. It is difficult to say what effect Jones had on giving added impetus to the Brisbane movement, but the act establishing the University of Queensland was passed the following year.

In Adelaide and Sydney Jones voiced his concerns about the Australian universities in general. It seemed to him that Australians had lost sight of the main purpose of a university, and that was to pursue research and create enthusiastic enquirers. The inquisitiveness of students can only be stimulated, Jones contended, by the example of those who are both great researchers and teachers. There were too many able people in the universities whose talents were being wasted because of the excessive teaching burdens they had to bear. These people should be allowed the leisure to further their own research and in doing so they would prove to be an inspiration to themselves and to their students.[85]

The lack of serious enquiry into social studies was an aspect of Australian universities that perturbed Jones. At Newcastle, Sydney, Wollongong, Melbourne and Adelaide, Jones tried to impress upon his audiences that society was the most complex and intricate piece of machinery that they could ever encounter, and instead of delving deeply into the character of the relations that integrated every moving part into the whole, Australians were content to allow their fortunes to be determined by accident and caprice, in the absence of enquirers whose sole business it would be to discover and understand the principles of social life. 'You expect this intricate and complex thing to grow right of itself', he told his Sydney audience, 'without anyone trying to understand it.'[86] Furthermore, it appeared to Jones that the care of society had been entrusted to persons who were as ignorant of political principles as the people who elected them. There was an urgent need, Jones argued, for professors of social economy and political science to turn out an army of educated students with some understanding of the social organism. But he was careful to remind his listeners that education should never primarily be for the sake of industry. Education must be for its own sake, and the benefits that flow through to society would be both indirect and bountiful.[87]

In the final two chapters of this book, seven and eight, we will look at Jones's views on nationalism, imperialism and international relations in the context of contemporaneous discussions. In both of these chapters, Hobhouse's criticisms of the implications of Idealism for imperialism and militarism prove to be inapplicable to Jones. Jones's political conclusions are, in fact, in sympathy with those of Hobhouse. It will be shown that Hobhouse was not unequivocally opposed to imperialism, and that he implied a certain degree of agreement with the sentiments expressed in Edmund Burke's view of the Empire. It is this view which informs the Idealist conception of imperialism, and which was itself opposed to the economic and social imperialism of which Hobson and Hobhouse were also vehement critics. Furthermore, it will be argued in chapter eight that the absolutist view of the state, with its diminutive and corrosive effect upon individual liberties, which Hobhouse and Hobson attributed to Hegel and suggested that it was an orthodoxy among British Idealists, with the exception of Green, was not an accurate account of their views in general, and a distortion of Jones's view in particular. In addition, their views on international morality and the possibility of greater international co-operation were far less 'Realist' and pessimistic than their critics wished to imply.

In conclusion, although only chapter five of this book directly addresses the theory of citizenship, it will soon become evident that all of Jones's concerns and preoccupations were directed towards the intellectual and moral improvement of every individual within the state. Citizenship therefore forms the key motif of Jones's thought. The attainment of freedom, that is the freedom to choose what is right, is a precondition to discharging the obligations and enjoying the privileges of citizenship. Freedom presupposes knowledge, and knowledge is itself a condition of morality. The good of the state depends upon a well-educated, morally developed, and therefore, free citizenry. The state's primary obligation to its citizens is to promote and sustain those conditions and institutions conducive to the attainment of one's personal potential. The state, which refers both to the offices and institutions of government and also, for the Idealist, to everything that we would encompass by using the terms 'country' or 'nation', is for Jones an educative state. Education in the principles of citizenship is not merely a formal process, but is accomplished, perhaps more importantly, by the good example of citizens around the hearth at home, and at the workbench in industry.

CHAPTER TWO

AN IDENTITY IN DIFFERENCE

As a prelude to discussing Jones's social and political concerns it is necessary to lay out the metaphysical and religious foundations which find expression in, and give force to, every facet of his practical and theoretical interests. It is the metaphysical principles which Jones applied to contemporary social and political problems which serve to unify his thought. This chapter examines his attitudes to the role and character of philosophy and then considers his conception of metaphysics.

The particular form of Idealism Jones promulgated was Absolute Idealism. The prime movers for this type of Idealism, in Jones's estimation, were Kant and Hegel. Jones felt, from his earliest student years, confident about the veracity of Hegelianism.[1] He regarded most other philosophies as either too thin and inadequate to stand up to philosophical criticism, or alternatively, in the case of philosophies like utilitarianism, in perceptible decline.[2] As Jones himself confessed, this particular assumption did not help him in dealing with other philosophies, some of which he dismissed in a surprisingly cursory manner.[3]

The roots to Jones's philosophy of Absolute Idealism lay, therefore, predominantly in the realms of late eighteenth- and early nineteeenth-century German philosophy. Kant was seen as the turning-point in modern thought, what Jones often referred to as the Copernican revolution in philosophy. Schelling, Fichte and Hegel were the main landmarks. Later neo-Kantian thinkers, like Hermann Lotze, in the neo-Kantian revival at the end of the nineteenth century, were also considered seriously by Jones, although usually in terms of a falling away from the truths of Idealism. Those in Britain influenced by the Germanic tradition, specifically thinkers like Edward Caird, Bernard Bosanquet and F. H. Bradley, were considered by Jones as powerful exponents of Idealism.

Very broadly philosophical Idealism in Britain can be differentiated into two main movements containing a number of sub-components.

Firstly, there was the more dominant and subsequently better known school of Absolute Idealism, exemplified by Bradley and Bosanquet; and secondly the less well-known and more diversified school of Subjective and/or Personal Idealism, whose exponents included Hastings Rashdall, Henry Sturt and C. C. J. Webb.

The Absolute Idealists shared certain fundamental ideas concerning the ontological monistic unity of the world and reality. Nothing short of the Absolute was adequate to explain or account for reality. However, certain deep fissures developed in the Absolutist movement, circling in some cases around issues which also divided the Personal from the Absolute Idealists. One strand of Absolute Idealism, particularly Francis Bradley's thought, contended that the Absolute was beyond description and that our only sense of it could be through immediate experience, a form of intuitive feeling, rather than rational knowledge. Anything short of the Absolute, including space, time, motion or the self, was seen as contradictory appearance. Even God was relegated to contradictory appearance and inadequate to account for the Absolute. This tendency of Absolutism had significant implications for notions of selfhood, finite individuality and the personality of God.

Another section within the Absolutists, headed by Caird and Jones, tended to emphasize the reality of the differentiated substance of the Absolute. Namely, it was considered that Bradley overplayed the unity of the Absolute at the expense of the rich and changing world of difference. In consequence the reality of selfhood and individuality were given particular emphasis; further, the notion of a personal theistic God was explicitly linked to the philosophical Absolute. The Absolute could be known and appreciated rationally through its complex manifestations in science, poetry, religion and philosophy.

The emphasis on personality and its relation to the Absolute has close links with the theories of Personal Idealism. There are various contentious subdivisions within this movement. Berkeley was usually regarded (even by some of the Personal Idealists) as distinctly idiosyncratic within Personal Idealism. A second element wished to retain Hegelianism and spiritualism, but focused on the indissoluble character and moral significance of individual persons. The more notable figures here were Andrew Seth Pringle Pattison, Clement C. J. Webb, Hastings Rashdall and Henry Sturt. The writings of Henry Martineau can also be incorporated into this general grouping, although he did not see himself as part of any such movement. A third element derived its sustenance from the neo-Kantian revival and critique of Hegelianism. This movement had a more significant effect in Germany, with Lotze as a leading light. Finally, there was the unique if strange output of John McTaggart Ellis McTaggart, which, although sharing important features of the Personal Idealists' argument, developed his own totally idiosyncratic doctrines. These movements in Britain paralleled developments in American philosophy specifically in Josiah Royce, William Hocking and Brand Blanchard.

Before considering Jones's place in this philosophical tradition it is worth mentioning some of the prominent philosophical tendencies which opposed Absolute Idealism. The opposition to Idealism at the time, as far as Jones was concerned, was loosely camped around four areas, although there were other components which were too loose to be described as schools, for example, naturalism and materialism. Firstly, there were elements of Personal Idealism which Jones felt to have either misunderstood Idealism or made basic philosophical blunders. Jones carried on a running battle with and commentary on Personal Idealist philosophers throughout his life, even after the movement's apparent demise. The one element which did survive was the neo-Kantian group in Germany, which had implications for the development of phenomenology, a movement which seems not to have touched Jones at all (unlike Bosanquet, who developed a correspondence with Husserl). In fact, after the turn of the century, Jones seemed to pay less attention to developments in European philosophy generally, apart from rare exceptions.[4]

Secondly, there was a vigorous Realist movement, which had been initially influenced by Lotze. It placed its emphasis on practical experience as a whole rather than theoretical thinking. The most well-known representative that Jones criticized was James Ward, whom Caird taught and admired, although he was eclipsed, at least in the eyes of posterity, by Samuel Alexander. Jones, unlike Bosanquet, paid little attention in his published work to Alexander.[5] Ward, however, came in for some passing critiques.

Thirdly, Jones, like Bradley, felt that the movement of philosophical Pragmatism needed refutation. His attention was mainly directed at William James. Even in his last work, *A Faith that Enquires*, Jones was concerned to criticize James's position; however the criticisms were never as fully developed as his critique of Lotze or the Personal Idealists. It is odd, also, that he did not address himself in any systematic way either to James's compatriots, John Dewey and C. S.

Pierce (although the latter admittedly did not like the title Pragmatist), or to some of the British admirers of Pragmatism, particularly F. C. S. Schiller.[6]

A final movement Jones only touched in passing, which was related to some aspects of Pragmatism, was Vitalism. The most notable representative, whom Jones could not ignore, but only mentions with barely disguised irritation, was Henri Bergson. Bergson's intuitivist philosophy, with its critique of rational intellectual endeavour, was having with Nietzsche and, to some degree, Schopenhauer, tremendous impact in some quarters of social, psychological and aesthetic theory in the Edwardian era.[7] Jones cannot have been unaware of this development. He was asked by Lloyd George to address, for example, the growth of syndicalism in the Welsh miners' lodges. He was too intelligent a man not to have identified the Sorelian intuitivist philosophy lurking behind many syndicalist intellectuals. In the case of Sorel himself it was a philosophy drawing upon Bergson. One of Jones's own philosophical assistants at Glasgow, J. W. Scott (later professor of Philosophy at Cardiff) wrote a book on this very influence entitled *Syndicalism and Philosophical Realism.*[8] Jones's impatience with Vitalism and other such intuitivist philosophies was precisely because of their emphasis on feeling, intuition, emotion and irrationalism, which he regarded as a sub-philosophical realm. Much of his more systematic critique of feeling is in fact developed in his earlier book on Lotze.

THE GENERAL CHARACTER OF PHILOSOPHY

Jones makes it clear that philosophy does not start from any sense of immediate experience, intuition or sceptical *cogito*. Philosophy begins for Jones with ordinary experience become reflective. It does not seek reality but alternatively starts with it and reflects upon it. As Jones contends, philosophy is 'the reflective interpretation of human experience, it must accept the laws of experience as its own. Experience is its starting point and whole datum'.[9] This, for Jones, is connected with one of the most fundamental misapprehensions of Hegel. Hegel did not need, as some of his critics implied, to leap out of the realm of thought into reality, mainly because, for Jones, he began with reality.[10] The above point gives rise to one of the most fundamental assumptions of Jones's thought, namely the unity of the world and experience. We begin with the unity and sense of reality.

However, as we grow, the world fragments. Thought or understanding breaks up the apparent unity. We see the world through the eyes of poets, scientists and philosophers, and all such views appear to be different, at least on the surface. Jones sees this fragmentation as a particular characteristic of the person starting to think philosophically. He comments that: 'In all ages of the world the young philosopher . . . is like the puppy-dog. He must tear things to pieces while he is teething.'[11] The struggle then takes place to recover the unity of experience, to make the implicit explicit, a task which is never accomplished, partly because reality is continually changing.[12]

The fact that philosophy begins in this domain of ordinary experience leads him to doubt that it should be regarded predominantly as a technical discipline. Despite the fact that some of the Idealist school in Britain had tried to professionalize philosophy in Oxford, Jones complains that philosophy has become too specialized, and concentrates on highly technical monographs.[13] He remarked ironically, at one point, that the philosopher is often confined 'to the exposition of a limited portion of the field of being . . . He insists, with a touch of nervous excitement, that he is not a "system-monger", that the last of these was Hegel.'[14] Philosophy should not be studied or done as a series of remote abstract systems. Jones did not teach it this way. Rather, philosophy was a way of comprehending and acting in the world, finding or postulating some principle to make reality intelligible. This endeavour, to a greater or lesser degree, was present implicitly in all thinking individuals. As Jones commented:

> all the activity of man, the practical as well as the theoretical, is an attempt to establish a *modus vivendi* between his environment and himself. And such an attempt rests on the assumption that there is some ground common to both of the struggling powers within and without, some principle that manifests itself both in man and in nature. So that all men are philosophers to the extent of postulating a unity, which is deeper than all differences; and all are alike trying to discover, in however limited or ignorant a way, what that unity is.[15]

Philosophy, in this reading, is part and parcel of being human, using reason, adjusting the understanding and making sense of one's environment.

Two further issues need to be noted in addition to the above: firstly, philosophy thinks through the medium of reason and concepts, which are the products of previous generations of thinkers. The philosopher tries to analyse the leading thoughts of the time, but through a medium saturated with historical traditions of thought and reflection.

Thus Jones remarks that reason evolves and amplifies 'the meaning of its own products. The movement from morality and religion to moral philosophy and the philosophy of religion, is thus a movement from reason to reason, from implicit to explicit.'[16] Secondly, each generation is condemned to begin this task anew. To understand the present and the past a struggle has to take place. As Jones comments: 'no generation, or individual, can enter upon its inheritance from the past except by making it its own. There is a sense in which human experience, begins again *de novo*, not only with every age and epoch, but with every individual.'[17] The path of spirit has to be traced in outline by each individual. Although Jones admired Burke and his emphasis on tradition, the Welshman in this case had much more faith in individual reason than the Irishman.

Philosophy reflected the need that all humans have for an intelligible account of the world, therefore it was intimately linked to self-consciousness and self-knowledge. For Jones: 'All alike endeavour to interpret experience.'[18] Such an endeavour was not a luxury, it was a necessity. It achieved its most adequate form in the various disciplines of human thought, more particularly in philosophy. As Jones argued: 'Self-consciousness is the working hypothesis of philosophy.'[19] Thus although philosophy was distinct from ordinary reflection and experience, it was not a categorial distinction, but rather one of thoroughness and degree. Philosophy was critical thought about thought, making systematic an essential constituent of our rational natures.

Jones deploys a number of arguments within the notion of self-consciousness. Firstly, he employs a form of transcendental argument. The unity of self-consciousness is the precondition to knowledge and experience. As Jones comments on the spiritual unity of self-consciousness: 'If . . . it [self-consciousness] is the condition of the possibility of *any* experience, it is more than a hypothesis: it is an absolute postulate.'[20] Self-consciousness is thus the truth of all things, their essential precondition. Jones suggests here a number of levels of unity. For example, space, time, substance, cause, evolution and so on act as unifying principles in themselves. They form the essential preconditions to experience in certain spheres of thought and activity. However, all of these varying principles which unify bodies of experience, presuppose the self-conscious agent or the ultimate unity of self-consciousness. As Jones remarked (his emphasis): '*The consciousness of reality is the consciousness of the unity of our psychical life.*'[21]

A second argument alludes to an explicitly Idealist theme, namely that the world is mind-dependent. As Jones comments: 'The great result of speculation since the time of Kant is to teach us to recognize that objects are essentially related to mind, and that the principles which rule our thought enter, so to speak, into the constitution of the things we know.'[22] This thesis is advanced against the basic empiricist claim that the world can and does exist independently of our conceiving it. Jones's position, like most Idealists, is not as straightforward as it first sounds. This will be examined in more detail in the section on 'Epistemology and Ontology'. The basic argument is that the objects which impress themselves on the mind are themselves mind-related. The subject implies the object and the object implies the subject, yet their difference as subject and object must be maintained as necessary elements. 'All science', as Jones argued, 'is nothing but an appeal to thought from ordinary sensuous opinion. It is an attempt to find the reality of things by thinking about them.'[23]

Kant's relation to the above arguments is somewhat ambiguous. Jones uses Kantian argumentation on the transcendental subject. Kant is also equated with the great Copernican revolution in philosophy. For Jones, he 'did more than anyone else to show that the object implied the subject'.[24] However, Kant was weaker on the subject implying the object. Paradoxically, for Jones, much of the distrust of thought and its relation to reality also derived from Kant. This distrust of thought in Kantian philosophy is traceable through theology.[25] It led to faulty theological distinctions between faith and reason. The upshot of the sceptical use of Kantian argument is that 'we can know thought or universals, but not things or particular existences'.[26] This is Kant's famed *ding an sich* argument, leading to the distinction between phenomenal and noumenal realms. For Jones, Kant had performed a remarkable feat in philosophy. He had identified thought and reality. He had shown that the object implied the subject. However, the great step implied in Kant, namely, that the distinction between *thought* and *reality* was contained within a broader unity, was never taken. This latter step was taken by Hegel. Kant, for Jones, thus never made the '*opposition* of the terms subordinate and secondary to their unity . . . Kant's task to the end was that of reconciling differences, that of Hegel was to differentiate a unity'.[27]

For Jones, therefore, self-consciousness and the world of objects are part of one differentiated unity. There is no 'world of ideas' in individuals constituting reality, rather reality is of the same self-differentiated substance as self-consciousness. The highest forms of such self-consciousness subsist in the disciplines of human thought, like natural science, art and philosophy. Self-consciousness is not, however, a static thing which can be articulated once and for all. The process of differentiation goes on. Self-consciousness thus develops slowly. The implication is of a hierarchy within self-consciousness. The higher stage integrates and gives a fuller account of the lower forms. As Jones argues 'each higher stage carrying within it the lower, the present storing up the past . . . the process is a self-enriching one'.[28] Self-consciousness is thus understood as a dialectical process.

Jones's account of this 'process' and development in self-consciousness and philosophical awareness is placed by him into the context of a teleological history of human thought and practice. Underlying this process and rich diversity is an unchanging substantial unity.[29] The process of differentiation is characterized by diverse ideas and philosophical systems, which become architectonic conceptions, linking up worlds of experience. Jones sees the concept evolution, for example, in this light, dominating much discussion in the latter part of the nineteenth century.[30] He remarks, in a somewhat grandiose style, that 'there are dynasties of great ideas . . . and these successively ascend to the throne of mind, and hold a sway over human thought which is well nigh absolute.'[31]

Jones saw these architectonic conceptions as part of a schematic development of thought from the Greeks. Hegel had argued, in his *Philosophy of History*, that there were periods in the development of civilization: oriental despotism, the Greek and Roman worlds and finally the Christian Germanic. These correspond to a speculative teleological pattern of history characterized by certain forms of thought and reflection. In some writings, Jones directly parallels this Hegelian categorization, although, interestingly, when he speaks of oriental despotism, he discusses the difficulties the British had in Imperial India. The basic thesis was that the Indians were still in the realm of historical oriental despotism, therefore could not be easily educated to a higher stage of consciousness and self-government. They were used to obedience 'as slaves'. Jones was extremely sceptical of the dubious pursuit of inculcating the Western spirit into Eastern peoples.[32]

As Hegel had enthused about the Greek world as a 'paradise of the human spirit', Jones contended that the Greek world, if doomed, was still 'the most momentous step in the history of man's spirit'.[33] The

Greeks represented the movement from sense to thought and from impulse to conscious will. In the Greeks 'sensuous knowledge and impulse blossom into self-conscious thought and purpose, man comes of age'.[34] The Greek world cultivated reason, which when 'set loose', as Jones put it, destroyed its creator. The Greek world was 'founded upon impulse, it could not stand the strain of thought. Hence the ethical enquiries of Socrates were fatal to the Greek state.'[35]

For Jones ideas become intelligible within a particular epoch and culture. Cultures are part of a developmental teleological pattern which was slowly evolving through the self-consciousness of individuals. Earlier ideas were embryonic of later forms of thought and practice. For example, Greek virtues were filled out and given substance by Christian virtue. Jones, therefore, viewed the history of philosophy as revealing features about particular cultures. For example, he remarks that the philosophy of Hobbes, Locke and Hume 'rendered intelligible to us the individualistic life of modern Europe, laying its fundamental principle bare, . . . they enabled us, thereby, to escape its limitations and to overcome its scepticism'.[36]

Philosophy is, therefore, a developmental process. Hume is corrected by Kant and Kant by Hegel. Writing in the 1890s, Jones remarked that no one with any philosophical acumen could subscribe to a Lockean or Humean view of mind.[37] Furthermore, events can have a role in refuting philosophical ideas. Jones comments that individualism 'received its practical refutation in the French Revolution'.[38] Similarly the failure of sensationalism and associationism in philosophy are seen to reflect upon the failure of individualism in politics.[39] This may sound strange to the modern reader, although it fits neatly with Jones's holistic interpretation of reality. This point also underlines the strong metaphysical character of Jones's view of politics.

Finally, Jones saw all individuals as the inheritors and interpreters of the history of ideas. Without this theoretically rich, densely-textured past, individuals would be empty husks. As Jones argued: 'what a man is he is in virtue of the traditions of his people. Strip him of all of these and he stands pitifully naked and helpless. For traditions are not possessions from which he can divest or disentangle himself. They are his experience.'[40] This has a strong and obvious Burkean ring to it, a point of which Jones was conscious. However, Jones places much greater emphasis on reason in tradition than Burke. There is a difference between thinking critically *within* a tradition (Jones) and simply living unquestioningly *through* traditions and prejudice (Burke).[41]

One of the major problems of Idealism for Jones derives from its virtue, namely, its comprehensive and all-inclusive character. Jones remarks that 'no philosophy ever offered to its votaries – and victims . . . so ample an opportunity for misapprehension and caricature.'[42] When Idealism, in its Absolutist format, tries to integrate the totality of experience, it is accused of a multitude of sins – losing God in man, or man in God, evaporating things into thought, matter into spirit, abolishing all right and wrong, and truth and error. Despite these dangers, Jones contends that the very fruitfulness of Idealism is that it does *not* settle upon any simple contrasts. It demands that justice be done to the complexity of reality. Its achievement is 'to hold *as difference* within its own unity, and to be able to manifest its own nature in a self-externalizing process, and by fortifying its opposite against itself'.[43]

As briefly as possible we will give a summary of certain elements of Jones's philosophical position before moving to an outline of his metaphysics. The points mentioned here will be of significance to the ensuing discussions.

Jones, like Bradley, was obsessed with the theme of unity in difference. He was neither satisfied with simple monism (unity itself), nor with pluralism. There had to be a combination which did justice to both terms; as he argued: 'To obliterate differences is not to explain them. But to insist on differences to the exclusion of their unity is equally futile.'[44] Such a doctrine led him to reject all forms of dualism. This was a position he inherited from Edward Caird. A. D. Lindsay reported that students of Caird at Balliol would often, in his classes, 'consign a philosopher to outer darkness with the fatal words, "He's a Dualist" '.[45] Jones pursued dualisms remorselessly throughout the philosophical field. One of the principle dualistic offenders was 'thought' and 'reality.' He considered that Hegel, taking the essential step beyond Kant, had solved this dualism once and for all. Hegel had pressed through the separation of thought and things 'to the unity which manifests itself in the activities of both subject and object; and the thoughts which *seem* to be purely subjective he regards as the products of the reality which energizes in *both* the subject and object'.[46] Thought, for Jones, does not move from some fixed datum and aggregation, but rather by differentiation and reintegration from within. In other words there is no dualism, rather a unity in difference. The datum of thought reveals itself progressively in the evolution of knowledge.

The choice that Jones puts before us is either between some form of associationism (which is floored by the fact that it cannot explain how a series, utterly unrelated and unknown by mind, can yet *be* related) or a related whole as a premise. As Jones argues: 'we must regard the whole as given at first, and watch its process of inward development.'[47] The interrelated unity also led Jones to the view that all objects are necessarily related. System lies at the heart of reality and philosophy. As he commented: 'every object declares itself to be part or element in a system, and we are referred to the system for its final reality and truth.'[48]

The emphasis on systematic unity connects up with four further points, which have already been covered. Self-consciousness was the systematic truth of all things. Reality was a developing process, evolving to a richer unity. Further, objects were all mind-dependent; thus empiricism, which was premised on the faulty dualistic separation of thought and things, was ruled out as a philosophical failure. Finally, reason was seen to be the measure of all things. This led Jones to a repudiation of feeling or emotion possessing any key role in philosophy. It might be argued that there is a lurking dualism within this separation between thought and feeling; however, Jones saw feeling as an inkling of what reason establishes in fact. They are not separate, but part of a continuum. Similarly, when philosophers point to intuition as a source of knowledge, what they are really drawing our attention to is the fact that past experience permeates our minds, but it needs rational self-consciousness to reveal its true character.[49] Emotion and intuition are thus not dualistically distinct from reason. Reason gradually evolves and amplifies, often from intuitive and emotive material, 'the meaning of its own products'.[50]

When Jones uses the concept 'idea' he means not merely thoughts, but also 'real principles, which manifest themselves in the objects of the outer world, as well as in the thinker's mind'.[51] This provides part of the answer to the regular contention against Idealism that surely the real world *must* exist independently of ideas? Jones argues that

> The question of the reality or the unreality of things cannot arise except in intelligence. Animals have neither illusions nor truths – unless they are self-conscious. The reality, which man sets over his own inadequate knowledge, is assumed by him; and it has no meaning whatsoever except in this contrast.[52]

In other words the separation betwen ideas and an external world is a distinction made *within* intelligence. It is perfectly feasible to make the distinction; however, if it is asserted as an absolute truth about reality, then it needs to be corrected by a broader perspective. The concept of an external world separate from ideas is itself 'an idea' which presupposes intelligence. If it were true of reality it would be absurd since it would be asserting the knowledge of the conception of a reality which no one knows. This, in essence, is asserting that both A and not A are true.

The above argument also combines with Jones's critique of Lotze. For Lotze the world of systematic thought is purely ideal. It is representational in character and the core of reality always escapes it. Conscious thought is thus a relating device. Ideas are not knowledge of reality. Sensation, perception, imagination and memory are not thought. Emotion and feeling are not reducible to ideas. Imagination, and the like, are independent sources of understanding from the intellectual faculty. Specifically, feeling in Lotze functions rather like reason in Kant's thought. Immediate feeling, in fact, teaches us far more about the world and reality than thought.[53]

Jones's basic response to this is to argue that if Lotze separates thought from reality how can thought provide any real knowledge? Also, the separation itself is a 'universal' premised upon intelligent thought. If thought is just a mediating and relating activity, where do universals arise from? Is there a clear distinction to be drawn between the sense manifold of reality and mental universals? There may be differences of degree, but a difference in degree is not a difference in kind. Conception is not always general and perception is not always concerned with particulars. Thus, Jones comments that: 'The individual object . . . resists the attempt to treat it either as particular or universal; it is a totality of concrete relations, a unity of universals and therefore explicable only in terms of thought and as the work of thought.'[54] Conception, judgement and the like are not separate from reality. The unity of reality, sense and understanding, thought and things, is prior to their separation. For Jones, 'reality expands with the thinking process and guides it.'[55]

Much of the previous discussion throws light on Jones's view of the relation between philosophical theory and practice. For Jones, the spectre of dualism lurks again since 'all human life is at once theoretical and practical'.[56] The basic idea that Jones works with is that the practical actions of rational beings are characterized by purposes (or intentions). It follows that action involves and is only explicable through the constitutive purpose, which is theoretical. For Jones it is only 'crude ignorance' which leads 'otherwise respectable people' to distinguish the practical from the theoretical.[57] He maintains that 'just as practice implies the theoretic activity of the intellect, so, on the other hand, the theoretic use of the intelligence implies the operation of powers deemed practical.'[58]

METAPHYSICS

Metaphysics is of central importance to Jones. It is not a question of choosing whether or not to have or engage in metaphysics, rather it is a question of whether one is conscious or not of employing metaphysical ideas. The choice, says Jones, is between 'a conscious metaphysics or an unconscious one'.[59] Many are, he believes, simply ignorant of the fact that they employ metaphysical notions. Thus metaphysics is a necessity in two senses. Firstly, metaphysical assumptions exist whether one knows it or not. One *cannot* wish them away or declare that one's own thought has no metaphysical characteristics; this is logically impossible to Jones. Secondly, it is better to be aware of one's metaphysical assumptions. One can then act in full self-consciousness.

Jones's major point is that every judgement we make about the world, whether in an abstruse philosophical argument, or in the most mundane practical activity, relies upon certain assumptions. Each judgement will in the end tie in with a diverse series of other judgements, forming some kind of systematic unity. Thus, he comments that 'there is no interpretation of an object which does not finally point to a theory of being . . . The history of the pebble can be given only in the light of the story of the earth . . . We must begin very far back, and bring our widest principles to bear upon the particular thing.'[60]

Jones suggests that our judgements are always based on suppositions and these more partial suppositions are traceable back to more deep-rooted assumptions. As he stated: 'All our knowledge, even the most broken and inconsistent, streams from some fundamental conception in virtue of which all the variety of objects constitutes one world, one orderly Kosmos, even to the meanest mind.'[61]

In practical life such assumptions are needed more desperately, since we have to act to survive. All human action is saturated with intelligence. The world itself, as Jones was fond of remarking, was 'thought-woven'. Thus he stated that 'wherever we touch the practical life of man, we are at once referred to a metaphysics.'[62] Every effort we make to act or understand will always assume certain things about the human self, the good and the universe in general. Thus we need a 'general theory of life' to do anything.[63]

All the disciplines, for Jones – ethics, psychology, natural science – must rest on metaphysical assumptions. It is the root of all forms of study. Metaphysics can be defined, rather as Collingwood was later to do far more systematically, as a science of absolute presuppositions. Jones thought that the Germans were probably the best at such study.[64] The French he considered to be fairly lightweight, if lucid. Thus, for Jones, 'Modern metaphysics, ... starts from a view of reality as a whole, and not from a fragment; and its task is to expound the inner articulation, the internal harmony of the whole.'[65] Such a metaphysics has no sense of completion or final synthesis to it. Finality in metaphysics was impossible to Jones. System after system fails for being too narrow to encompass a changing reality. Thus the study of metaphysics becomes a continual, but necessary, process.[66]

One of the terms which appears continuously in Jones's metaphysical writings is 'colligating hypothesis'.[67] Its use parallels a number of other terms in his various texts, namely, 'absolute presupposition or postulate', 'fundamental assumption', 'conjectures' and 'working hypothesis' or 'faith.' The basic point, as suggested above, is that every discipline develops out of certain fundamental presuppositions. The more basic of such assumptions link up the component parts of a discipline or body of ideas. They thus *colligate* ideas. All significant thinkers and systems of thought are ruled by such 'great conceptions' or 'colligating ideas'.[68]

The interesting point here is what Jones attributes to these colligating hypotheses. Firstly, they are not limited to the great philosophical and scientific systems. Jones remarks that:

> we err greatly in confining our notions of hypotheses to those great scientific occasions in which a new science is born ... as when a Copernicus, Newton or Darwin makes his revolutionary contributions ... The same miracle happens whenever the puzzled mind extricates itself from a difficulty, masters a problem and cries, 'I see'.[69]

Thus every judgement we make relates to some form of colligating hypothesis. Secondly, there is a distinction drawn, as previously indicated, between more relative and absolute hypotheses. Jones contends that all reasoning rests upon hypotheses. An absolute hypothesis is usually more than a guess. It is suggested to the intellect by the world whose intelligibility is sought, and is held 'only so long as the realm of reality seems to support it'.[70] Jones maintained, many years later, that 'except for hypotheses, facts and events would seem to us to stand in no relation of any kind to one another.'[71] Hypotheses are never ultimately proven, but always in the process of being proved. A hypothesis, while lacking certainty, 'commends itself to our notice by the range and the clearness of the light it seems to throw on the manifold data of our experience'.[72] Some hypotheses so thoroughly permeate our rational life that their denial would entail the destruction of experience.[73] Hypotheses of this character attain the status of absolute postulates.[74]

The distinction which Jones makes between relative and absolute hypotheses is remarkably similar to the distinction which Collingwood was later to make between relative and absolute presuppositions. Collingwood argued that every statement is in fact an answer to a question, and every question involves a presupposition which is either relative or absolute. A relative presupposition is one which is both an answer relative to one question, and a presupposition relative to another. Relative presuppositions are propositions which can be verified. Absolute presuppositions, however, are never answers to prior questions; they are always presupposed by the question to which they are related. They are not propositions about which you seek truth or falsity, rather you ask if they are being absolutely presupposed. Constellations of such absolute presuppositions provide the manifold to which the whole thought pattern of an age is related.[75] There is no direct evidence that Collingwood's views are derived from, or modifications of, those of Jones. Collingwood was never one for expressing his intellectual debts, but he does on one occasion refer to Jones as 'one of our most eminent philosophers'.[76]

Jones does elaborate upon the distinction between absolute and relative postulates, although the upshot of the arguments is not always clear. At one point he argues that the philosopher's function is both to articulate and explicate such absolute hypotheses or colligating ideas. They should, says Jones, 'bring the ultimate colligating principles of thought into clear consciousness'.[77] This too was the historical role which Collingwood envisaged for the metaphysician.[78] Jones is, though, at odds with Collingwood in believing that some of the absolute postulates or colligating principles may be empty or false.[79]

For example, Jones felt that the Hobbesian/Humean colligating hypothesis of individualism needed analysis and ultimately rejection.[80] Since absolute hypotheses are viewed as ontologically true, it is important that they be subject to such critical scrutiny.[81] Jones speaks, for example, of the rapid revolutionary changes in science, via Newton and Einstein, coming about through 'the substitution of one hypothesis for another'.[82] Colligating principles or hypotheses are, he says, equivalent to critical 'conjectures' or 'guesses'. He therefore states that a 'hypothesis is a conjecture on trial. Its existence is threatened by every relevant fact which it cannot explain . . . It is liable at every moment to be supplanted by some simpler, more fundamental or far-reaching hypothesis.'[83]

In sum, colligating principles or hypotheses are conjectures, intellectual constructs which allow us to make the world intelligible. These can be refuted by new constructs or guesses.[84] Relative hypotheses are distinct from colligating hypotheses or absolute postulates to which we can feel unconditionally and ontologically committed.

Jones contends that much of the time we do not bring these colligating assumptions into explicit consciousness. Yet they still underpin our activity in the world. It is also the fact that we live in a common society and that we are 'heirs of the same social inheritance, tradition, or other, fashioned by the same creeds and habits'.[85] It is in virtue of these habits that we 'understand one another'. Jones remarks in this argument that all our judgements are rooted in our memory. Where there is no memory there is no judgement. Memory and judgement are in the end rooted in coherence. Thus it is the colligating ideas which, through our memory, form the substance to our judgements. Tradition can be intepreted as a body of colligating assumptions. When we speak of intuition, it is really intimations of these colligating ideas which are at the core. Tradition is thus implicitly rational. We only have to articulate the idea, bring it into explicit consciousness, to know its rational nature. This particular idea would be one way of distancing Jones from conservative thought. Many conservative writers try to distinguish practical habits and reason from theoretic reasoning. Jones's intuitions, however, when recalled, fall directly into the domain of theoretic metaphysical reason, which would be anathema to many conservative philosophers. Such rationality will be tested in the end by the standard of coherence. We can also begin to see here the glimmerings of the metaphysical roots to Jones's social and political philosophy.

EPISTEMOLOGY AND ONTOLOGY

Jones became involved in a number of metaphysical debates during his academic career. One of these was concerned with the status of epistemology. He wrote two tightly argued articles on this issue, published in *Mind*, 1893. Jones appeared to take some delight in controversy, in this case mainly with the ideas of Andrew Seth, later Andrew Seth Pringle Pattison.[86] This particular debate is also connected to another concerning the nature of individuality, which, for the sake of clarity will be kept distinct.

Seth's basic contention is that Idealism, specifically Hegelian Absolute Idealism, is guilty of confusing thought with reality. The abstract character of our thought takes on flesh and blood. Logical categories thicken into real existences. Logic and thought leap uninvited into nature. The world becomes thought. Human experience is then seen as a process whereby the Absolute thinks through finite self-consciousness. Hegelians thus mistake their own consciousness with reality. Logic becomes ontology and epistemology is swamped in a sea of metaphysics. It is this last point which Jones focused on.

Seth was not alone in this accusation. It was also echoed in the work of Lotze. One of Lotze's main arguments against Idealism was that thought was not an ontological principle and that it did not constitute reality; rather thought represents or mirrors the world of being. His case against Idealism, however, is far broader than that of Seth and the Personal Idealists.

For Jones, the source for Seth's and Lotze's arguments lay in the sceptical use of Kantian philosophy. Kant, in fact, teetered between the ontological and epistemological claims. In Kant 'things-in-themselves were gradually deprived of all significance . . . He left nothing to distinguish his theory of knowledge from a theory of reality except the disguise of the word "phenomena".'[87] Kant generated the dispute on the status of epistemology, but he never really settled on any position. Francis Bradley is also brought into this argument by Jones.[88] Bradley had spoken critically of the Hegelian system as an unearthly ballet of bloodless categories, thought being appearance and separate from reality. For Jones, the same kind of point is being made by Bradley, Seth and Lotze, although the direction and nature of Bradley's argument was different. Interestingly though, at points in his study of Lotze, Jones quotes Bradley to elucidate Lotze's arguments.[89] There is a much stronger connection here between Lotze's philosophy and Bradley's than has often been realized.

Jones suggests that the critics have misunderstood the claims of Idealism. They contend that Hegelian Idealism views the universe as a system of cohering worlds of ideas which are said to be at once unstable and insubstantial. The floating worlds, the critics contended, need to be anchored at both ends to reality; at the one end to individuals whose thoughts they are, and at the other end to the external facts which thoughts represent. Philosophy, for the critics, must therefore be divided into three spheres: psychology which deals with the thinking person; ontology, which is concerned with the nature of things, which includes thinkers; and, epistemology which focuses upon the relation between thoughts and reality.[90]

When Jones was writing, epistemology was a relatively new branch of philosophy although the basic idea itself goes back to Locke, Descartes and Kant. Its purpose was to distinguish certain types of questions from those legitimately associated with psychology.[91] The questions that epistemology sought to answer were, of course, always part of the philosophical enterprise. However, they had been inadequately answered due to insufficient clarity in their demarcation from quite different questions in psychology. By 1891, the term epistemology was becoming accepted in Britain as the least cumbrous name for that type of enquiry, which Andrew Seth described in his Balfour Lectures on Realism as 'an investigation of knowledge as knowledge, or, in other words, of the relation of knowledge to reality, of the validity of knowledge'.[92]

It was this new preoccupation with epistemology that constituted a threat to Idealism. The critics, including the Personal Idealists and Lotze, thought they detected a fatal flaw in Hegelianism. The unpardonable defect was simply the fact that Absolute Idealists had no epistemology, or still continued to confuse it with metaphysics and ontology. Lotze's attack on Idealism in these terms had, in Jones's view, 'stemmed the tide of Idealism and given pause to that ambitious Monism which seemed to have confused the old boundaries of thought'.[93]

Jones's reply to these criticisms is extremely forceful. He launches an all-out assault on the discipline of epistemology. The gist of the argument is that Seth, and other like-minded epistemologists, give no adequate account of the connection between thought and the world. Furthermore, if it can be established that there is no world of thought to be investigated, *vis-à-vis* reality (epistemology), then there is therefore no need for epistemology. It is a non-subject. If there is anything residually there, it is better studied by empirical psychologists.[94]

For Seth, the psychological datum of the existence of an idea is distinct from its meaning. The former is fleeting and transient and is dealt with by psychology; the latter is objective and universal and dealt with by epistemology. Therefore there can be no objective science of subjective meanings. Epistemology must deal with objective universal meaning. For Jones there are problems here. In omitting any objective reference for the psychologist 'the whole task of [the] science would be to mark the time of psychical occurrences, none of them having any character'.[95] In this case the epistemology would swamp the psychology. Yet would epistemology have any objective reference? As Jones claims, if Seth associates ideas with individual consciousness, then they become transient pyschical phenomena. Psychology is here in danger of swamping epistemology.

More fundamentally, for Jones, the edifice of epistemology rests upon a contradiction. Epistemology must not assume any reality in the first place, since this is its problem. Ideas, as psychical occurrences, are also ignored since that is the domain of pyschology. Epistemology is therefore *not* connected to reality, either as meaning or as a psychical occurrence. In other words it treats its starting-point 'as both real and unreal'.[96]

Epistemologists argue that we must deal with the nature of knowledge before any philosophical enquiry. We need to explain the transition from conscious states *to* reality. We therefore start from subjective states of consciousness. The idea is distinct from the actual event. But, as Jones asks, where does epistemology gain a foothold in this analysis – reality or the knowledge of reality? The actual psychical event is not knowledge of it, and the knowledge of it cannot be the real psychical event. As Jones notes: 'The one is the object known, the other is the knowledge of the object.'[97] Which of these is the datum of epistemology? He continues: 'Is it in the reality, or is it in the knowledge of it? Is it the subjective state as a psychical occurrence, or is it the reflective knowledge of the psychical state?'[98] Where does the epistemologist reside, in the 'knowledge' or 'reality'? For Jones epistemology is caught in an insoluble dilemma:

> It cannot deal with the subjective state as real, for, *ex hypothesi*, it has first to pronounce on the possibility of knowing any reality . . . And, on the other hand, it cannot deal with the subjective state as mere idea; because if it begins with an idea it must end with ideas. There would be no outlet from the sphere of ideas, for surely it is preposterous to seek such an outlet by having more ideas.[99]

If epistemology starts with the ideal sphere and tries to get to reality it has an impossible task. It must remain shut up in an ideal sphere. If, on the other hand, it starts with the facts of psychical occurrences, then it does not tell us about knowledge or the relation of knowledge to reality. Thus epistemology, in Seth, rests on an insoluble contradiction. 'It both must assume and must not assume reality.'[100] Jones concludes from this that epistemology is a total non-subject.

For Jones, Idealism had no epistemology, in fact it denied the very possibility of having one. The charge that Idealism had been unable to account for the link between thought and reality, because it made the latter the product of the former, was, in Jones's view, fundamentally misconceived. No Idealist, Jones argued, would want to deny the distinction between thought and reality, nor maintain that knowledge of a fact or event *is* that fact or event. Such an idea 'is inconsistent with the possibility of knowledge that it should *be* the reality it represents'.[101] Indeed, reality itself is indifferent to our activities, by which Jones meant that it would be preposterous to claim that the earth only began to orbit the sun as a result of modern astronomical theory. He is most emphatic on this point.[102]

Jones denies that Absolute Idealism entails the assertion that experience is a world, or worlds, of cohering ideas. It is the critics themselves who want to maintain the existence of a world of ideas which mediates between psychic states (which act as indubitable data) and the reality we seek to know. The problem of epistemology, as Jones sees it, is to explain how we make the transition from our conscious states to the reality of which we are conscious. In viewing the problem from this subjectivist standpoint the critics themselves have been unable to transcend the dichotomy between thought and reality.[103]

In Jones's view, Idealism arose from the consciousness of this insurmountable gulf which frustrates the 'movement from within outwards, or from ideality to reality'.[104] All reasoning, as we saw earlier in this chapter, rests upon hypotheses. To postulate the knowing subject as the starting-point of philosophy has proved, Jones contends, to be an untenable hypothesis. Kant, as we mentioned in the section on Metaphysics, wondered whether the world could be made more intelligible if we dispensed with the view that 'thought must correspond to things' and assumed instead 'that things must correspond to thought'.[105] However, in failing to resolve the dualisms between thought and reality, and the noumenal and phenomenal, Kant does not succeed in showing how thought can ultimately reconcile itself with things. To compound the problem, things are unable to reveal their central character in thought.[106]

It was Hegel who, for Jones, completed the Copernican revolution, and instead of reconciling differences as Kant had attempted to do, began with the hypothesis of unity and sought to explain its differentiations. For Hegel, reality is an all-inclusive unity whose manifestations reveal themselves in the knowing subject and the known object. The starting-point of his philosophy is the conception of reality as Absolute self-consciousness, or Spirit, which finds expression and knows itself in all things. Reality, or Spirit, is an active principle in all thinking and being. Ideas do not interpose between the subject and the object, they are themselves reality expressing itself. Thus it is a mistake, Jones contends, to understand Hegel as leaping from thought to reality. To attribute such a dualism is to deny Hegel's starting-point, and to repudiate the contribution he made to resolving the intractable problem of escaping the world of thought by means of thought. For Hegel, ideas do not stand between the thinking intelligence and the world of reality; the ideas are reality expressing itself in the thinker, who in that expression makes it his own. Essentially, then, critics of Absolute Idealism, like Lotze and the Personal Idealists, take a retrograde step in beginning not with unity, but with the opposition between thought and reality, and once again entangle themselves in escaping from thought into reality by means of thought.

Jones's solution to the above problems, therefore, is not to make a total separation between the realms of ideality and reality, but rather to see these as aspects of a deeper ontological unity. There is no problem as such of reconciling thought and reality, since Jones contends we should refuse to begin from their opposition. What remains for philosophy is the problem of a single principle which appears in the forms of knower and objects known. Philosophical discussion is premised on an ontological unity. There is no 'world of ideas' imposed on or related to reality. Rather the universe is the activity of mind, its diverse workings and epiphanies. Reality is imbued with the rich differences of spirit.

INDIVIDUALITY AND THE ABSOLUTE

One closely related metaphysical debate to that on epistemology and ontology forms a central theme in the critique of Absolute Idealism. This debate centred on the idea of individuality in Hegelian thought. Bradley and Bosanquet used the concept 'individual' in a logical sense. It implied a comprehensive unity, completeness, wholeness and coherence. If it was applied to the person, then individuality again, logically, implied non-contradiction. This was of course, *prima facie*, at odds with the more ordinary language usage of the term individual, which implied some degree of uniqueness and idiosyncracy.

One important implication of this argument was that individual persons, because of their limitations and finiteness, could not really be classed properly as individuals. Individuality, as Bosanquet was fond of remarking, was not empty eccentricity. However, certain institutions and practices, because of their comprehensiveness, could be described as more individual than others. For Bosanquet, finite self 'qua finite, is the centre of an awakening of a determinate world which is its presupposition'.[107] The Absolute is the high watermark of an effort 'in which our minds actually consist and have their being'.[108] It follows that the most complete self-comprehensive individual is the Absolute. As Bradley put it: 'There is nothing which, to speak properly, is individual or perfect, except only the Absolute.'[109]

The central theme of the above arguments is that the Absolute is the most complete individual. This monistic trend leads to the claims that the distinctness of individuals, the finite difference, is a result of imperfect individuality. Selves exist as parts of an objective order, bare points of existence which only obtain value in so far as they manifest features of the Absolute. What is desirable is that the individual progressively blends and merges with the complete individual. The finite self is limited, powerless, inadequate and contradictory. Thus Bosanquet remarked: 'All the great contents of the developed human self – truth, beauty, religion and social morality – are all of them but modes of expression of the Ideal self.'[110]

One upshot of this Absolutist argument was a vociferous body of criticism stemming from the Personal Idealists. The debate, which rumbled along for twenty years, spilled over into a meeting of the Aristotelian Society in London in 1918 devoted to the question: 'Do Finite Individuals Possess a Substantive or an Adjectival Mode of Being?' The papers were later published in a volume from the Aristotelian Society entitled *Life and Finite Individuality*.

The initial starting-point for the debate was Andrew Seth's 1887 Balfour Lectures.[111] However, it was the publication of Bosanquet's and Seth's *Gifford Lectures*, which really sparked the debate into flame.[112] The basic gist of the Personal Idealist criticism was that individual persons were being denied significance and moral worth. Finite individuality was seen of secondary signifance to the Absolute. As Seth (Pringle Pattison) argued: 'The universal is no less an abstraction, if it is taken as real, or as possessing substantive existence, independently of the individuals whose living tissue it is.'[113] Individuals in Bradley, Bosanquet and Hegel were becoming 'a negligible feature of the world'.[114] A similar argument is repeated, with slight variations, in the writings of C. C. J. Webb, Hastings Rashdall, Henry Sturt and even McTaggart.[115] McTaggart's *Studies in Hegelian Cosmology* (1901), however, mainly directs the fire at Hegel as the source of the problem.

Jones's response to this debate is interesting, but nevertheless characteristic, in so far as he does not come down on either side. On the one hand he appears to be in substantial agreement with the claims of Seth and others. He comments on a number of occasions on the solitariness and uniqueness of the human self.[116] For example, he stated that 'the self-conscious subject is the one reality which in possessing its world of objects holds itself apart from it. It is the supreme instance of a universal which is immanent in all its differences.' [117] However, as argued in the previous section, it is clear that Jones was fundamentally at odds with philosophers like Seth. In fact, the root of Seth's critique of the Absolutist notion of the individual is integrally related to his separation of epistemology from ontology. It was the ontological dominance of the Absolute, and the crushing together of thought and the world, that led to the absorption of the individual. Jones could not accept this argument. He had previously addressed a similar question in relation to Martineau, criticizing him for contending that Absolute Idealism is morally inimical to the individual, because it loses the person by merging the individual into the unity of God and nature. Jones, invoking his ideas of the role of hypotheses in thought, argues that Martineau's charge that Absolute Idealism is pantheistic and involves a denial of human free will is based upon a faulty hypothesis. Martineau assumes that to suggest that there is a binding connection between persons and the broader world of reality is to deprive the individual of his, or her, freedom. On the contrary, Jones contends, the relation between the self and not-self needs to be interpreted differently. The not-self only finds meaning in the self, which unites and then identifies the not-self with itself. Spirit incorporates differences without annulling them.

The important point to grasp in this argument is the manner in which Jones established the importance of the self. This can in fact be observed more clearly through his critique of the Absolutism of Bosanquet and Bradley.[118]

In a nutshell, Jones's argument against Bradley's and Bosanquet's Absolute was that, like Spinoza's, it was too static, monistic and consequently ignored essential differences. As he commented, specifically in relation to the Bradleian Absolute: 'A unity which in transcending the differences obliterates them is not their unity. A unity which becomes itself unknowable, or lies beyond the reach of predication, holds no differences together, but sinks itself into an empty affirmation of the all-in-allness of everything.'[119] This entails that the finite 'is either lost, or transmuted beyond recognition'.[120] The argument is thus that there is neither simple unity nor difference. The Absolute is a unity in difference. If too much stress is laid on the unity and the infinity then all claims to finitude are relegated. It is this trend in Absolute Idealism which Seth used to refer to as 'unity *ad nauseam*'.

Furthermore, bringing into play his usual critique of dualism, Jones complains that Bosanquet has artificially separated the finite from the infinite. In Bosanquet the infinite becomes an ever-receding ideal, an infinite source of human despair. Individuals must always pass beyond themselves for infinitude. This argument, for Jones, is premised upon a false dualism and misses the point that the individual *is* an infinite process. The self is a growing and becoming process; the Absolute expresses itself in individuals and their strivings. The individual is neither exclusively finite nor infinite. Individual persons, for Jones, 'are infinite by nature and therefore all-comprehensive, although hindered and limited by littleness of their medium'.[121] Bosanquet and Bradley could not assign individuality to man and the Absolute, since they were caught in a false dualism. Their Absolute must, of necessity, extinguish individual selves or persons. 'But', as Jones argues, 'on the view I have tried to set forth, the indwelling of God *constitutes* the personality; for . . . what is done to his world by the individual is done by the use of his powers . . . By his immanence in man God empowers man. The constituent elements break into consciousness in him, and are focused in his self-consciousness.'[122]

For Jones the Absolute needs persons *qua* persons. It is a comprehensive whole enriched by such differences. Such differences express the unity in difference character of the Absolute.[123] There were more debates at work here which we will touch upon in the next chapter. For example, Bradley denied that the Absolute was God and secondly, that the Absolute possessed personality. Jones fundamentally disagreed with both these claims.

In sum, Jones may be described as an Absolute Idealist. His primary assumption was the monistic ontological unity of reality. This was not a simple monism, which he saw in thinkers like Bradley and Bosanquet. Nothing short of the Absolute was acceptable: however, such an Absolute could only be appreciated through its complex differentiations. This appreciation of the differentiations was essential for grasping the nature of the Absolute. The Absolute was an 'identity of differences'. This point also led him to attack the Personal Idealists from the opposite end of the argument, namely, that they focused too intently on the differentiations at the expense of the the unity. For Jones, all forms of dualism and fragmentation had to be overcome. For example, there was no ultimate separation between thought and reality. They were regarded as differentiations of the Absolute. There was no world of objects separate from thought. This did not mean that either thought was reduced to objects or objects were reduced to thought. Both were differentiations of a deeper unity. Self-consciousness was the truth of all things and human reason was also the measure of all things. This point led Jones to oppose the discipline of epistemology. His fundamental objection to epistemology was that epistemology assumed at the outset the separation of ideas and reality. It is the premise to the discipline. In so far as it starts with this assumption it remains fatally flawed. For Jones, the psychical event of an idea is not knowledge of the idea, and the knowledge of an event is not the psychical event itself. Epistemology both must assume and must not assume reality. Despite its appearance, philosophy is not for Jones an abstruse discipline. Philosophy is ordinary human self-consciousness and experience become reflective. Metaphysics is therefore not viewed as an esoteric discipline. For Jones, we are all metaphysicians, whether we know it or not. Metaphysical assumptions (or colligating hypotheses) are part of the very texture of our lives. Every judgement embodied, in the final analysis, metaphysical assumptions.

Having now examined the basic constituents of Jones's Idealistic philosophy and metaphysics, which underpin the other dimensions of his thought, we will turn in the next chapter to a review of Jones's conception of religion. This can be dealt with briefly because the arguments will relate closely to much that has already been discussed.

CHAPTER THREE

A FAITH THAT ENQUIRES

To acquire a more complete picture of Jones's philosophy it is necessary to have some acquaintance with his views on poetry and religion. This discussion can be relatively brief, especially on poetry, given the strong links of both these topics to his general metaphysics. Both were of importance to Jones, although he interpreted them in a philosophical manner.

Like Caird, Jones had a strong feeling for poetry. He was an enthusiastic admirer of Welsh hymns, but this artistic bent did not stretch in any systematic way to the fine arts or painting. Poetry was his first love. His earliest book was on Browning's poetry and throughout his working life he contributed articles and commentaries on various (usually Victorian) poets. For Jones the aesthetic realm is not the highest realm, but it is necessary and systematically related to other elements. As for Hegel, 'Art, religion and philosophy fail or flourish together.'[1] Art, like religion, deals with the same material but in a different manner. For Jones, 'neither can be subordinated to the use of the other.'[2] The overt separation, though, between these realms should be resisted. They are linked within the Absolute. The same material is present in all. Any separation 'rests upon the [same] psychology which broke up the mind into separate faculties'.[3]

The relation between poetry and philosophy is problematic. On the one hand Jones argues that each discipline illumines the other. Poetry, however, usually comes before philosophy, temporally and systematically. Poets anticipate the ruling conceptions (colligating hypotheses) of an age before philosophy has arisen to reflect on them. As Jones put it: 'The poets are the best exponents of their time; they give utterance, as no others can, to the dim thoughts that blindly move . . . the public heart.'[4] For Jones, Browning, like Carlyle, exhibited this prophetic quality. By understanding such figures, Jones says, 'we shall, to some degree, understand ourselves'.[5] In fact the poets of Britain are, for Jones, more informative, of a higher calibre and more uplifting than many moral philosophers.

Yet despite maintaining the autonomy of poetry, Jones does contend that philosophy deals more adequately and thoroughly with the colligating ideas. Poetry *shows* us what philosophy *analyses*. Philosophy, for Jones, is art made conscious of itself. In one essay Jones put this point bluntly: 'poetry reaches the results of philosophy by short cuts and without the endless argumentation.'[6] However much Jones talks of the autonomy of art and its necessary place in the realization of Spirit, this argument still appears to lower the significance of art and poetry to a search for something which can only become fully articulated and understood in philosophy.

A similar difficulty haunts Jones's writings on religion, although, unlike poetry, it is much more difficult to disentangle his philosophy from his religious sentiments. Jones's particular emphases are part of a broader movement of liberal theological thinking in the nineteenth century. The two main elements of this liberal theology which preoccupied Jones were Hegelian immanentism and neo-Kantianism. In the case of theologians like Albrecht Ritschl, the neo-Kantianism was premised on a rejection of Idealist metaphysics. T. H. Green had most influence (even if his legacy is ambiguous) in the area of Hegelian immanentism in Britain, particularly as a backgound to works on liberal theology like the *Lux Mundi* essays, published in 1889.[7] Jones's religious views are, however, more directly influenced by Hegel, mediated through the work of John and Edward Caird.

One obvious point concerning Jones's reading of religion is that it is immensely optimistic. Even at the end of his life, after the carnage of the First World War, with one son killed in combat, and himself suffering intense pain from cancer, writing his *Gifford Lectures*, he could still state: 'The truth I would impress is *the friendliness* of the world to man, the co-operative and final identity of the purposes of nature and spirit.'[8] It is too easy to dismiss this as cosy, *ersatz* optimism. Much of the speculation of his final lectures is taken up with the dual themes that religion can be investigated by reason and, most importantly, reason has answers to the problems of pain, evil and suffering. Some of these speculations are intense reflections on his own suffering and the attempt to make sense of it.

Jones's attitude to the Christian Churches of his time was both unorthodox and critical.[9] He favoured Protestantism over Catholicism, but felt that the element of private judgement and the use of reason within Protestantism had been swamped by official dogmatism.[10] At times, he even appears optimistic about the future educative role of churches, commenting that the ordinary church 'instead of being a place where the deliverances of ancient religious authorities are expounded, . . . would be a place where the validity of spiritual convictions are discussed on their merits'.[11] In his own day Jones came up continually against the rigidity and official dogmatism of the Nonconformist and Established churches. He suffered from innuendo and outright theological condemnation from many of his fellow churchmen. For Jones, dogmatic religion of any kind, premising itself upon authority or mystical intuition, was a halfway house to agnosticism and the negation of reason. Deism, for example, he described as 'negation arrested in mid-career'.[12]

For Jones, there were certain crucial points to establish on the question of religion. Religion emphatically did not mean the death of thought or reason. As he stated: 'The religion that can maintain itself only by limiting the uses of reason, and the reason that can make good its rights only by extinguishing religion, may both be the products of abstract thought, falsified by clinging to antiquated presuppositions.'[13] Religionists should encourage exactly the same spirit of critical thought as is seen in other humanistic and scientific disciplines. Doubts cannot be sidestepped through faith, intuition or authority. Making God unknowable by reason is foolhardy. As Jones remarked: 'I doubt whether there can be anything unintelligible except that which is irrational, and I doubt if anything real is irrational except as misunderstood.'[14]

Jones's judgement went totally against the prevailing theology and philosophy of the back-to-Kant movement. One of the implications of the Kantian position on knowledge in general was to distinguish the spheres of theoretic from practical reason. The distinction, which has ancient roots, in Kant's hands became an immensely influential and pregnant idea. Theoretic pure reason was demonstrable. The categories of thought, intuition, space, time, quality, quantity and causality, referred to the interrelation between finite things and objects. Such categories were valid for the natural physical sciences; however, for Kant they are not appropriate in the sphere of religion. Humans are finite and their cognition and reason are linked to their finiteness. Infinite categories, like God, morality and freedom, cannot be demonstrated by finite terms. This argument effectively undermined natural theology.

At this point in the argument theologians like Schleiermacher appealed to feeling and other theologians to authority. However, for Kant, the only way out of this impasse was the postulate of practical reason, primarily in morality. Humans, unlike animals, can have knowledge of themselves and can give themselves an unconditional imperative of duty. In performing self-legislated unconditional duty we raise ourselves above our finiteness. Yet we could never *know* anything above the finite. Religion however is not destroyed by Kant; rather it appears as an appendix to the moral philosophy and practical reason. We can *know* nothing of God, miracles or revelation. However, we can act 'as if' God exists and is linked to moral conduct. If knowledge is removed, for Kant, it makes room for faith. Religion is, in essence, the recognition of moral duties as divine commands.

Lotze was deeply affected by Kant's arguments on religion, and while at Göttingen, from the mid-1860s, had a profound influence on the theologian Albrecht Ritschl, who subsequently transferred his allegiance from Hegelianism (Ritschl had been a disciple of the Hegelian theologian F. C. Baur) to Kantianism. Kant's distinction between the theoretic and practical/value became central to Ritschl's whole theology and to that of his disciples, for example, Wilhelm Herrman, Theodor Haering, Adolf von Harnack and Walter Rauschenbusch. Ritschl felt that Christianity had to be purified of its metaphysical Hegelian accretions. His theology was probably the most dominant force in Germany, and later the USA, till after the First World War. In Britain the impact of Ritschl was much less pronounced.

For Ritschl, theology cannot articulate the infinite or divine. Religion, as in Kant, is a support to the ethical personality. Ontology thus gives way to morality. Christianity cannot make rational ontological statements, but only comment upon practical/value judgements. Christianity liberates humans, via practical reason, from their passions and from the natural world, through the assertion of moral personality. We judge Christ *by* his ethical personality as historically revealed. Christianity is thus tied into ethics and value judgement.

The upshot of the Ritschlian theology, for Jones, was another series of false dualisms. Religion was no longer a subject for reasoned discussion.[15] Despite not being mystical it was none the less still in the realm of emotion and value. Reason and emotion, reason and value, fact and value, such dualities were all implicit in the Kant/Lotze/Ritschl theology. Although it was an attempt to salvage religion from the encroachment of science, such theology was still flawed. For Jones, religion should distance itself from the espousal of emotion or feeling. For Jones, Kantian theologians, like Ritschl, were fundamentally wrong to separate the heart/values and the head. Emotional religion is just a warm afterglow. It should matter to us whether religion is true or false. Emotion is an intimation of what reason establishes as fact. Faith is not distinct from reason, as Kant had suggested. All intellectual systems, even the most complex and abstruse, rest upon assumptions which cannot be proved, and are accepted by faith. Absolute postulates which are taken in faith are the roots of all intellectual endeavour.

The point we should be affirming is not a dualism between faith and reason, but how rationally coherent is the religious form of life? Jones is careful here not to identify religious knowledge with religion itself. Knowledge may be a 'condition of spiritual experience', but religion is a way of life.[16] Religion is 'thus not only practical in its essence, it *is* practice; it is experience, it is life'.[17] Similarly nature is not distinct from religion as a subject for scientific study. Nature is rather 'the other aspect of spirit'.[18]

Jones also places religion into a historical framework. It has evolved from the Greeks. Christianity is part of a historical pattern which ultimately culminates in the expression of religion in the secular circumstances of daily life. This is the summation of Jones's theological immanentism.[19] At that point, says Jones, 'Mankind will be engaged in the spiritual business even when it is handling the so-called secular concerns of life.'[20]

The overall perspective that Jones develops here is the unity of the divine and human. The story of Jones being asked whether he denied the divinity of Jesus and responding that 'he was not prepared to deny the divinity of any man' catches the whole sense of his position. God is incarnated in the mind of humans. If this were put in logical format it would be that 'the universal is in the individual'.[21] It is the perfected human character which reveals the divine. The individual is 'a spiritual being in a physical frame'.[22] As Jones stated:

> Surely the essential message of Christianity is that perfect humanity is the most perfect revelation of God; or that the humanity of God and the divinity of man are two aspects of the same truth. The Idealist . . . also accepts this doctrine but he employs it to correct the original abstraction which sets man and God in relations so exclusive that we can only proceed from one to the other, as if they were originally *separate*.[24]

In this reading of religion, humans find God in the world that they know intimately on a day-by-day basis. There is no separation of religious and secular concerns, value and science. The kingdom of God is manifest upon the earth. Spirit exists in the institutions and practices of everyday lives. Thus Jones comments: 'His "Kingdom will come" *pari passu* with the development of more secular forces.'[24]

Underpinning the above account of the divine and human is Jones's attitude to the doctrines of immanence and transcendence. A totally immanent God, spiritualizing nature, social and moral life, runs the extreme danger of pantheism.[25] In such pantheism finite existence and personality also become shadowy and problematic – an implication that Jones saw in the work of Bradley and Bosanquet. Alternatively, a totally transcendent God appears to separate God from the real world of humanity and nature and make him intrinsically unknowable. God becomes, as in the theology of Karl Barth, infinitely other. Neither tendency appealed to Jones. Hardly surprisingly it is the dualism which he wishes to overcome. 'Divine Immanence', says Jones, 'implies Divine Transcendence, that God who manifests *Himself* in the Universe, not only fills it with His presence, but in filling it excels it.'[26]

The above contention throws light on his views on a number of theological issues. The incarnation is identified with the doctrine of divine immanence. God is existent within self-conscious agency. A divine life is a moral life, one which is lived in the service of a broader purpose. As Jones argued: 'The good life is one continuous dedication to great causes.'[27] Conversion is a process whereby the individual 'reinterprets every incident in his past life, and revalues every fact and purpose, setting them in quite a new order of preference'.[28] Conversion in fact relates to the idea of renewal through change in the colligating idea. Further, for Jones there is no overt need for miracles. Miracles are irrational and superstitious. As he argued: 'The moment religious faith is made to rest upon the spiritual and superhuman, the moment that things divine do not express themselves in the ordinary world and ordinary life of man, – religion becomes indistinguishable from superstition.'[29] Faith is not a matter of unreasoned belief. It is the precise opposite.

The above argument also places Jones clearly on the issue of Christology. The Father/Son relation or Christ/Man relation is another false dualism. Jones maintained that the theory of Christ which totally separates him from humankind is mistaken. For Jones, 'the unity of the divine and human nature . . . is the essence of the Idealism of

Jesus.'[30] The humanity of Christ and the divinity of man are obscured in Christological controversies. Jesus is ideal man. He is perfected humanity. In the early days of the Christian church theologians could not accept the true sense of the sonship of God. For Jones their presuppositions prevented them from entertaining the idea.[31] Judaism, for example, was trapped in a transcendent conception of God and had no place for such ideas. However, with the growth and maturation of ideas, the notion of divine humanity was slowly gaining ground.

Redemption and atonement also become transformed in this argument. Redemption is the process of revaluing one's life. Edward Caird's favourite phrase, which Jones took over, 'dying to live', implied that each individual dies to 'the temporal interests and narrow ends of the exclusive self and lives an ever-expanding life in the life of others'.[32] The individual does not need to atone or be punished. In fact, Jones claims that such eschatological speculations are utterly redundant, if not abhorrent.[33]

One of the most difficult and intractable issues, which derives from Jones's conception of religion, focuses on the problem of sin, evil and error. The problem is an old theological issue, but it is particularly pressing in the case of Idealism. The debate centres on the question: is the rational character of the world and the perfection of God undermined by evil, pain and error? If Idealism does offer an all-inclusive explanation of reality, how does it account for these? This was a pressing theoretical and personal issue for Jones. Not only did he suffer great personal pain and loss during his life, but he also interpreted evil in a wider social context, which made the arguments more problematic. For example, he commented:

> It is difficult to become familiar with the slums of our big cities without being convinced that there are many thousands who neither in themselves nor in their environment give evidence of any such divine operation . . . Children born into the world bringing with them inherited diseases or physical and mental feebleness: . . . they are brought up in a social environment in which moral judgement is hopelessly perverted.[34]

Such comments as these are linked to the wider issues of citizenship and poverty which are discussed in chapter five; at the moment the theological issues are our primary interest.

Jones, despite a strong emphasis on spiritual process and change, believed strongly in the notion of a more static divine perfection. Such perfection appeared *prima facie* to be undermined by the mass of evidence of evil and pain in the world. Jones's response to this issue is, however, far from consistent. The primary claim, which appears in a number of writings, is that evil is the *condition* of goodness.[35] Evil is seen as a necessary precondition or means to the achievement of goodness. In fact, for Jones, evil is the *only* means which calls into existence the divine good in human beings. One of the implications of this conviction is that evil is not a positive force or reality, but rather a resistance or negative obstacle to goodness. 'Evil', says Jones, 'is the resistance which makes progress possible, the negative which gives meaning to the positive'; and again, evil '*is* resistance; it *is* a negative'.[36] This argument contends, therefore, that evil, as such, has no reality.

However, in his *Gifford Lectures* he does admit that 'even if evil . . . is overcome, abolished, or turned into its opposite in a way which Good is not, it does not follow that it lacks reality in any sense or degree'.[37] The reality of evil is part of a more inclusive reality in the Absolute. In this argument to hold good and evil apart, one as reality and the other as unreality, is to fall into a dualism. They are premised on a deeper sundered unity. Without the negative there would be no positive. Without, in fact, the existence of the negative there could be no free choice. For Jones, 'That which is ultimate . . . operates in such a way as to permit the possibility of moral choice and therefore moral evil.'[38]

Jones adds to the above arguments a number of observations on evil. For example, he asserts that good and evil are not absolute standards but relative estimates of actions. We may believe an act is evil, but there are limitations on any such judgement. Can one ever have full enough knowledge actually to know something is completely evil? For Jones:

> neither evil nor good exist in this sense. They are characteristics of what is real but not themselves separate realities. In short, moral good and moral evil are ways in which the will operates, characteristics of man's aims and efforts. They are evaluations, or estimates of facts, true or false; and they exist only when and as long as, the process of willing goes on.[39]

Jones uses this argument to meet the problematic example, cited earlier, of the slum-dweller. He contends that we cannot have full knowledge of what has given rise to the slum and those who live in them. We also cannot estimate what good might arise from such a situation. Jones draws a parallel here with the scientist, to try to reveal his point. The scientist 'knows that to fail to trace the law is one thing and to deny its existence is another'; he goes on, 'the religious man can justly make a strictly analogous claim in the case of the slum child'.[40] We do not know enough of the inner workings and complexities of such a situation to enable us to pronounce that something is definitely good or evil.

Jones also adds to the above points the observation that right behaviour brings physical well-being. Pain, suffering and the loss of well-being become natural warning systems. He comments: 'Physical pain, I believe, is nature's way of indicating that a law of physical well-being has been violated.'[41] This point, which is mentioned on a number of occasions, appears peculiarly animistic and odd, particularly when placed beside Jones's contention that natural events are neither good nor bad in themselves but only through contact with the human will.

In the end Jones wants to argue that good behaviour ties into the moral, teleological and rational purpose of the world. Moral evil involves 'the wrong use of gifts that are good. It is a turning of them against themselves.' Nature *per se* has a bent toward rationality and goodness, therefore evil action is always intrinsically irrational and self-contradictory.[42] The problem with this argument, which is occasionally used by Jones and at other points denied, is that the development of rationality itself is a moral enterprise. Namely, to become more rational entails moral growth. Growth of rational capability might mean the ability to appreciate moral issues, but it surely does not necessarily entail moral growth in the person. Jones was as conscious as any one else that there were very intelligent, rational but amoral or immoral individuals, individuals who could choose rationally to be evil. A similar point haunts Kant's arguments on 'radical evil' in *Religion within the Limits of Reason Alone*.[43] Can a truly rational human being freely choose evil? Neither Kant nor Jones provided a wholly satisfactory answer to this problem.

Another important theological issue in Jones's thought, which we briefly mentioned at the close of chapter two, is the relationship of the Absolute to God. A number of theories were present within Idealism on this point. The whole debate though, for Jones, revolved around the question of the nature of the finite and infinite. For Jones, it is clear that 'the god of religion is the same as the Absolute of philosophy; and for both alike the universe in the last resort is the scene of a self-manifesting perfection'.[44] Some of Jones's final arguments on this question are to be found in Lecture XVII of his *Giffords*.

On the one hand, Francis Bradley presents the position that God is separate from the Absolute. In *Truth and Reality* Bradley argues trenchantly that:

> God for me has no meaning outside of the religious consciousness . . . The Absolute for me cannot be God, because in the end the Absolute is related to nothing, and there cannot be a practical relation between it and the finite will. When you begin to worship the Absolute . . . and make it the object of religion, you in that moment have transformed it. It has become something forthwith which is less than the Universe.[45]

For Bradley, therefore, God is short of complete reality. This is particularly the case if God is made into a person. Nothing can stand over against the Absolute. To worship an Absolute is to portray it as an object. In so doing it becomes less than the whole. Religion, thus, both demands and rejects a perfect God. Personality, since it always means 'I' as against 'you', cannot be the complete truth. In religion, Bradley maintains, we rest with contradiction. If humans and God are separate persons, there can be no perfection.

In Bradley, however, individuality becomes merged into the Absolute. Pantheism looms large here, where every finite being becomes a shadowy trace of the totality – a night where all the cows are black – to use Hegel's phrase. For Jones religion becomes impossible in this argument, since it minimally requires independence. In Jones's reading Bradley 'cannot reconcile this "pantheism", . . . with a God who is personal and individual'.[46]

One response to the Bradleian argument, taken by the Personal Idealists, was to heed the claim that personality implies 'I' as against 'you', and thus finiteness and limitation. As one of the group argued, 'Do you say that all this makes God finite? Be it so, if you will. Everything that is real is in that sense finite. God is certainly limited by all other beings in the Universe.'[47] In this case, the Absolute might be regarded as a society of persons plus God. The personality of God is retained, but at the cost of finiteness. Such a finite God makes the question of evil easier to handle. God, in this limited sense, cannot be held responsible for imperfection or evil. Rashdall remarks on Bradley: 'We don't really solve difficulties by chucking contradictions into the Absolute and saying "Be ye reconciled".'[48] Bradley's philosophy is thus seen to be a confused matrix of Idealistic and Spinozist themes.[49]

However, if one denies the omnicompetence of God and emphasizes the finiteness then other problems arise. The idea of an infinite person is difficult to understand; on the other hand, a finite God is inadequate to explain the world. McTaggart pointed out here that although souls exist as a society in the Absolute (in fact pre-exist and exist after death for McTaggart), there is no need or no adequate account of why God exists apart from these souls. McTaggart thus developed the theme of Idealist atheism out of this argument on God's finite limited personality. As Rashdall noted, the implication of McTaggart's argument is a 'reality which consists of eternal souls without God'.[50]

In the case of William James's pragmatist position, ideas are seen to need a cash value. Pragmatists are primarily concerned with the application of ideas. Ideas are our plans of action. Humans are seen as actors informed by reason. As James argued: 'for rationalism reality is ready-made and complete . . . while for pragmatism it is still in the making, and awaits part of its complexion from the future.'[51] Pragmatists thus argued that knowledge was not fixed, but open to perpetual critical change. There were no absolute monistic solutions to problems. We could thus be said not to have a universe but a 'multiverse'. As James comments, 'For pluralistic pragmatism truth grows up inside of all finite experiences. They lean on each other, but the whole of them, if such a whole there be, leans on nothing . . . Nothing outside of the flux secures the issue of it.' [52] This is the major theme behind James's book *The Pluralistic Universe*. Truth is not a matter of either coherence within an intellectual system or correspondence with some objective world. Rather the crucial question is do ideas work, provide solace or function for humans? Religious truths are judged in the same manner. They are not dependent on metaphysical beliefs, rather they function in individual lives. James examines this function in detail in his famous *Gifford Lectures, The Varieties of Religious Experience* (1901–2),[53] in which, remarking on Idealists, he says: 'from the point of view of practical religion, the metaphysical monster which they offer to our worship is an absolutely worthless invention of the scholarly mind.'[54] The Jamesian God is thus both finite, imperfect and multiple, as in the Personal Idealists, although for manifestly different reasons.

Jones, remarking on James's God, writes: 'This is a most restrained testimonial to the Divine Being. Would it, one wonders, secure him a College Fellowship or an American degree in divinity?'[55] Jones felt that the mistake of these various positions was to concentrate too heavily on the finite or infinite. In the case of Bradley, the argument is premised on the concept of infinite unity. Unity implies a unity of something whose opposition must be assumed. Jones comments, 'Affirm nothing but the unity of the divine and human will, or, on the other hand, affirm nothing but their independence of each other, and religion becomes impossible.'[56] Whereas Bradley argues that the Absolute absorbs individuals, Jones contends that the difference and personality of individuals is essential to genuine unity. As Jones stated: 'Only wills that are free can truly unite'; the common life in fact 'deepens their individuality'.[57] Personality is not destroyed in the Absolute but, as an expression of difference, is essential to its unity. 'The Absolute', says Jones, 'realizes itself in finite centres; and more fully in that finite centres are spiritual, and that man is man only in virtue of the indwelling of his God.'[58] The personality of God and man are thus both essential.

On the other hand in philosophers like Rashdall, McTaggart and William James, there is a sacrifice of unity for the sake of upholding finite difference. The upshot of this is to make God finite or non-existent. The final result is spiritual pluralism. It is good, for Jones, that the Personal Idealists and Pragmatists emphasized the importance of finite centres. However to over-emphasize finiteness carries equal dangers. A limited imperfect God is not acceptable to Jones.[59] Such spiritual pluralism fragments the world. It leads to the denial of any ontological unity and of the unifying indwelling God. Religion 'is the life given away as particular and exclusive in its ends, and taken up again as universal and comprehensive'.[60] A purely exclusive individualism forbids all communion. Unity and difference, transcendence and immanence, must be considered together. Jones argues that: 'a piece of music is not an aggregate of sounds; nor is a picture a collection of colours; nor is a geometrical demonstration a succession of statements.' The whole cannot be separated completely from the parts.[61]

In sum, for Jones, religion should be articulated through reason. Doubts could not be sidestepped through assertions of faith or intuition. God was knowable. Religion was at the very heart of our experience of the world. The essential message of Christianity was that God was incarnated in the self-conscious minds of human beings. Perfected humanity was the perfect revelation of God. Jesus Christ was the expression of ideal humanity. Human beings could actually find God in the world they knew on a day by day basis. The kingdom of God was therefore actually manifest upon earth. Political institutions and the moral life of individuals were regarded as the epiphanies of the divine. As we have seen, unlike other Absolute Idealists, Jones was not concerned that the Absolute should actually be decribed as both a person and God. The personality of both human beings and God had to be preserved by the philosophy of religion. This particular argument did make it difficult for Jones to account for the existence of evil and error which he ultimately tried to overcome dialectically within the unity of the Absolute. How successful this argument was remains questionable.

Having now reviewed the basic outline of Jones's philosophy and religion, and placed his Hegelian immanentism into the more general context of nineteenth- and early twentieth-century religious thought, we will turn in the next chapter to consider another crucial concept in his thought, namely that of evolution. We contend that Jones's concept of evolution is underpinned by the metaphysical and religious themes that we have been discussing in the previous two chapters. Indeed, evolution, one may say, was the conceptual tool in terms of which all experience could be comprehended and rendered rational.

CHAPTER FOUR

THE EVOLUTION OF SPIRIT

In the course of the previous two chapters the principles and assumptions concerning philosophy and religion, which are the foundation of Henry Jones's social and political thought, were articulated and related to some of the concerns of his contemporaries. In summary, Jones's philosophical position amounts to this: all knowledge including science, poetry, religion and philosophy must begin, not with indubitable data, but with hypothetical conjectures which act as the organizing principles in terms of which the universe can be made intelligible. They are regulative conceptions without which 'experience would have no systematic coherence, and even perception would be blind'.[1] If reality is to be intelligible we must hypothesize that it is a rational system: 'a system of interrelated elements in which every part sustains every other part',[2] and whose organizing principle is immanent, or reveals itself, in each of the parts.[3] The principle of systematic unity in the universe is the idea of God who saturates reality with a spiritual significance, and who is the ideal known through and expressed in the individual spirit. The spiritual life of man is a process of development in which the ideal and the actual, the divine and human, constitute a rational unity striving towards higher levels of rational freedom. God, then, is the absolute postulate who provides for us the principle in terms of which the universe can be comprehended as a coherent and systematic unity.

To assume rational unity entails the denial of any absolute distinctions between the different idiomatic modes in terms of which experience is organized. The modes of science, poetry, religion and philosophy complement each other and are mutually inclusive.[4] Testimony to their ultimate affinity was discerned by Jones in their common convergence upon the same hypotheses, and indicated to him that knowledge was approaching more closely than ever before to the heart of reality. It was no coincidence, Jones suggested, that the hypothesis of evolution had become the dominant organizing principle of the day. It enabled both spiritual growth and the rational development of character to be understood in terms of an organic process, which exhibited, in turn, the Idealist principle of unity in diversity, or identity in difference.[5] Evolution as a hypothetical conjecture constituted, for Jones, an absolute postulate exercising 'subtle dominion'[6] in every sphere of life. If it were to be discredited the natural and historical sciences would be reduced to a 'mass of contingent particulars waiting to be colligated'.[7]

The purpose of this chapter is to explore Jones's understanding of evolution, and to demonstrate its centrality to his conception of individual and social development as the manifestation and growth of spiritual freedom. The idea of evolution transcends the intractable dualism of Spirit and Nature by showing that 'the natural and social orders are in some way or other continuous and constitute one cosmos'.[8] Spiritual principles are immanent in nature, and evolutionary growth, for Jones, entails conceiving society, like the individuals who comprise it, as an organic unit maintaining its sameness throughout change. The individual and society, in their organic unity, develop as one through higher levels of rational freedom. In other words, Jones rejects the naturalistic hypothesis of evolution as a competitive struggle for existence, or the survival of the fittest, in favour of co-operative and self-conscious, as opposed to blind, social progress. Furthermore he denies Herbert Spencer's parallel between the organic unity of a natural body and the body politic, arguing instead that social relations are moral in character, constituting a spiritual, as opposed to a mechanistic, unity. It is by regarding evolution as a spiritual process, and God as its unifying principle, that Jones is able to reconcile religion with what many regarded as an irreligious doctrine. In capitalizing upon Weissman's theory of inheritance, Jones dismisses the idea of hereditary character, upon which many of the common ignorant prejudices of the day regarding the futility of state action in improving the conditions of the children of degenerate parents, and of the poor, were based.

THE DIMENSIONS OF EVOLUTIONARY THINKING

Although sociobiological arguments of social phenomena flourish, evolutionary ideas are only occasionally invoked in modern social and political theory.[9] It is difficult to imagine the extent to which biological and social evolution so thoroughly impregnated all levels of discourse in the latter part of the nineteenth century in Great Britain, continental Europe, Australia and America. Joseph le Conte, for example, estimated in 1894 that evolutionary perspectives on the development of organisms, animals, the earth, the solar system, and society constitute 'nearly one half of the whole domain of modern thought'.[10] As early as 1860, the year after Darwin published *The Origin of Species*, the issues involved had already overflowed the bounds of scientific circles, and shared with 'Italy and the Volunteers the attention of general society'.[11] While there can be no doubt that Darwin's influence upon theories of social evolution has been greatly exaggerated,[12] evolutionary forms of explanation, derived from a variety of sources, became the predominant hypothesis in terms of which society came to be understood. Herbert Spencer, the most notorious of the nineteenth-century social evolutionists, formulated many of his ideas independently of Darwin and gave much more emphasis to the role of hereditary characteristics (a theory identified with Lamarck) than to natural selection, for which Spencer preferred the term 'survival of the fittest', and which Darwin himself came to favour. It was common to acknowledge both Spencer and Darwin, not as the progenitors of evolution, but as the two men most responsible for making it a familiar conception.[13]

Henry Jones readily applauded Darwin's achievement of being the first to apply evolution systematically, that is with extensive observation and scientific imagination, to a particular field. Darwin's success and stimulus to apply the idea to other areas of knowledge had made evolution a convincing and compelling hypothesis.[14] Jones was, however, less disposed to be civil to, and more inclined to be disparaging about Spencer. Jones called into question Spencer's credentials as a scientist and philosopher, claiming that specialists in neither field could take him seriously.[15] Jones also detested Spencer's agnosticism and ridiculed the doctrine of the 'Unknowable' upon which it is premised, by suggesting that it is a 'masterpiece of confused thinking',[16] and 'the maddest of all the projects propounded to suffering mankind'.[17] In a lecture given in Australia Jones went as far as to suggest that Spencer was 'the philosopher who more than any other represented the stupidity of the English people'.[18]

The contribution of evolutionary theory to nineteenth-century social thought was to demonstrate the continuity of the natural and spiritual spheres: the difference between man and the animals was one of degree rather than kind. Because of this purported continuity, evolution held out the possibility of a real unity, or unifying principle, in the natural and social sciences. In this respect, while denying the political implications of the evolutionary mechanism of natural selection, or the survival of the fittest, such social theorists as L. T. Hobhouse and J. A. Hobson applauded the contribution that Darwin and Spencer made to overcoming the seemingly intractable philosophical dualism between man and nature.[19] However, it was the very suggestion that man and nature constitute a continuous process that offended the sensibilities of those who objected to evolution on religious grounds. Evolution, for these critics, implied the degradation of man to the level of the animals, and the explanation of the spiritual in terms of the natural.

While Darwin's theory of the origin of species undermined the creationist theory derived from Genesis, it was not necessarily incompatible with the religious point of view in general. Of course there were those who contended that the first book of Genesis constituted the only firm foundation upon which to build scientific knowledge, and when defences of this view were given they were often poorly argued and insubstantial.[20] Darwin himself tried to avoid becoming embroiled in religious controversy. He suggested, for example, that his view of the origin of species appeared to correspond to what observation tells us about the 'laws impressed on matter by the Creator',[21] and he refused to allow Marx to dedicate a revised edition of *Das Kapital* to him in order to avoid being publicly linked with an attack on Christianity.[22] While Spencer's social evolution supported agnosticism, there were many thinkers who tried to reconcile evolution and religion. Le Conte argued that the ultimate end of evolution is the divine plane, from which the process began, and towards which man is evolving to become the ideal, or divine man.[23] Emma Marie Caillard put forward a similar view in arguing that: 'The goal of man's evolution, the perfect type of manhood is Christ. He exists and has always existed potentially in the race and in the individual, equally before as after His visible Incarnation, equally in the millions of those who do not, as in the far fewer millions of those who do, bear His name.'[24] Caillard went even further and applied the idea of evolution to the development of Christianity. Using Spencer's definition of evolution she argues that Christianity complies perfectly with it, and constitutes a striking illustration of the principle of the survival of the fittest in its ability to convert the most hostile forces to the faith.[25]

Jones acknowledged the extent to which all forms of thought were employing the hypothesis of evolution, including religion itself, and this indicated to him that there was a general intellectual convergence towards a truer understanding of the universe. We saw in the previous chapter the importance of religion in his philosophy as a whole. Reality is thoroughly saturated with spiritual significance, and God reveals Himself as the spiritual principle, in unity with man, manifest in the process of developing rational consciousness and freedom. The development of the human character, on the way to attaining the ideal immanent in all reality, is a process of spiritual evolution. 'The idea of Evolution', Jones contends, 'is itself the hypothesis, the methodizing conception which we employ to render intelligible to ourselves the process which Spirit follows in becoming free.'[26] It is, in other words, 'the subtle presupposition which suffuses all our endeavour, whether in the sphere of knowledge or in that of social and moral practice'.[27]

The significance of the idea of evolution for Jones is that it implies the necessary identity in difference that the hypothesis of the spiritual unity of experience demands:[28] 'Evolution', he argues, 'implies not only an unbroken identity, but also change, newness, acquisition.'[29] Evolution involves continuity and has convinced people 'that the natural and social orders are in some way or other continuous and constitute one cosmos'.[30] It is this unity which allows the Idealist to insist upon the immanence of the spiritual in the natural, and upon the all-encompassing character of religious principles.[31] This may give the impression that Jones is attributing to nature more than it can bear, that is, a nascent or latent form of intelligence residing in inorganic matter. Jones, however, wishes to convey something different. Consciousness, for the Idealist, is the ultimate truth of reality which entails an anthropomorphic interpretation of nature in that 'what constitutes thought constitutes things, and, therefore, that the key to nature is man'.[32] Jones expressed his argument most clearly when, in the Dunkin Lectures on Sociology delivered at Manchester College, Oxford, in November 1904, he contended that we cannot assume inorganic things to be spiritual by attributing thoughts and feelings to them. Inorganic things 'are spiritual not in that they are intelligent, but in that they are intelligible'.[33]

TWO TYPES OF EVOLUTION

Jones saw two ways of viewing evolution. The first, which he calls the 'ordinary' or 'scientific' view,[34] is incompatible with morality and religion in that it attempts to account for the spiritual in terms of the material. It is the conception of evolution which tends 'to animalise' man and despiritualize the world.[35] Jones believed that Darwin, Spencer, Huxley and Tyndall were all guilty, in their different ways, of levelling down humanity by over-emphasizing the common origins of mankind in the lower animals.[36] Religious objections to evolution often mistakenly took the positivistic or materialist view as definitive. Jones believed though that there is another view – one which is compatible with morality and religion. It has its roots, not in the geological and biological sciences of the eighteenth and nineteenth centuries, but in the writings of Aristotle and the great German poet philosophers – Lessing, Goethe, Kant, Hegel, Fichte, Schelling and Schiller.[37]

Hegel, for example, was familiar with the term 'evolution'. Yet he rejected it as a form of explanation. It was unable to explain the higher stages of development in terms of the lower. The method which Hegel employed was that of 'emanation', that is, the explanation of the lower forms in terms of the higher.[38] Jones, in common with a number of British Idealists and Neo-Idealist Liberals, appropriated the sense of evolution equivalent to Hegel's notion of emanation. Edward Caird, for example, deplored the prevalent tendency to trace backwards from the more complex to the less, with its consequent implication that the former really has nothing more in it than the latter. He argued that: 'we must not only deny that matter can explain spirit, but we must say that even matter itself cannot be fully understood, except as an element in a spiritual world.'[39] David Ritchie also takes Spencer to task for suggesting that 'we must interpret the more developed by the less developed'. On the contrary, Ritchie argues, Spencer would do well to acknowledge with Aristotle that 'the true nature of a thing is to be found, not in its origin, but in its end'.[40] Furthermore, L. T. Hobhouse, who deplored the political implications of Hegelianism,[41] but who was, in Jones's view, an Idealist, 'after a fashion',[42] was critical of the tendency to trace the higher back to the lower, and explain the former in terms of the latter. 'The study of mind', Hobhouse argues, 'takes us at once to the highest thing that evolution has produced, and when we compare the different phases of mental growth, we get into the way of judging the lower by the higher, and viewing the process in relation to the result.'[43]

For Jones, the tracing of a variety of entities back to a common source does not entail 'equality of worth'.[44] In a lecture delivered in Sydney, Jones contended that the nature of something is not revealed in its rudimentary form, but instead in its most perfect examples.[45] The highest exemplar, however, cannot arise from nothing; it is immanent in the lower forms. In his moral philosophy lectures he put the same point as follows: 'We cannot get out of a thing by evolution that which is not in it.'[46] The implication of this, Jones told a Brisbane audience, was that, 'the idea of evolution rightly used was not to materialise man, but to spiritualise nature'.[47] Jones claims therefore that it was modern Idealism which refuted 'all theories that account for results by origins, and which try to explain the last in terms of the first'.[48]

Evolution as a regulative concept is, in Jones's view, the most optimistic that the sciences and philosophy have ever employed. In relation to morality, spiritual principles can be shown to develop out of the trials posed by nature to humanity. Physical needs lead us to develop and ultimately to overcome material problems. Such problems are opportunities or impediments depending upon how one harnesses them or converts them into allies of the evolutionary development of society. In this respect the material problems can be raised to a higher level. By applying our moral principles, we infuse materiality with beauty and truth. We spiritualize nature with our values and consequently our physical circumstances 'are made working partners in the evolution of man'.[49]

Furthermore, for Idealism it is the 'absolute postulate' of evolutionary change that holds out the hope of resolving all dualisms, for example, between spirit and nature, and between the mind and its objects. Such a vehicle of analysis is crucial for Idealism since it sustains the hypothesis of unity, from which all enquiry must begin. Bosanquet, for example, maintained that all experience exhibits an 'impulse towards unity and coherence',[50] and it is evolution, for Jones, which is able to explain and demonstrate the reality of the universe as a genuine identity in difference, or unity in diversity. Evolution 'makes the identity express itself in the differences, and it deepens both the identity and differences as it proceeds'.[51]

So far we have tried to establish the prevalence of evolutionary theory. We have also suggested that although Jones shared the general enthusiasm for its form of 'historical' explanation, the source from which he drew for inspiration was not biology or geology, but Aristotle and the great poets and philosophers of Germany. Strictly speaking, Jones favoured Hegel's method of emanation, the understanding of the lower in terms of the higher, rather than the method of evolution, which understands the higher in terms of the lower. Most importantly, however, evolution could be used to establish the unity of existence, the fundamental presupposition from which Absolute Idealism begins.

UNITY OF EXISTENCE

Society, from the point of view of evolution, is thus viewed as a continuous unity whose modifications look to the future, but nevertheless always retain something of the past. Jones's vision of society as a continuous unity in diversity has strong echoes of Burke. Society for Jones, as it was for Burke, is a moral partnership between those who are living, those who are dead, and those who are yet to be born.[52] Evolution enables us to place on a firmer foundation Burke's insights.

> For evolution is not only a conception that opens out into the future a boundless vista: it also redeems the past. Instead of the wide waste of lost causes that human history presented, each little life reaching at best its little ends and then, so far as its earthly career went, perishing forever, we find that its meaning and substance are carried forward into the very structure of the present.[53]

Whereas Burke contended, in the name of conservatism, that social and institutional changes should always comply with, or conform to, those principles which are deeply embedded in the traditions, and which, to put it in Oakeshott's terms, intimate the changes to be made, Jones invoked the same conception in the name of reform. In anticipation of the discussions in subsequent chapters, it suffices to say here that Jones saw genuine social reform closely related to loyalty to one's state and society. A precondition of loyalty is a reverence for that to which loyalty is given, and one cannot revere that which is not striving towards goodness and perfection. The social reformer detects in his, or her, society inadequacies inviting transformation, and this entails a knowledge of, and a building upon, social conditions as they exist. In other words, the evolutionary frame of mind predisposes one to reform rather than revolution; 'and the better we understand revolutions, the clearer we shall see that, so far as they have lasting value, they were simply evolution, with its steps somewhat hastened'.[54]

If the idea of evolution was to be applied to social development, then society itself had to be conceived in such a way that it could comply with, or exhibit, the laws of evolution. In other words, individuals within society had to be characterized as standing in a certain relation to each other and to the whole. This relation, Herbert Spencer believed, was continuous with those of the development of biological and human organisms.[55] Social and organic development were subject to the same laws of evolution; hence society should be conceived as an organism. Spencer went to considerable lengths to establish the identity between the biological and social organisms. His most famous attempt was in the *Westminster Review* of 1860.[56] Undeterred by penetrating criticism,[57] he reiterated the same analogies and arguments in his *Principles of Sociology*.[58] It will be instructive to look at Spencer's argument and the responses of some of his critics. It is within the context of this debate that Jones formulated his views on the relations which constitute an organic unity.

Spencer's article 'The Social Organism' is ostensibly a review of the works of Hobbes, and volume II of the works of Plato. He praises both writers for recognizing that there is a correspondence between the natural body and society, but criticizes them for believing that the latter is the creation of human artifice. Societies are neither created, nor changed, by the wills of individuals, 'but are consequent on general natural causes'.[59] Spencer claims that it is only with the advances in biological generalization that we are able 'to trace out the real relations of social organizations to organizations of another order'.[60] There are three clear ways in which a society can be compared to an organism or a living body. First, both begin as small aggregations and develop into augmented masses; second, they evolve from a simple to an increasingly more complex structure; and, third, from relative independence and autonomy the parts become mutually dependent, and the activity of one part has implications for the life of the rest. The most conspicuous difference between the body politic and the biological organism is the fact that in the latter only some of the parts are endowed with feeling, and all are subservient to the central nervous system whose pleasures and pains constitute the good and evil in life. Thus the parts of a biological organism are merged into a corporate consciousness which is capable of being both happy and miserable. In a society, however, the individual consciousness is a living unit, or component, in the corporate consciousness which is not itself distinct from its components.

> And this is an everlasting reason why the welfare of citizens cannot rightly be sacrificed to some supposed benefit of the State; but why, on the other hand, the State must be regarded as existing solely for the benefit of the citizens. The corporate life must here be subservient to the life of the parts.[61]

On the basis of the principle of the 'survival of the fittest', which was an ethical conception, Spencer was able to argue that government 'interference' (a word which he preferred to 'intervention' in order to convey the maximum pejorative import), was impractical. The complexity of society made it unsuitable material for government manipulation. Such interference would result in catastrophic unintended consequences, which would exacerbate the problem that government action itself was meant to alleviate. Interference is also immoral. It distorts the mechanism of the ethical principle of the survival of the fittest and encourages and perpetuates weak strains. It is a long-established law of nature, Spencer contends, that each creature receives both the benefits and evil consequences of its activities, whether these consequences are attendant upon one's ancestry, or the result of self-modification. This is the means by which life has so far evolved, and 'whatever qualifications this natural course of action may now or hereafter undergo, are qualifications that cannot, without fatal results, essentially change it'.[62] The theory of justice which this implies is not one of desert, because Spencer is well aware that rewards are not always commensurate with effort. Instead, it is a view of justice based upon entitlement. In other words, whatever the consequences of our actions we are entitled to enjoy, or suffer, them. In this respect, there are those whose skills, perhaps, have been superseded by technology, and who have fallen into poverty not through any physical or moral defect, but through misfortune. These are the deserving, as opposed to the undeserving, poor whom charity may legitimately help out of their difficulties.[63]

Spencer's naturalistic ethic, based upon the principles of pleasure and pain motivating the organism, assumes a unity between nature, humanity and society. It was therefore imperative that he establish this unity. Spencer goes to considerable lengths to substantiate his hypothesis that the social organism is analogous to the biological organism. For example, he suggests that the circulation of blood and the distribution of nutriments around the body are equivalent to the distribution of goods throughout the body politic. The blood corpuscles are analogous to the circulation of money in society. Spencer develops the analogy, which he borrowed from Liebig, and argues that in many species of the lower animals there are no corpuscles in the blood, just as 'in societies of low civilization there is no money'.[64] Spencer's most famous analogy, however, is that between nerve-bundles travelling alongside the great arteries, and the groups of telegraph wires running alongside railway lines.[65] In essence, the unity which Spencer detects is biological rather than spiritual, and is demonstrated by means of comparing how human beings have advanced from savagery to the highest levels of civilization, to the process by which simple structureless organisms develop into highly structured and complex organisms.

Of Spencer's many detractors T. H. Huxley is of particular interest here. Jones rejected Spencer's biological analogy, but he could not reconcile himself with the dualism which Huxley had opened up between what Huxley called the cosmic and ethical evolutionary processes. In what is perhaps the most famous criticism of Spencer's biological analogy, Huxley argues that if we accept nature as the criterion of ethics, far from condemning state interference, the implication is that we should have more. 'The fact is', Huxley says, 'that the sovereign power of the body thinks for the physiological organism, acts for it, and rules the individual components with a rod of iron.'[66] Huxley did not subscribe to this analogy. Society, he argues, unlike a physiological organism, depends upon expressed or implied contracts between the individuals who comprise it. In this respect the social organism is comparable to a chemical synthesis in which complex aggregates are comprised of independent elements subordinate to the whole, each one of which having 'given up something, in order that the atomic society, or molecule, may subsist'.[67] Similarly, in a society each individual has to suppress, or renounce, certain freedoms which are anti-social in order that society may continue to subsist and other freedoms be enjoyed. The business of government should not only be to 'enforce the renunciation of the anti-social desires, but, wherever it may be necessary to promote the satisfaction of those which are conducive to progress'.[68] In other words, Huxley denies nature as a standard for morality; acknowledges the human propensity for anti-social aggression, and contends that society and social progress depend upon its amelioration.

In his *Romanes Lectures* Huxley develops his argument by denying that the idea of the fittest could constitute an ethical standard, because what is 'fit' is a purely circumstantial condition of variable nature.[69] He argues that the struggle for existence, or the principle of the survival of the fittest, belongs to the cosmic process by which nature and the human organism have developed. However, the capacities which equip one for this competitive and ruthless process ill equip one for social existence. The struggle for survival enacted in the cosmic process may be able to elucidate how good and evil characteristics have arisen, but it does not explain why what we call 'good' is preferable to what we call evil. The cosmic or evolutionary process may explain the occasion for the emergence of morality, but it cannot be a guide to conduct, otherwise ethics would simply be 'applied Natural History'.[70] The cosmic process is in fact anti-social, and such tendencies are restrained by fear of the opinions of others. From the time that social progress begins, shame and sympathy restrain the anti-social tendencies in human nature. The moral code arises in the course of the development of our feelings of approbation and disapprobation, and we become accustomed to think about conduct in terms of 'the acquired dialect of morals'.[71] The natural character of man, then, is countered by an 'artificial personality', or conscience. In other words:

> Social progress means a checking of the cosmic process at every step and the substitution for it of another, which may be called the ethical process; the end of which is not the survival of those who may happen to be the fittest, in respect of the whole of the conditions which obtain, but of those who are ethically the best.[72]

The more advanced a civilization, that is, in terms of securing the means of existence for all its members, the more diminished is the role of the cosmic process internal to that society.[73]

THE SOCIAL ORGANISM

Before we show how Jones conceived the social organism and developed his views in opposition to those of Spencer, the terms of reference of the discussion are best drawn by discussing the responses to Huxley's dualism between the cosmic and ethical processes. Both Herbert Spencer and Leslie Stephen, from their different points of view, wished to deny the dualism and maintain the unity of nature and society.[74] Huxley himself had introduced an ambiguity in his argument when he confessed, in 'Evolution and Ethics', that 'strictly speaking, social life, and the ethical process in virtue of which it advances towards perfection, are part and parcel of the general process of evolution.' Spencer immediately seized upon Huxley's equivocation and asked rhetorically where ethical man might spring from if it is not the cosmic process.[75] Leslie Stephen, who argued against Huxley, was convinced of the necessity of the struggle for existence and suggested that at each stage of evolution a new condition of equilibrium arises with its own mechanisms of selection. In modern societies, he argued, the need for the elimination of the unfit was not obviated; it was the methods by which the process was effected which changed.[76]

The Idealist response was to apply the familiar hypothesis of unity, and the spiritual nature of reality, to the problem. Andrew Seth, for example, argued that the fatal flaw in Huxley's argument is the apparent denial of the unity of the cosmos, which for the former was not so much a conclusion requiring proof, as 'an inevitable assumption'.[77] In this respect he could sympathize with Spencer and Stephen in believing that human nature must be part of the wider cosmic nature. However he differed from them in their tendency to identify nature with the laws and processes of the non-human world. In other words, they sought to explain the higher in terms of the lower, namely, the effect in terms of the cause; whereas 'the true nature of the cause only becomes apparent in the effect'.[78] If we are really serious about unity, Seth argues, we must read the most recent 'consequent' into the most distant 'antecedent', and only then can one truly say that the one is the cause of the other.

Although Jones rejected Seth's Personal Idealism, he was nevertheless at one with him in opposing Huxley's dualism. Jones chose the occasion of his inaugural address at Glasgow University to confront Huxley's argument. He expressed his bewilderment as to how one could intelligibly represent a collision between two forces so different in character, the one unconscious and purely natural, the other exhibiting intelligence and morality. Unless there is some common ground between them, the ethical could not combat the cosmic process. For Huxley, the law that produces primitive man becomes transformed to produce ethical man. The latter is born of the former, while possessing the ethical element which nature does not. While modern biology recognizes quite dramatic changes, by means of spontaneous variation, Jones argues that there is no metamorphosis in the natural order so abrupt as that which Huxley posits between nature and spirit. If evolution implies any continuity it must show how the ultimate ends of man are in some way nascent from the beginning. But this does not mean that we should minimize the differences between organic and physical processes, and rational life, nor should we deny the role of nature in human achievements. Huxley's argument, Jones contends, attributes too much to man and too little to nature: 'In fact, knowledge and morality are not the achievements of either man or of the world in which he lives. Into each of these products both enter as indispensable factors.'[79] Nature is a partner in all of man's endeavours, though it knows none of them. Nature itself is amoral, but morality assumes knowledge, and knowledge presupposes a world and an intelligence to interpret it, and thus nature shares in the moral achievements of man, and 'his intelligence is her instrument for self-expression'.[80] Each is intimately related, and neither can exist without the other. Nature is essential to man, and mind is essential to the possibility of conceiving a world. Nature, as we suggested earlier, while not intelligent, is intelligible; whereas we cannot attribute love and hate to it, or any moral attributes, the progress of man depends upon its co-operation:

> The majesty of the natural world is the result of a combined endeavour. And the still more solemn majesty of the world of goodness is the product of the interaction of man with man, and of all men with nature. Hence the cosmic process which contributes to these surpassingly great ends, guiding the struggling intellect at every step, furnishing it with all it owns, casting before him all its inexhaustible wealth, is not man's foe, but his ever-constant friend, attending him in all his battles, and sharing in all his victories.[81]

The unity which Jones speaks of moralizes nature. Nature is an accomplice in all of humanity's enterprises, and the social organism, far from cohering on material principles, is unified by moral and spiritual relations. Thus whereas Spencer materialized spirit, Jones, without wishing to deny the differences between nature and spirit, spiritualized nature. We now turn, then, to the question of how Jones distinguished his conception of a social organism from that of Spencer.

We have already suggested that Jones's conception of evolution has its roots in German Idealism, and particularly in Hegel's idea of emanation (the explanation of the lower in terms of the higher). The question remains, how can one relate the idea of an organism to this view? J. M. E. McTaggart, the Cambridge Idealist philosopher, suggested that the ordinary view of an organic unity is one which 'binds together the different parts of a living body',[82] and upon whatever principle of unity a society exists it cannot, on the Hegelian understanding, be analogous to the unity of a natural body. Hegel wished to oppose the view that society and the state should be looked upon as external means by which to promote the welfare of the individual citizens, but, McTaggart argues, there is nothing in Hegel's metaphysics that logically involves the view that society is anything more than external means.[83] In other words, if society is to be viewed as an organism, it must be conceived as an end for those who comprise it. Yet, Hegel's metaphysics do not entitle us to claim that society is, or ought to be, such an end.

Bosanquet, while not claiming to refute McTaggart's argument, suggests that Hegel may be understood differently. For Hegel, an organism may possess the organic essence in differing degrees. The character of an organism is that it is internally related, that is, containing its substance within itself; self-sustaining; and, even though in contact with things external to itself, is in fact self-determined. Bosanquet sums this up by suggesting that the social organism 'is an inward process, a circular course, in which a whole maintains itself in a relatively perfect identity throughout differences which itself creates and does not accept from without'.[84] The state as a spiritual unity of body and soul is an actualized and harmonized self-consciousness, that is, a free will developing its freedom. The end, or self-end, Bosanquet asserts, is 'freedom, or the will which is adequate to the notion of will'.[85] McTaggart's interpretation, as far as Bosanquet is concerned, is contrary to the spirit of the remarks which Hegel offers us, especially in the *Philosophy of Right*.[86] Notwithstanding the merits of McTaggart's criticisms of Hegel, Jones, the avowed Hegelian, took society to be an organically related unity whose evolution is towards the mutual development of freedom. Society which is a unity of the individuals who comprise it, is assisted in this evolution by the activity of the state, that is, the manifestation and the expression of the will of the whole.

Jones, although often caustically dismissive of Spencer, went to considerable lengths to acquaint himself with Spencer's arguments, and, indeed, Jones's contribution to the British Idealists' testament was a critique of Spencer's ideas on the analogy between the biological and the social organism.[87] Jones consistently warned against the use of misleading metaphors in the human sciences. Metaphors are often used to make the unfamiliar intelligible in terms of the familiar, which having been serviceable in shedding light on different terrain, are believed to be illuminating media through which to interpret the social sphere. Metaphors, on Jones's understanding, are only metaphors when something of relevance is omitted, and something of irrelevance is introduced. Metaphors, he argues, 'cannot give the truth any more than analogies can disprove'.[88] This is neither to suggest that metaphors are entirely misleading, nor that they do not afford degrees of intelligibility. Viewing society as a biological organism is indeed an advance on understanding it as a mechanism, with the excessive individualism which it implies. At least there is the implication of the mutual interdependence and welfare of the parts.[89] One of the main difficulties with Spencer's characterization was that he wanted to retain the excessive individualism of the mechanistic view, upon organic principles which were incompatible with it. For Spencer society is nothing more than an aggregate of individuals, and the organism of which he speaks is the resultant of 'a mechanical and temporal equipoise produced by the opposition and collision of individuals'.[90] Society is not an end in itself but merely a means to the welfare of the individuals who compose it. Yet, Jones argues, if it is to be a means, society must stand apart from the individuals who compose it, and this is something that no one wants to admit. In fact, means and end are inapplicable to the idea of an organism because, instead of conveying the intimacy and complex unity of the relations among the parts, they are separated into discrete entities, which the idea of organic unity was itself meant to overcome.

The biological metaphor misleads us because in emphasizing the physical analogies between natural organisms and society, it omits the spiritual element which makes a social unity possible. Indeed, 'the organic metaphor . . . implies too remote, rather than too close, a connexion.'[91] The scientific, or biological, metaphor must be superseded by the philosophical conception of organic unity. Society is a living organism, and experiences organic change which has a bearing upon, and implications for, the whole structure,[92] not 'because it is like an animal. . . but because the individual realises himself as an ethical being in society, and society realises itself in the individual'.[93] The unity of a social organism is not metaphorical, but more real than that of a biological organism,[94] and this is because there is a greater intensity in the relations which as self-conscious 'facts of mind interpenetrate more intimately than physical facts and events'.[95]

Jones read Hegel's *Philosophy of Right* in preparation for developing a different conception of a social organism from that of Spencer.[96] Like

Hegel, Jones argues that the social bond must be an internal relation and not imposed upon a society from outside, nor is it accidental, but essential in that should the bond be broken the parts degenerate into abstractions with no meaning.[97] In other words:

> The social organism is thus a concrete, living, self-integrating, self-differentiating whole, apart from which neither the universal – the abstract society, nor the particular – the abstract individual, can be. Isolated from each other they are but names; sunder their relations and they cease to exist. They exist in and through each other, and are constituted by their relation.[98]

This, according to Jones, is not a denial of the individuality of the parts, but an affirmation of their mutual implication in the whole, and the realization that the welfare of each, and the welfare of the whole are inseparable.

BIOLOGICAL AND SOCIAL HEREDITY

In order to appreciate what Jones meant by the unity of a social organism, and the relation of the parts to the whole, we must first distinguish between biological and social heredity in order to understand how society can evolve towards its ideal. It was intimated earlier in this chapter that although Herbert Spencer believed that natural selection and the principle of the survival of the fittest to be important evolutionary mechanisms, he nevertheless believed that they were insufficient in themselves to explain the process of evolution. In opposition to the increasingly popular theories of August Weismann, Spencer tenaciously attributed more and more importance to the Lamarckian idea of inherited characters in the explanation of evolution.[99] An acquired character is one which is modified by factors external to the organism, and believed to be transmittable to the offspring: the little toe, for instance, whose functional purpose appears to have declined considerably, and whose apparent deformity, commonly attributed to the pressure of wearing shoes, was believed to be inherited.[100] Extreme neo-Lamarckians, like Spencer, accounted for well-developed moral sentiments and a strong sense of obligation in terms of the transmission of inherited characters.[101] Darwin, whom Spencer readily invokes as an ally on this question,[102] gradually diminished the importance of the Lamarckian principle in his system as a whole, whereas Spencer, during the last thirty years of his life, insisted upon its centrality to his system, and to the efficacy of his political conclusions. The question of whether acquired characters are transmitted became for Spencer the most important which the scientific community faced, because of its implications for 'influencing men's views about Education, Ethics, Sociology, and Politics'.[103] In Spencer's view, the 'inheritance of acquired characters becomes an important, if not the chief, cause of evolution'; it is not only 'a factor', but 'an all-important factor'.[104]

The advances made in discovering the common properties of cells in the work of cytologists was drawn upon and systematized by Weismann in formulating his germ plasm theory. This considerably undermined the scientific basis for adhering to the theory of inherited characters. Weismann argued that the reproductive germ cells contain within themselves that which is to be transmitted, and do not become modified, or transformed, by changes in the environment.[105] Weismann therefore argued against the view propounded by Darwin, that cells received in a host body give off gemmules capable of impregnating the alien cells with transmittable characteristics from the donor.

The view that acquired characters could be transmitted by parents to their children was shared by popular opinion, and even among the Idealists Bradley appears to have subscribed to a variation of it.[106] Evolutionary theories, however, could be commandeered in support of almost any political conclusion,[107] and even the idea of inherited acquired characters which Spencer used to argue against government interference in alleviating the distress of degenerate persons, could be invoked to substantiate quite different conclusions. H. I. Jensen, for instance, using the pseudonym of H. Ingemann, claimed that 'all the good habits and lofty ideals gradually introduced for the common good by the advance of socialism will become hereditary propensities in the human race'.[108]

On the whole, however, Weismann's views began to prevail over those of Spencer. Huxley, L. H. Morgan, Benjamin Kidd, A. R. Wallace and David Ritchie, to name only a few, supported, in varying degrees, Weismann's arguments. David Ritchie, for instance, could suggest in 1896 that the 'Lamarckian doctrine is tending to disappear from the evolution theory', and that 'it seems very doubtful whether, except in fairy tales or romances, the child brought up away from its parents and in complete ignorance of them (for this is essential to a fair experiment) would present any of their moral characteristics'.[109]

Jones was thoroughly familiar with the terms of reference of the debate between those who affirmed the transmission of acquired characters, and those who denied such inheritance on genetic grounds. He appraised hundreds of manuscripts for Macmillan, many of which were concerned with aspects of the evolutionary question.[110] The answers to the questions raised by the heredity debate were, for Jones, of crucial importance because upon them hinged our very conception of a rational responsible person, and his, or her, relation to society.[111] The biological sciences had, he argued, pronounced the case for the inheritance of acquired characters inconclusive and unsubstantiated,[112] and on the whole the tendency was towards the denial of the hypothesis. In other words, the conclusion to be drawn is that the environment has no significant impact upon the child, who is to a large extent the manifestation of the potential encoded in the genetic make-up of his, or her, ancestors. The environment, then, provides the occasion for the development, or flourishing, of inherent traits, but cannot initiate anything new, nor provide the opportunity for development beyond an inherited capacity, which may over the course of generations have become accentuated by means of natural selection, resulting in internal genetic modifications, but which are ostensibly unaffected by environmental factors. In other words, the denial of the inheritance of acquired characters does not minimize the significance of heredity: on the contrary it asserts the importance of the inheritance of all other aspects of character.[113]

We have, then, a dualism between a character which is genetically fixed, and one which is plastic to environmental factors, that is, what Martin Hollis has called, the Nature and Nurture views of the human character.[114] Both views, Jones contends, are inimical to the conception of the person as a free and rational agent, and in effect deny the possibility of a moral character capable of self-improvement. The idea of character in the Victorian period was a moral conception implying individual consciousness, and self-improvement. Self-realization in the context of social relations was the very essence of individuality.[115] 'Character,' Collini tells us, 'the constantly reinforced disposition to restrain one's animal instincts, was both the prerequisite and the expression of responsible independent behaviour.'[116]

How, then, could the opposition between character and environment be overcome, while at the same time rescuing the idea of free moral agency? In common with most Idealists Jones believed that the individual divorced from society is an artifical abstraction. Ritchie, for example, argued that 'the individual, apart from all relations to a community is a negation'.[117] We owe everything, Jones argues, to the society into which we are born, and the country in which we live. Our language, religion, ways of thinking, and even the manner in which we greet our parents we owe to the social environment. The sustenance of both our mind and spirit we receive from society,[118] and whether we are born in the modern age, or during the time of the lake-dwellers,[119] the social inheritance is the only intermediary between us and 'helpless idiocy'.[120] 'Organized Society', Jones maintained, 'is the means of all our knowing and the impelling power of all our doing'; indeed, 'we literally owe our soul to our environment'.[121] Every child as a moral entity begins anew,[122] but none is a mere receptacle into which the social inheritance is poured. Any moral theory worth its salt must retain the good which was to be found in individualism and reconcile it with the social character of our being.

No theory of the individual's relation to society can ignore the category of self-consciousness:[123] 'There may be misery in the palace, and the affluence of contentment in the hut; for the mind is its own home.'[124] Character and environment, or the individual and society, are not opposed to each other. Biological evolutionism, of the Darwinian kind, has, in emphasizing the extent to which we adapt to the environment, minimized the degree to which we adapt the environment to our own character.[125] The relationship between character and environment is not one of mutual exclusion, but one of mutual implication: 'The entire meaning and power of both lies in their relation.'[126] Although the human spirit must borrow from its surroundings it must also translate:[127]

> For the conditions imposed upon a man by his environment are nothing to him until they have penetrated into his consciousness, and when they have done that they have subjected themselves to a power which has transmuted them. They are no longer mere conditions but thoughts – parts of the power which understands them.[128]

We are saturated by the social world of which we are the makers, and which itself is the maker of us.[129] Life, Jones argues, is a continuous process of internalizing and making the world our own; it is a process by which the environment is constituted anew in every individual's mind and will.[130] It is we who, internalizing the world, infuse it with spiritual significance,[131] elevating it to a higher level, and at the same time achieving our own selves in the process.[132]

If we do not inherit our characters, what is it that enables us to develop them in conjunction with the environment? Jones does not want to deny heredity outright, he wants to claim that only certain things are capable of transmission. Our moral attributes, those which constitute character, are not able to be transmitted. Good and evil are not structures and functions of the body, nor are they the qualities or modes of such functions; neither can they be described as organic, nor faculties of the mind. Instead, they are values in terms of which individuals organize their lives, and have no existence, or persistence apart from the people who will them, and apart from a will which is 'not only potentially but, in some degree, actually rational'.[133] To call a person 'good' implies that the character will from time to time be expressed in the doing of good acts. Both good and evil are constantly being recreated and perish with the act which characterizes them; they are therefore incapable of transmission even in the form of a tendency or disposition towards performing good or evil acts. In this respect, 'not even the most unfortunate of human beings is born with a moral taint.'[134] What we do inherit are varying capacities, or powers – we may call it a constitution – realizable only when in contact with the social and physical environment. In addition, we inherit the social, cultural and intellectual heritage of our ancestors, which is as little or as much as we will to make of it, depending upon the opportunities which our small corner of the environment afford us, and upon our potential to seize and use them in enhancing our own well-being. The tradition which lives within us is recreated in the act of appropriation,[135] and constitutes a partnership between the generations who are dead, those who are living, and those yet to be born.[136] Society is a moral partnership, and each person who is at once shaped by, and shaper of, the social environment is his, or her, own 'society individuated'.[137] That which constitutes the organic relation among individuals in society is rational self-consciousness whose thoughts interpenetrate more deeply than any physical components,[138] and which makes moral life possible in that the social whole, and the state which is a reflection of it, 'is a system of obligations; [and] the organic filaments which hold it together are duties'.[139] These social relations are not 'addenda' to the personality of the individual, 'but the inmost content and reality of it'.[140]

If morality presupposes a rational self-consciousness capable of choosing freely that which is good, then the essence of the individual and of society in their mutual implication, or inclusion, is that freedom, which is at once that of the individual conceiving his own purposes, and in doing so realizing a social purpose. It is, to put it in Hegel's terms, 'the free will which wills the free will'.[141] This new Hegelian freedom, Jones suggests, is 'to will in accordance with the nature of things, to will the right'.[142] The individual and the common good coincide in a unity of purpose, or to put it in Bosanquet's words, freedom is the self-end of the social organism.[143] Freedom, as the condition of morality, and, by necessity, of the consequent system of obligations and duties, is that which gives cohesiveness to society. For Jones, 'the bond of the social organism, that which is self-differentiating, self-integrating life, is freedom', and 'freedom is the life which forms the unity of the moral organism'.[144] The social organism, then, is not a mechanical, or biological, entity whose components collide, but a self-conscious unity in which the components realize themselves as ethical beings, and society realizes itself in them. In Jones's view, the welfare of the individual and that of society are inseparable. The aims and purposes of the individual are inseparable from social aims and purposes.[145]

If society is an evolving ethical organism, how is this evolution to be conceived? Biological evolutionism and the social variants derived from it, as Ritchie observed, had a tendency to become fatalistic, but freedom on the Idealist conception was the struggle for the emancipation from fate,[146] or as Hegel suggested, 'none other than the progress of the consciousness of freedom'.[147] Jones was vehemently opposed to any form of determinism in ethics. The idea of free will is circumvented if it is allowed that antecedent hereditary character, or the external environment, in any way determines it. Consciousness always intervenes converting the antecedent and external into the self, and in doing so makes all rational action self-determined.[148] Freedom is not an implicit aspect of our character, but an achievement, which has to be acquired or won.[149] We are not born free, but capable of becoming progressively more free by our relationships with others, and experience of life. Freedom is a power, or capability, which is not hindered by the environment, but which uses it to become more free, the first signs of which appear when we endow facts with our own interpretation and attribute to them our own value. Just as we are neither rational, nor irrational, but in the process, or on the way, to becoming more rational, we are also in the process of becoming free:[150] 'the freedom and reason which makes us men is not realized but realizing.'[151]

We saw in the previous chapter that Jones believed that rational experience depends upon the absolute postulate of the existence of God, and that God reveals Himself as Spirit, and knows Himself in and through the expressions of his children. The love and truth that are God's are the ideals manifest in us, and which we are 'on the way' to realizing. In opposition to Bradley and Bosanquet, Jones maintains that the personality of the individual is not destroyed by God dwelling within, but actually constitutes the personality, and by being immanent in it empowers man to conceive purposes and carry them out. The Divine Spirit cannot surpass the limits of the individual's free choice, but realizes itself in the person's self-conscious striving for the attainment of greater and greater degrees of freedom.[152] Evolution, on this understanding, 'suggests that expansion, that victory of the living thing over its own limits, that conversion of things external which bound and restrain, into elements within its own life, that determination not from without but from within, which Freedom is'.[153] Freedom, then, is the manifestation of the progress of Spirit, expressing itself in, and being expressed by, individuals in their ethical unity with the social organism.

Like Hegel, Jones in articulating Spirit's progress towards the ideal, believes that the ascent can never be direct. Every ideal can be differentiated into two complementary instances, and in our advance we first emphasize one to the neglect of the other, whereupon we realize the consequent one-sidedness and contradiction, and put a similar degree of weight behind the other, until eventually we unite the two at a higher level of understanding.[154] In Jones's view freedom has evolved through three stages: the receptive, recalcitrant, and reconciliatory.[155] The embryonic stage of freedom is that when order is imposed on our lives by means of external forces. We are dependent upon that which we perceive as other, and its laws reduce rudimentary and capricious sensuous life into a semblance of coherence. Nature's laws are harsh teachers and swiftly administer their punishments and rewards for digression from, or conformity with, its precepts. The gods of religions demand obedience and conformity, and even the worst of them have elements of moral value in that they provide guidance to individuals by looking upon life as a whole; focusing the future on the present moment and giving 'new depth of significance to every act'.[156] Furthermore, society, in the face of ethically immature and capricious will, moulds the individual by means of customs and traditions. These traditions are assimilated and constitute the experience of the person;

he, or she, owes everything to society, and even in criticism of it, that person does so in terms of conditions which society has determined and with a mind which it has formed.[157]

The individual must always initially, whatever society he or she is born into, accept the beliefs and assimilate the traditions of the society uncritically. Without developing the rational element which society is able to impart, the individual would have no facility to examine the received opinions, challenge them, and press for reforms.[158] To acquire that reason necessary for criticism the individual is totally dependent upon society, or the environment,[159] but as we have already seen, there can be no absolute distinction between man and the environment, and from the first, consciousness intervenes and impresses itself upon a world which it makes its own. There comes a time when every man 'ceases to be the docile medium of the traditions of his people'.[160] Spirit subjects itself to self-examination in the minds of those who comprise the society it has built up, and in the process attains freedom.

The initial cost of this attainment is a diminution of social authority. The social institutions and constraints, whose authority appeared to be of divine sanction, are seen to be of man's artifice; the product of conflict and flickering reason, devised for convenience to minimize disorder. What men have made for their own utility, they can also destroy:

> Thus, there gradually grows up an inner world of personal conviction and of private rights. The individual constitutes himself into the measure of all things, and the arbiter of all values. The standard of truth and error is his own judgement, and of right and wrong is his own conscience.[161]

This is the stage in the evolution of freedom which Jones calls 'recalcitrance' or 'independence'. It is manifest at certain times, in certain individuals who decry all social constraints as artificial impediments which must be cast off in order to let the inner light of innate right and reason shine. The value of this spirit of independence is that it asserts the radical subjectivity of action, attributing to inner conscience a supreme authority, but in doing so failing to recognize the debt owed to the society against which it rebels: 'no man can rise above his age except by means of it.'[162] A true reformer is not one who comes to destroy, but one who takes society's institutions as they are, denounces their corruption and demands they correspond to their ideal. Such a will is reluctantly in opposition to the authorities who cannot acknowledge the wrongs he, or she, exposes. Jones argues that the person 'is his society individuated, so far as he is an individual at all;

hence social criticism is the most difficult of all criticism, for it is self-criticism'.[163]

To the man who is ethically immature, all of society's constraints are undesirable, and the only demands the state can make upon him are negative.[164] Such a person is not free, but capricious; unable to perfect a rational will, because he, or she, has no will, only chaotic desires subject to no rule other than personal pleasure.[165] Such a person repudiates all external influences and recognizes no demands other than those which emanate from the inner self. However, all motives are made one's own through consciousness of a condition beyond a current state. Consciousness looks to the future, an ideal, however inadequate, outside the self, which it seeks to incorporate into the self through action. There can be no motive found inside the self and subjective freedom leads to no action at all.[166] States, too, are capricious when they rule by mere force, and do not govern through the medium of the wills of those over whom they preside. Such capricious states disregard freedom, treating individuals not as persons, but as things. They do not seek to promote the good of their citizens, but deprive them of the conditions by which such good could be attained. Instead of aiding the development of their capabilities, they frustrate them by denying them the possibility of exercising their free will.[167]

For Jones, freedom is at once both subjective and objective: neither can be elevated to a primary position without compromising the 'infinite value' of the other; 'both the inner and the outer law must be supreme'.[168] In the third evolutionary stage of 'reconciliation' the individual and the state are not opposed. Any increase in the sphere of activity of the one does not diminish the sphere of the other. The state is itself free and the means by which its members attain freedom. There is a common good in which the state and the individual share. Thus, for Jones, 'the authority that was alien and external becomes a personal conviction, and the rule of behaviour is self-imposed.'[169] The will of the individual and the will of the state are one social will, and neither is a means to the end of the other. Both are ends in themselves.[170] We will see in chapters five and six how Jones conceives the role of the state in advancing the freedom of its citizens.

This chapter has shown how Jones's notion of evolution enabled him to sustain the postulate of unity, which is itself the foundation of all rational activity. The principle of unity was employed to resolve what he took to be false oppositions in the evolution debate. Evolution entails a unity between Nature and Spirit. Instead of materializing

Spirit, evolution spiritualizes the material world. The material world is not attributed with intelligence, but with 'intelligibility', thus emphasizing the intricate partnership of Nature and Spirit in every achievement of the mind. Jones denies Huxley's distinction between the cosmic and ethical processes, maintaining that far from being opposed, they are one and the same process. In opposition to Spencer, Jones speaks of 'organic unity' as an ethical and not a biological metaphor, but an ethical unity with rational self-consciousness as the central cohesive force. Furthermore, we saw how Jones believed that both sides of the debate over whether acquired characters are inherited undermined the principle of rational self-consciousness and could therefore not accommodate the growth, or evolution, of spiritual freedom.

CHAPTER FIVE

CITIZENSHIP, THE ENABLING STATE AND EDUCATION

Having outlined Jones's concept of evolution and its social implications, against the background of his metaphysical and religious thought, we now turn, over the next four chapters, to a detailed investigation of aspects of Jones's social and political thought. This particular chapter looks at two related issues. The first section outlines the context and substance of his philosophy of citizenship. Jones's notion of citizenship is seen as part of the symbiotic moral and spiritual evolution of the state and individuals comprising it. In advance of tracing the details of Jones's views we wish initially to put his ideas on citizenship into a broader conceptual and historical framework. The second section examines the central position of education in Jones's social and political theory. Essentially, education in the broadest sense is seen to provide the necessary preconditions for adequate citizenship.

CITIZENSHIP AND THE STATE

The term citizenship derives from the Latin *civis* and the Greek equivalent *polites*. Its simplest and earliest definition is membership of a city. In Greek life it usually denoted an identification with a place or city by birth; a collection of duties and claims; and an equal eligibility to participate in the adjudication processes of the city (at least in larger cities like Athens).[1] The moral, cultural and personal good of man (literally) was tied to his citizenship, although the idealization of Greek communal life can be considerably exaggerated. The English cognates of citizenship – civil and civility – still illustrate aspects of this more personal and moral usage.

The breakdown of the Greek city states and the rise of large empires, like Rome, introduced a less personal and moral sense of citizenship. The early Roman Republic had cultivated an idea (which inspired later Civic Republicans, like Machiavelli), where citizenship denoted self-discipline, patriotism, piety and devotion to the common good. However, citizenship under the Roman Empire usually denoted a more juristic notion – a body of legal entitlements. This was an idea which prevailed during much of the Middle Ages in various guises.

Many of the above notions are implicit in eighteenth- and nineteenth-century understanding of citizenship. We wish to suggest a fairly rough conceptual dichotomy of forms of citizenship under which rubric we can locate Jones's views. This dichotomy is between *active* and *passive* conceptions of the citizen. This distinction encompasses a number of diverse views. The activistic notion entailed involvement and participation in the polity. Such an idea can be found in the earlier doctrines of Aristotelianism, Civic Republicanism and later Jacobinism; and in the nineteenth and twentieth centuries, in doctrines like Blanquism, Communism, Fascism, Leninism – the *bêtes noires* of statism to theorists like Karl Popper or J. L. Talmon. Passive citizenship is a more conventional classical liberal bourgeois view, implying, conversely, negative rights to protection of one's person, property and liberty.

Active citizenship in the Jacobins implied unstinting participation. It presupposed a positive conception of an objective common good – a general will – which is the basis of our true freedom. Citizenship transcended all other loyalties, like family or religion. Freedom, in this latter sense, would be more positive in character; passive citizenship, on the other hand, ties in conventionally with a more negative understanding of freedom as an absence of constraints.

Arguments for passive citizenship are usually premised upon a distinction between the public and private realms. Although not all classical liberals follow this line of reasoning with precision, none the less, the conventional classical liberal interpretation argues that individuals choose their own senses of the good life, within their own sphere of interest, as long as it does not infringe a like freedom for others. Value (specifically moral value) is largely an individual matter. Many liberals have admittedly wanted, or seen the importance of, some kind of broad regulative moral consensus in society. Such an idea is present, for example, in writers like John Locke or Adam Smith. *Prima facie,* however, this value consensus is not generated by government. Value is a matter of individual choice (within a broad rule of law framework). It is not impossible for a consensus on certain values to evolve in a classical liberal society, but it could not be a publicly or communally generated moral goal (or set of goals). If the government were to define the moral goals of individuals, something very significant would have been undermined in liberal thought, namely the private/public dichotomy. If there is one thing the passive sense of citizenship is not meant to conjure, it is a common objective moral good by which all ought to abide. This would be a category mistake. Rather, passive citizenship represents the minimal rule of law framework (as a concrete value and practice) *within* which individuals choose their own good. In other words, passive citizenship is an instrumental practice which is one of the constitutive elements of the formal legal and moral framework of a classical liberal society.

Another of the crucial factors of the classical liberal vision (given that we acknowledge many variations on a theme) is the idea of a free economy. Production and consumption to a large degree are rooted in individual freedom of choice. All individuals must be able to pursue their own interests and have certain guarantees of property and the like. Passive citizenship, which upholds certain basic civil rights to freedom, independence and property, is the precise precondition required. A passive notion of citizenship is thus a necessary prerequisite for the adequate functioning of a commercial market society. Civic order is not an intrinsic value, as it might appear in some traditional conservative writers; rather it contributes to the end of human liberty. In the same way as the market order must be considered an amoral and impersonal entity by many of its proponents, so the legal/civil aspect of citizenship is also amoral. It provides the parameters within which individual moral choices can be made. The vision of human nature expressed in many classical market liberal writers is that of the producing, consuming, self-interested and competitive creature seeking to further its interests and powers. This vision of human nature is closely linked to passive citizenship.

The older sense of citizenship, as stated earlier, relates back to the Greeks. Political science, or politics *per se*, was the science or study of life in the *polis*. The *polis* embraced the life of the individual. Citizenship was part of the integrated life of the city-state. In thinkers like Aristotle and Plato, the good of the individual was related to the good of society. Ethics was integral to politics. There was little recognition of any separate realm apart from society. There were no clearly established realms of privacy, personal rights or freedoms, and little conception of a separation between public and private law. The virtues of Greek life were integral to the social practices of the *polis*. The end of the political life, at least for the more leisured citizens (who in fact were the minority), was moral and, coterminously, intellectual. Human nature was fulfilled in social life. The ethical end of the individual was to realize the end of society. For Aristotle, citizenship was not only membership of the city-state, and all that implied, but also an inner disposition of rational virtue, entailing the internalization of communal norms.

The Aristotelian theory formed the groundwork for the now much discussed Civic Republican tradition.[2] Civic Republicanism, which is identified with writers like Machiavelli and Harrington, is a language of civic virtue, piety, patriotism, community and civic liberty, often embodying a clear and unequivocal fear of corruption by the loss of such virtues. Citizenship was a shared communal activity and an involvement in the adjudication processes of political rule. Citizens were seen to be independent propertied individuals who identified fully with the public ends of community. They thus freely identified their interests with the community. Liberty was identified with the tranquillity and security of life under such regimes. Some contemporary writers, like Quentin Skinner, see this Civic Republican theory as a language of virtue contrasting with the language of rights embodied in the liberal perspective.[3] In this sense Civic Republicanism is seen as a competitor to classical liberalism, contrasting active virtuous citizenship with the negative individualism of liberalism. Such an idea can be grossly overdone. It also overemphasizes the unanimity of Civic Republican political life. However, it is clear that both Aristotelian and the Civic Republican notions of active virtuous citizenship do not rest easily with some of the cherished nostrums of market and rights-based classical liberalism.

The Hegelian tradition, from which Henry Jones derives, like the Aristotelian, with which it has affinities, is also premised upon the possibility of a communal consensus on values. Such an idea of citizenship embodied the well-established notions of civil rights; however it was also integrally involved in the much stronger normative ends of the state.[4] The state was premised upon the ethical end of individual development and freedom (in a positive sense). Citizenship embodied a consciousness of the ends of human life as embodied in the institutional forms of the state, in other words a clear consciousness of a common good. The state is the body within which this consciousness functions. There is thus a synonymity between the individual will and the outward laws and institutions. The individual acquires the most fundamental norms by participating in social life, since social life expresses the the basic structure of human nature. To deny one's citizenship was in essence to deny one's humanity. The social world *was* the concrete structure of human will. This active notion of citizenship, at least for Hegel, was the fruition of a long and tortured historical development from the Greeks. It was, however, a qualitative development on the Greek and Roman citizens. True freedom was becoming realized in the modern ethical state. Such an active citizenship implied the internalization of fundamental communal norms, through self-conscious development, and thus loyalty to the normative ends of the state.[5]

Since the 1950s the rather crude discussions of totalitarianism and its origins are often rooted in a critique of the above type of argument. The liberal *Rechtsstaat* is usually contrasted with the more activist state. Rousseau and Hegel are often seen as guilty parties in such activistic accounts.

Most scholars of citizenship have noted a development (and dominance) of the more passive entitlement-based citizenship in the last two centuries. This development has in fact marked out a subdivision within the liberal tradition. The earliest classical liberals were concerned to extend certain civil/constitutional rights to citizens. These rights primarily were concerned to protect certain basic freedoms from interference by arbitrary authority – as in freedom of worship, speech, conscience and private property. Citizenship was encapsulated in certain negative civil entitlements.

One of the important extensions of such citizenship rights, which might be considered an independent stage in the development of the idea, is the political right to enfranchisement – sometimes called political citizenship.[6] This idea was already causing many problems for some classical liberals by the mid-nineteenth century, who believed that extending political rights of citizenship was pandering to mass mediocrity. Liberals like J. S. Mill were not exempt from such reflections. Political citizenship is concerned with the right of participation in the political process, mainly via voting in a representational democracy.

Finally, there is a stage made famous by T. H. Marshall this century, namely social citizenship.[7] Social citizenship, for Marshall, opened up with the late nineteenth and early twentieth century, and implied the right to a modicum of economic welfare and security and a share in the heritage of civilized life. In other words, the chance to live according to the prevailing civilized standards of life. This dimension of entitlement, which linked the rights and development of individual citizens with the possession of adequate resources, undermined the consensus of liberalism. Social citizenship became the mark of social liberals, social democrats and reformist socialists this century. It was a conception of liberalism which is related to the more continental *étatiste* tradition of liberalism. This point will be explored in the next chapter.

Marshall noticed that social citizenship existed in a tense relationship with a classical liberal market vision of society. He saw Britain, for example, in the 1950s as a democratic-welfare-capitalism – what he called a hyphenated society. Despite the manifest need for a flourishing market society, poverty and deprivation could not be tolerated. The poor are those who are prevented from participation or enjoyment of our common civilization. Without social rights individuals are excluded from genuine citizenship. Such an exclusion endangers the legitimacy and stability of society. Such rights do not entail equalizing incomes, rather guaranteeing to all citizens the possibility of enriching their lives. For Marshall unequal material income becomes relatively insignificant once individuals have social rights. The problems and ideological debates of many industrialized democracies in the last decade have in fact utilized this conception of citizenship. There has been a growth both of the entitled (with accompanying political pressures) and of the entitlements themselves. Fears of government overload and legitimation pressures have been indissolubly linked. Political action and political recipience go hand in hand.

Henry Jones's Hegelianized notion of citizenship corresponds more precisely to the active citizen tradition. It is not, however, a totally precise fit. Jones has his feet in both camps. His dissatisfaction with the older classical liberal individualism, and notions of passive citizenship, drew upon the activist Hegelian tradition. This tradition also provided him with intellectual resources for his qualified acceptance of a social liberalism (a point that will be returned to in chapter six). However, there are ambiguities here. He was not totally at odds with traditional liberalism and he was not prepared to abandon all of its assumptions. He saw an aspect of the truth about social life present in classical liberalism, for example, the emphasis on values of privacy, liberty and private property. Further, despite his acceptance of much of the social liberal case (which involved extending entitlements), he also had a more radical activistic theory of an organic, ethical and dutiful citizenry and consensual community. This latter notion made some social liberals and social democrats feel uncomfortable. The Fabian Webbs, for example, had very little interest at all in the ethical dimensions of citizenship.

Like many of the British Idealists, Jones had been involved deeply in both the theory and practice of citizenship. He saw no distinction between the metaphysics and actual practice of citizenship. Any hard and fast distinction between the theory and practice of citizenship, Jones would have regarded as false dualism.[8] Jones lectured extensively on the duties of citizenship, giving a short lecture series on the topic in Sheffield, Newcastle and Oxford, and never ceased, in his speeches for the Parliamentary Recruitment Committee around Wales, to remind miners and slate-workers of their obligations as citizens during time of war. At Merthyr, for example, he made his plea: 'I implore of you my lads to stand by your country. It has been more generous to you than your father or your mother, for your fathers and your mothers have been nursed on its knees and suckled on its breast.'[9]

Jones, in Henry Hadow's view (Hadow was the Director of Education for the YMCA), was the natural choice to write a book on citizenship for the education of army officers, who would then pass on the principles to their men. Jones enthusiastically accepted the invitation and told Hadow that it would be like no handbook he had seen before, 'but I'll tempt the men to think of the State as built to the music of the stars'.[10] Jones himself, though, thought the book might be 'too hard for its purpose', a view which was later shared by Hadow.[11] To understand his views on citizenship it is necessary to identify briefly some of the metaphysical ideas underpinning it.

The argument on citizenship is part of a series of ongoing themes in Jones's thought. The individual citizen is not an isolated particular. To isolate particular citizens is as faulty as isolating any object, ontologically, in the world as simply particular. As Jones put it: 'to insist on differences to the exclusion of their unity is . . . futile.'[12] The particular develops in the context of the universal. There is a metaphysical identity in difference. The particular citizen is both a particular person *and* a focus of a deeper unity. As Jones contends: 'It is the spirit which has built up the social world that becomes in its own members aware of what it has achieved.'[13] The citizen develops through assimilating and reflecting upon the substance of the society, culture, traditions and so forth. Thus the citizen is suckled and weaned, as Jones liked to say, at the breast of the universal.[14]

When Jones discussed the 'universal' in society he employed the term tradition.[15] The gist of his argument is that the tradition of a society embodies the accumulated wisdom of *Reason*. Tradition is 'continuous and cumulative'.[16] It grows organically and teleologically and is assimilated by the growing individual. As Jones comments:

> If man did not at first accept the beliefs and customs of his people; if he were not for a considerable part of his life docile, assimilating and uncritical of the rational habitudes of his time, receiving his nutriment prepared, simplified and made innocent from the larger life of the social organism . . . reason could not be fostered within him.[17]

The substance of individual nature is thus assimilated through social life. However, it is not a blind assimilation. The substance of critical reason becomes embodied in this process. Eventually the citizen can contribute to the reform and restructuring process of society. For Jones the ' "now" of an individual or a nation is a very complex affair. It is the moving point in which the echoes of their past deeds are converted . . . into the duties and opportunities of the present. Man is always reminiscent when he acts: his past lives in him whether he knows it or not.'[18] Thus Jones sees citizenship as a borrowed inheritance. It is a body of ideas which, when assimilated, become actions. For Jones, it must be remembered, 'an idea *is* an act'.[19] The entailed inheritance of the idea of citizenship, assimilated from the traditions of society, modifies the perceptions and activity of individuals. For Jones 'tradition . . . has its value; but only when it is taken up and made to live again in the individual's thought and will.'[20]

The implication of the above arguments on the nature of the self is that it cannot be dissociated from the tradition. This argument is underpinned by those in chapter two on the nature of individuality – where the more complete individuality denotes greater universality – and in chapter four on the evolution of the interdependence of man and his environment, The self is not an isolated abstraction, soul or character idiosyncracy, nor a psychological continuity. Rather it is a focus of reason, bringing together the tradition of a society. As Jones put it, the self 'is the organised and living system of . . . past acts of willing, desiring, knowing and feeling . . . The self, in a word, is a living and operative memory: a memory which, so far from being the resuscitation of dead or sleeping ideas, is experience repeating itself, the very self iterating its operations.'[21] Jones claims that the self is not absorbed into society or tradition. This is as absurd as contending that the individual is completely independent.

Jones indicates that the above process, of gradual modification of individuals by the assimilation of the traditions of citizenship, is one of evolution. This is not a naturalistic evolution, but a moral and spiritual one, as we established in the previous chapter. As Jones comments: 'The application of moral principles to natural or physical circumstances injects new values into them – beauty, truth and worth. They are made working partners in the evolution of man.'[22] When the past develops through the individual mind – it evolves. When we reason through traditions we evolve and experience the world in new ways. In other words the citizen is not a static entity with unchanging interests. Moral growth and development are seen as necessary.

Citizenship is thus not just a political or legal category. It is a state of mind and being. Individual citizens are seen to be rational and moral agents able to advance arguments and to deliberate and judge between ends. This point links up with Jones's theory of colligating ideas, outlined in chapter two. Each individual has a *Weltanshauung*, colligating idea or working hypothesis, which 'defines the relation of his ends, determines the ranks of his needs, decides the content of his desires. It is the interpreter of his circumstances'.[23] Jones also calls it occasionally the 'deeper self'. The colligating idea or working hypothesis is embodied in the will, that is the activity of citizens, and determines the character of their experience. For Jones, 'thought inevitably breaks out into practice, and ideas are deeds in the making.'[24]

Change and reform ultimately denote a change of ideas and will. Jones had a powerful sense of the role of ideas in reforming social reality.[25] The breadth and character of a citizen's life will be determined by the nature of the purposes. The 'petty life has petty and secluded interests', whereas 'the interests of his neighbourhood, his city . . . thud in the arteries of the good man'.[26] Moral conduct is ultimately dependent on the nature of the purposes and ideas adopted by the agent. The most comprehensive of such ideas are communal and consensual in nature and thus express common values and sense of identity. Morality is a social practice, but not thereby simply relative to social forms. Underlying the changing practices of social and historical existence Jones detects a static universal substance which makes teleological and universal sense of moral conduct. For Jones a person's own good is at the same time a universal good. This argument again parallels those in his metaphysics. As Jones commented: 'Moral good is like truth in this respect.'[27] However the unchanging character of truth and moral good are fairly clearly upheld – 'The "good" maintains its character of being ultimate and necessary . . . for it is the object of every desire.' He continues: 'The whole of the activities of mankind which together make up "history" is the self-evolution and gradual manifestation of the good.'[28]

Although in some of his discussions he appears to be rejecting individualism wholesale, Jones does make a distinction between an old and new individualism. These terms correspond to some degree with the notions of active and passive citizenship. For Jones genuine 'law, order, continuity, in human action, . . . were beyond the reach of an individualistic theory. It left ethical writers no choice but that of either sacrificing man to law, or law to man.'[29] The old individualism, which envisaged society as an aggregation of atoms or particulars, gave a thin reading of social life. Thin individualism is inadequate, given that its units of analysis are empty asocial individuals. Such individualism is also dangerous since its vacuity lays down no limitations to conduct. Following Hegel, Jones saw the terror of the French Revolution, which 'rent asunder every political and social bond', as rooted in such thin individualism.[30] Thin individualism, which was both abstract and false (whether it appeared in revolutionaries or abstract liberal political economy), was the root to many expressions of passive citizenship.

For Jones, thick individualism recognized the social nature of humans. It was rooted in the idea of citizens having a common social identity and substance and recognizing a common good. Individuality expressed universality. The more truly individual entailed the more universality. For Jones, 'The least investigation will show that the tissue of the individual's soul is social in every fibre.'[31]

The old individualism's appeal to character cut no ice with Jones. Character is not something which flourishes in glorious isolation, rather, 'the interpreter of *character* can no longer rely on the old individualism: he must study it in relation to the social life, of which it is both cause and effect, both expression and product'.[32] This doctrine put him into a difficult situation with groups like the Charity Organization Society. Yet, he certainly was not rejecting the case of such groups, only the logic of their arguments.[33]

It was relatively simple to conclude from this argument that Jones rejected any clear distinction being drawn between the state and the citizen. For Jones it is another of the false dualisms presented to us by social theory. The state and citizen are compared by Jones to the concave and convex sides of a circle. They are 'ultimately nothing but different manifestations of one self-revealing, self-realizing spirit, the spirit of *man*'.[34] Both share the same destiny. In fact, for Jones, it is the aim of the social sciences to demonstrate this fact.[35] The state exists to provide the conditions and means for the development of citizens. The good citizen is not harmed by legislation. As Jones comments: 'The good citizen does not wish to send women to work in pits, to employ little children in factories, or to sweat employees. He is not wronged by any legislation that prohibits these methods of making wealth.'[36]

The relationship between the individual and the state is one of mutual inclusion: it is an organic relationship, and thus the state is a living unity. Not only is it a living thing, but like the individual, the state has a moral character, which, for Jones, necessarily means that it is a personality.[37] If this is the case, the state is capable of being free and of promoting the freedom of its citizens. As Jones remarks, the state is 'the Kingdom of heaven upon Earth . . . the temple of rational life'.[38] In such an organic unity the welfare of the whole and of the individual are inseparable.[39] It is no longer possible, Jones argues, to think in terms of individual good apart from the social good, and in this respect the opposition between individualism and collectivism turns out to be false. The latter had taken the former up into itself, because all reconciliations are effected by one of the opposites absorbing the other, and only in this heightened form of collectivism, or socialism, was there to be found 'any consciousness of the deepened solidarity of modern citizenship'.[40] The opposition was false because both individualists and collectivists made the same mistaken assumption. They believed that an extension of the activity of states necessarily entailed a consequent curtailment or limitation of opportunities for individual enterprise. Given that the individual, as we saw, is saturated with social relations, and is nothing without them, the controversy over the desirability of extending state activity was simply absurd. It was clear to Jones that the enhancement of individual freedom and the extension of the activities of the state had grown concurrently. There was no evidence to suggest that with the development of state intervention there had been any diminution of competition between private enterprises, nor any decrease in its activities. This new liberal belief actually empowers the citizen and provides more opportunities for an advanced moral and social life. The limits of state intervention could not be fixed by abstract principles, and each proposed extension of its sphere of influence had to be assessed in terms of the criterion of whether the personality of the citizen was being presented with greater opportunities to develop, and on the condition that no weakening of individual responsibility was involved.[41]

It follows from the above arguments that any complete separation between the public and private realms or private rights as against public was viewed as false by Jones. The communal and private always grow together. As he stated:

> I should accord to individuals every item claimed for them, in the way of privacy, sacredness, independence . . . But I would point out that all these rights that we attribute to persons exist only on a certain condition. And that condition appears to do the exact opposite of their private and individual character. They must be recognized as not less social than they are individual! – nay! that they are individual, private, personal, *because in the first place they are social*. Rights are social institutions.[42]

Jones in fact clearly denies the whole natural rights perspective. Rights are liberties, claims and powers bestowed on individuals by society. A society 'extends to its citizens genuine rights, thereby widening the compass of their private effective wills and enlarging the significance of their personality, knits them together'.[43]

One of the implications of Jones's views here is that he expected and argued for a high standard of public ethics. Citizenship in public office was a high calling and should be taken with immense responsibility.[44] Jones also was keen to advance education courses and degrees in citizenship.[45]

There are a number of propositions in Jones's Hegelian perspective which rest uneasily with a more classical liberal vision of passive citizenship. The public/private dichotomy is not accepted or is at least severely modified; totally private individual goods are seen as arbitrary and socially divisive; value and an objective common good are defined publicly; law is integrally involved in morality; freedom is defined via communal moral goals; human nature is seen to be social, rational, and developing in ethical awareness; and finally, the state is part of an enterprise to make humans more virtuous. This is not an exhaustive list. It indicates, however, the general ethos within which active citizenship has functioned. Finally, it is worth pointing out that this particular notion of citizenship was more concerned with duties than rights and, given its concern for the public interest and common good, it stressed common resources of moral identity and culture.

For Jones, citizenship is thus not limited in any way to extending civil, economic or social entitlements. Jones is looking for a common ethical identity amongst citizens. Citizenship is seen as an integrative experience allowing the individual to attain a higher moral ground to review his or her community and personal life. We can thus see the importance that Jones attaches to education in citizenship.

A SCHOOL OF VIRTUE

Given the emphasis which philosophical Idealism places on the attainment of knowledge as a precondition of freedom, and that freedom itself is a precondition of virtuous action and active citizenship, education must of necessity be one of the paramount concerns of the state. Education is too precious an instrument, and the good it is called upon to procure is of such enormous significance for the common good of society, that decisions about who are to be the recipients cannot be entrusted to the whims of parents. The responsibility of the state for educating its citizens, and indeed, the very conception of an all-encompassing educative state, entrusted with the physical and spiritual care of its citizens, and whose purpose is to facilitate provisions for the promotion of the good life, lay at the heart of the political philosophies of Plato and Aristotle. It was inconceivable to Aristotle, for example, that anyone could deny 'that education should be regulated by law and should be an affair of the state'.[46] Education moulds the character appropriate to the particular constitution and the neglect of imparting its principles is bound to be harmful to the state.

Hegel, and the British Idealists in general, of course, found considerable inspiration in the classical Greeks, and while disagreeing with their conceptions of what constituted the good life, the Idealists could concur with the Greeks on the responsibility of the state to promote it. Jones is no exception in this respect. A state, whether it does it well or ill, is unavoidably engaged in educating its citizens, and 'as an individual agent, must have some aim, that is, some notion of a common good; and it cannot divest itself of the responsibility of inducing its adoption as an end to be realised by its citizens'.[47] The purview of the state's vision extends beyond that of formal instruction and encompasses the much broader conception of an educative society. It provides the exemplars of conduct in the everyday activities of its citizens to be emulated by those who are 'on the way' to a virtuous character. State intervention is necessary to improve family, social, and economic conditions, as well as to provide a more formal system of instruction to discharge its educative obligations.

The interest of the state in the educative welfare of its citizens entailed the extension of state activity. This meant that questions relating to the state's legitimate province were integral to the more general terms of reference of the individualist versus collectivist debate.[48] Individualists argued that any attempt to make education compulsory, or to extend its scope, necessarily entailed an encroachment upon, or denial of, the liberties of parents. In opposition to this view T. H. Green argued that to compel parents to educate their children removes an obstacle to the effective growth of the capacity in the next generation to exercise their rights beneficially. In so far as the compulsion is sensitive to the particular ecclesiastical or other preferences of the parent, there is no interference with the moral duty of the parent, nor with social spontaneity, and is therefore felt as compulsion only by those in whom that spontaneity is absent. The following generation, having acquired the capacity by means of education of beneficially exercising its rights, will not, even though the law with its penal sanctions is still in place, feel the compulsion backed by penalties which law implies.[49]

Variations of such arguments were prevalent among educational reformers, many of whom had direct links with Idealism.[50] H. A. L. Fisher, for example, who was vice-chancellor of Sheffield University, a member of the Coalition Government of 1916–1922, served as president of the Board of Education and held a seat in the Cabinet, was a personal friend of Henry Jones. He was also deeply interested in the philosophy of Hegel and Green when a student at New College, Oxford.[51] He argued, in familiar Idealist terms, when trying to convince the country of the efficacy of the 1917 Education Bill, which included among its provisions the raising of the school-leaving age, continuing education, restrictions on child employment and increased government education funding. In support of his scheme Fisher argued that 'the compulsion proposed in this Bill will be no sterilizing restriction on wholesome liberty, but an essential condition of a larger and more enlightened freedom'.[52] In Jones's view Fisher was 'a leader calling us forth to renew the battle against ignorance',[53] who was 'like the voice of a hero on the battle-fields of old'.[54] This is not to say that Jones thought that the 1918 Education Act was entirely satisfactory, but he fully concurred with Fisher's view that state compulsion in such matters enhanced rather than diminished individual liberty.

In his 1905 address, 'The Function of the University in the State', Jones argued that the state, by making education compulsory, had not subverted but transformed the voluntary actions of its citizens. The compulsion of law had not displaced the individual will, but simply given it a clearer and more forceful expression. Good laws were, in fact, nothing else but the free desires of the people expressed and enacted in legislation. This expression of the general will 'is just the will of each, organized, universalized, strengthened'.[55] For Jones, the case of compulsory education illustrated yet another illusory antithesis, namely, between voluntary and compulsory action in the context of the relation of the individual to the state.

Jones developed his views further in *The Principles of Citizenship*. He argued that the interest of those who valued education highly was not lessened by the introduction of compulsory elementary education – just as the person who is charitably disposed to hospitals does not cease to have that disposition with the introduction of a tax to support them. In this respect, spontaneity is not being invaded, but rather endorsed by the state. For Jones the view, propounded by Mill, that law and liberty are inconsistent and mutually exclusive spheres which require us to distinguish between actions which chiefly concern the individual, and those which are chiefly of social interest, is mere abstract thinking. He argues that there are no personal interests which are not also either immediately or remotely social, and no social interests which are not personal.[56] On a narrow view of the state, as the legislative and judicial power of society, there is no doubt a distinction between, for example, a policeman being drunk at home and being drunk on duty. However, Jones argues that such a distinction is made on different grounds from those of Mill. The state refrains from interference with supposedly private acts because of the possible inconvenience and social wrongs that might be occasioned by attempting to execute such laws. Furthermore, Jones contends that if the state may punish the actions of those who damage, or risk damaging, other individuals or the public, as Mill allows on his assumptions, then liberty itself becomes a casualty, because, on the broader view of the state, that 'of being the organized will of society to the common good', every wrong committed damages both to the individual and to society. On this meaning, the state is concerned about the policeman who gets drunk at home, in so far as it knows of his activity, and will feel less confident about his capacity to carry out his duties. The policeman's drunkenness at once damages his own personality and does harm to the state.[57]

It was commonplace among Idealists, and those influenced by them, to suggest that education, like the state, has a formal, or institutional meaning, and a broader sense in which the organized will of society fulfils an educative function in all aspects of life.[58] This, of course, was merely echoing Hegel and the Greeks. For Hegel education is a process of liberation from ignorance towards the realization that the laws of the state, which at first appeared to be externally imposed, are in fact the expression of one's own will and a self-imposition. In this process the family, formal instruction in school, and the exemplars provided by the wider society all play their role. The public spectacle of the Estates' Assemblies in deliberation, for example, constitutes in Hegel's view 'an excellent education for the citizens' in that 'it is here that there first began to develop the virtues, abilities, dexterities, which have to serve as examples to the public'.[59] The purpose of the educative state, in Plato's view, is to 'produce citizens of good character'.[60] Plato goes on to imply that such virtues are inherited and, by means of education, built upon by succeeding generations of children.

We saw in chapter four that Henry Jones rejected the idea of inherited character in favour of the view that what parents transmit to their children are powers and capacities which are realized only when in contact with particular circumstances. In every other respect the child begins anew along the pathway to virtue unaffected, as far as internal conditions go, by the fact that he or she is the progeny of wicked or virtuous parents. It is the environment, especially the social environment, which is of crucial importance in the development of character. Even though the education of the child towards the attainment of virtue may differ according to the powers and capacities of the children, Jones was still of the firm conviction that 'such education is more or less possible in the case of every rational being'.[61]

What, then, is the relation between morality and education? Jones, while visiting America with the British Education Mission, told an audience at the Rice Institute on 27 November 1918 that he subscribed to a creed with only one article; namely, that human well-being depended on doing what is right, and right-doing is conditional on knowledge of the truth.[62] This is a conviction that permeates the whole of Jones's philosophy. In 1895, for example, at the closing of the session of University College of North Wales, he argued that in the world of spirit 'Truth and Goodness are twin powers'.[63] Indeed, knowledge facilitates, and is the condition of good conduct. Elsewhere he argued that human freedom depends upon education and is the condition of all the virtues. Knowledge emancipates and gives us the power to conquer the natural and spiritual world.[64] In other words, the virtues which make for good character, and responsible citizenship, and which comprise the good life, are an attainment rather than an endowment. They must learn from the educative exemplars of the social environment and by formal instruction in schools. If the purpose of the state is to promote the good life, and ignorance constitutes an obstacle to its enjoyment, then it is bound to make available to its citizens the means by which they can develop their minds. The state cannot confine itself to the provision and maintenance of institutional arrangements for education. It must also provide moral guidance in pointing the way to a true, rather than false, good.[65] It can achieve this through the conduct of its officers and good laws. But, in the broader sense of being the organized will of society, it can work at the constant improvement of the social environment and the moralization of the relations within its purview. For Jones, 'the question of surrounding the child with influences calculated to evolve its powers is thus of transcendent importance'.[66]

In speaking of the broad conception of education, the practice rather than the precept of moral conduct was emphasized by Jones. The power of the community to educate its own children could only be measured by the extent to which its customary conduct was permeated with virtue and wisdom. If opportunities for the good life are not evident at the fundamental level of relations between employer and employee, then, neither charity nor legal compulsion can penetrate the social evils inherent in the condition.[67] This is why, for Jones, 'every industry in the land is meant to be a school of virtue',[68] and why he was so disillusioned and angry when he heard the evidence of the south Wales coal owners before the Commission on Welsh Higher Education who cared as much for educating their employees as they did for educating their pit-ponies. Jones was well aware that the large industries were 'not educational institutions or schools of art or of gentleness as the little workshops were'.[69] These conditions, he argued, should be changed and instead of destroying the working man they should ennoble him. To this end Capital had to acknowledge its duties.[70] In a letter to H. A. L. Fisher, dated 16 July 1916, Jones went as far as to suggest 'uneducated and selfish men cannot lead in such a cause. There is no need of the times more pressing and more important than that of keeping intellectually stunted and morally marred men out of industrial captainship.'[71]

In relation to formal education, the German system was much studied and admired both for its transmission of cultural values to the intellectually inclined, and for the contribution it made to industry. The German system prepared the more technically orientated pupil for the performance of highly valued skills necessary to the operation of business. The former was the work of the '*Gymnasium*' and the latter of the '*Realschule*'. Futhermore, there was a good deal of co-operation between the universities and industrial enterprises designed to apply the advances made in knowledge to commercial ventures. In Germany the state took an active interest in developing and funding the education system. T. H. Green and R. B. Haldane, among the Idealists, both wrote in praise of the German system, indicating that Britain could fruitfully adopt certain of its aspects. Green thought the German division of schools the only rational one to be made at secondary level, and Haldane was impressed both by the dual purpose of the system, that is the promotion of pure culture and the application of research to commercial enterprise, and by the extent to which the state interested itself in education.[72] The Government, too, looked to Germany for educational ideas. In 1895 it set up the office of Special Inquiries in the Education Department under the directorship of Michael Sadler, who was an Oxford man deeply moved by the ideas of Green. Sadler wrote a special study of German education under the auspices of the office of Special Inquiries.[73]

Most of the Idealists, of course, had first-hand knowledge of the German system in that it was a matter of course for them to travel the beloved country of Kant, Goethe and Hegel, and study philosophy under a German professor. Jones was no exception in this respect. In arguing for an integrated system of education in which the state fully acknowledges its responsibility for the mental as well as the physical health of the nation, Jones argued that the individualist point of view had gradually been transcended in the provision of state elementary education, but it still prevailed in matters of higher learning. Unlike the Germans, the British were averse to converting their institutions into organs of the state, but nevertheless the very success of German universities and technical institutions invited close scrutiny for the lessons that might be learned. Whatever freedoms may have been restricted by state control in other areas, the universities, Jones claimed, enjoyed a greater degree of independence after the failure of methods of direct control of internal university affairs. Like Hegel and Green, he was not suggesting that any institution could be imported wholescale from another country. Each people developed institutions appropriate to its character. What he was suggesting was that the principles which informed the German experience and led to progress in higher education were instructive for the future development of the British system. The Germans had realized that upon the investment of the resources of the Empire in the universities, as well as in their army and navy, the nation's prosperity and welfare depended. Furthermore, they had allowed the internal freedom and independence necessary for the special service that institutions of higher learning could perform for the state.[74]

Although Jones always had his reservations about the German system, with the advent of the First World War he became vociferously critical of the way the German state had abused the power of education. It was not the control of education by the state, nor the success with which it fashioned the German mind, of which Jones was critical, but of the purpose for which education was being used. The German state had wilfully disregarded the supreme Kantian principle of treating every person as an end and never as a means.[75] Germany provided an example of the deliberate and systematic use of education for the promotion of the efficiency of the state:[76] 'it is education *by* the state *for the sake* of the State'.[77]

For Jones, the ultimate purpose of education was the moral development of the individual. It must therefore be education for its own sake, rather than as a means to an end.[78] The president of the Board of Education was himself partially sympathetic to this view, although in practice the 1918 Education Act was rather more geared to industry than many social liberals and Labour supporters would have liked. Fisher contended that, 'I feel to the full the strength of the contention that young people, whatever may be their station in life, should primarily be regarded as subjects for education and not as parts of the industrial machine.'[79] Far from the German example deterring the Coalition Government from wishing to take control of an integrated education system, the concrete demonstration of how the state could mould national character and improve industrial efficiency gave it a greater resolve to take education into its care.

Jones was not worried by greater state intervention. The German example showed that a state, inspired by nobler ideals of a rational moral life and universal humanitarian principles, could just as easily foster unlimited devotion in its people to this higher good.[80] He was, however, concerned that education should not, in the light of

Germany's industrial success, become the handmaiden of the squalid morals of industrialism and economic greed. In 1917 Jones expressed satisfaction at the prospect of the government making greater use of the instrument of education. There was no doubt that the pursuit of science could make the foundations of industry more secure, and that more emphasis upon modern languages could contribute to the opening of wider markets. These, he acknowledged, were necessary motives in the economic and industrial struggle with Germany, but they were not the highest conceivable motives. Jones argued that:

> it is better to love knowledge for the sake of economic prosperity than to be content with ignorance. And the process of education will by and by raise the motive to a better level; so that the sciences may be valued by the many, as they are now by the few, for their own sake, and Modern Languages may be studied for the sake of the literary treasures which they hold.[81]

Moral education at school would, in his view, precipitate such an elevation of motive.[82] This moral education at first must be primarily practical, and whether the teacher imparts his or her knowledge of Greek, or the lessons are more vocational or technically orientated, the teacher must by the example of moral demeanour liberate the potential character of the pupils. Only later does the pupil come to share self-consciously the ethical purpose of the teacher in being exposed to moral theory.

Education for Idealists was not to be viewed as the means to economic ends. It was for them the great social healer and class leveller which would ultimately lead to the evaporation of social evils associated with moral depravation, and class antagonism born of privilege. If the ladder of learning were genuinely open to all irrespective of background, social conflict would largely disappear. Green, for example, believed that all questions concerning education in Britain were complicated by class. The distinctions of occupation, natural in any society, were exacerbated and deepened by the fact that there was no fusion of classes within the schools or universities. A common education, he believed, would contribute to the levelling of the classes. If something other than the accident of birth was to determine the provision of education to the nation a levelling up, rather than a levelling down, would result from a properly organized system of schools. Such a system, where all classes were educated side by side, would cure the 'unconscious social insolence' of the gentleman, and 'cure others of social jealousy'. Furthermore, Green argues:

> It would heal the division between those who look complacently down on others as vulgar, and those who angrily look up to others as having the social reputation which they themselves have not, uniting both classes by the freemasonry of a common education.[83]

Haldane was also optimistic about the efficacious power of education to solve social problems,[84] and the 1918 Education Act itself was ostensibly designed as a class levelling and social healing measure. Fisher argued that the bill he wished to have enacted was 'a people's measure' meant to benefit those members of the community who comprised the labouring classes. In a country with such a huge responsibility for governing over five hundred million human beings throughout the world, there should be no proletariat, because each citizen should bear his, or her, share of 'the heaviest burden of civic responsibility which has ever been devolved upon an organised community of human beings'.[85]

Given Jones's social background and the pathway by which he was elevated in civic stature, it is not surprising to find him arguing that the pernicious effects of class could be eradicated by an open education system, and devising schemes to ensure the wider dissemination of knowledge throughout the whole community. In the following chapter we will see that Jones's opposition to the Labour Party was based upon his presumption that by promoting the interests of the working man it actually exacerbated rather than alleviated class conflict. That discussion will be foreshadowed here by briefly introducing his views on class in relation to education. Jones, as we know, was of the view that by means of education the working class should be elevated to the level of responsible citizenship. In this respect education could recognize no class distinctions, because all those who travel its road are 'pilgrims on the same journey'.[86] Education, Jones believed, should be used to guide the working man to a better use of his leisure. He should be educated to such a level that he would continue all his life to enjoy the pleasures of history or literature.[87] Class could not be allowed to determine who was to be educated. Jones argued that:

> This *immoral* conception of 'class', has to be fought *in* the schools and colleges; and especially in the latter by educating folk together. And, for that reason in part (and many others) I've actually resolved to put my whole face, if necessary, into throwing the Colleges open without fee in Wales.[88]

The scheme to which he refers was supported, after some hesitation, by Jones's fellow Commissioners on University Education in Wales, and also gained the approval of Lloyd George.[89] Jones was confident, after every county adopted the 'penny rate', that Wales would lead the Empire in abolishing university fees. Although the counties voluntarily and generously supported the scheme, and their example was followed by many counties in England, the devaluation of money frustrated the total abolition of fees. Nevertheless, Jones reflected, 'I am sure it was a great step in advance . . . and I have no doubt that, as time goes on, considerations of material wealth will have less and less to do with deciding whether a man shall or shall not enter a university.'[90]

Jones devoted much of his energies during the last four or five years of his life trying to persuade universities and politicians to extend extra-mural teaching and make education more widely available to the population as a whole in order to arrest what he saw to be a decline in moral standards occasioned by the war. He had always been a strong supporter of the work of the Workers' Educational Association and the Adult Education Committee, but thought that their efforts could be supplemented with the involvement of churches and chapels. Jones was wholeheartedly committed to Green's view that 'if the people are to be made scholars, the scholar must go to the people, not wait for them to come to him'.[91] He firmly believed that 'College education should be available to the majority of the people and within their reach throughout their life'.[92] At a public meeting in Corwen, August 1919, Jones outlined a scheme which would bring the universities, churches and people into closer harmony, and make higher learning available even in the smallest market town. Following that meeting a committee was established under the chairmanship of William George of Cricieth, to whom Jones sent a printed outline of his scheme.[93] Jones proposed that in every market town in Wales a committee should be established, representative of all the churches, which should be responsible for organizing classes in at least one of the sciences and one of the humanities, and made available on a weekly basis during the evenings, for three winters, conducted by the ablest young college tutors, and taught at university standard. In this way the churches would once again serve the youth of the country who were disillusioned by the war, and 'Wales would be transformed both religiously and educationally in twenty years or so'.[94] In an interview for *Yr Herald Gymraeg* he argued that 'it is incumbent on religious leaders to face up to their responsibilities in trying to develop the character and mind of young people'.[95]

The scheme required government and church funding, and in the end came to little, but it does illustrate once again the practical ways in which Jones believed that the class barriers, standing as an impediment to education, could be surmounted, and the highest-quality education, for its own sake, be made available to all for the purpose of virtuous development and responsible active citizenship. Having now examined the central motif of citizenship against its metaphysical and moral background, and reviewed the directly practical ways in which Jones wished to establish the educational preconditions for citizenship, we will now turn in the next chapter to his views on domestic Edwardian politics and ideologies.

CHAPTER SIX

POLITICAL REFLECTIONS: SOCIALISM, LIBERALISM AND SYNDICALISM

In this chapter we wish to undertake a more detailed scrutiny of Jones's perception of contemporary Edwardian political movements. The basic structure of the discussion will begin with a more general introduction to Jones's political views, followed by an examination of his opinions on socialism, liberalism and syndicalism.

We need not rehearse the major points of Jones's biography which have already been discussed, apart from briefly reiterating that Jones was a Liberal Party member for most of his active life. He campaigned for Asquith and was a personal friend of a number of Liberal Party figures, probably most significantly David Lloyd George.[1] He had, however, a deep if qualified sympathy for the growing Labour movement. In fact there were attempts in the Labour movement and Fabian circles, before the First World War, to encourage him to join the Labour Party. As regards syndicalism, this was a doctrine which affected him in a number of ways. Syndicalism was a revolutionary and deeply anti-statist doctrine, and it was having some *prima facie* success in Jones's own stamping-ground, Wales. Jones, as an ardent statist and Welshman, felt a double duty, philosophical and cultural, to take up active lecturing against syndicalism. In the case of syndicalism he had no overtly systematic writings to confront, therefore he presented his doctrine of citizenship as a philosophical and political antidote.[2]

Before discussing his interpretations of these movements we wish to make some more general observations on Jones's political stance. It is worth noting immediately that his vision of the British state and national character was not wholly sanguine. In his articles in the *Contemporary Review*, responding to Hobhouse's book *Democracy and Reaction*, Jones commented:

> [The British] moral and intellectual temper is not all that could be desired. We verily are an ill-educated, or, rather, a half-educated people. Our pursuit of truth is not serious or sustained. We are 'general readers' who gain from the journalistic Press and the novel that slack knowledge and smattering

> acquaintance with the principles of science and philosophy which cheapens them and makes them stale.[3]

On a number of occasions he bewailed and inveighed against this state of mind in Britain, particularly that of the commercial business mentality. In one of his private letters in 1916, commenting on a visit of mineowners to the Reconstruction Committee, Jones remarked that the employers' contributions to the discussion were

> an appalling exposure of their souls. They had no more thought of educating the youth than of educating their pit-ponies. It was all a question of converting human raw-material into productive machinery. It was the *unconscious* background of their minds that was overwhelming . . . All that you and I think of when we hear of 'Citizenship' or 'Ethics' . . . all that is pure jargon for them, within the whole domain of their business and intercourse with the workers and with the markets of the world . . . I am despairing! The layers and layers that have to be dug through.[4]

Jones felt that the general character of the average British mind was limited by a philistine commercial mentality.[5]

He noted that the British at the turn of the century tended to mistrust the state. In an inaugural lecture in 1905 he complained that this view was particularly damaging in the field of education. Education generally, and higher education in particular, were caught up in the peculiarly British mania for private enterprise. However, Germany's singular public commitment to higher education, as Jones noted, was bearing fruit in Germany's industrial pre-eminence over Britain. He thus noted that: 'Our repugnance to state organisation and state maintenance and management is to a certain extent irrational.'[6] State policy on education does not necessarily mean any loss of autonomy; it can in fact enable citizens and enterprises to succeed. For Jones we should also be aware that '*laissez-faire* is as dangerous a policy in public as in private affairs'.[7] It could damage both the industrial and cultural future of Britain. What the private commercial mentality did not grasp was that 'taxation in support of the institutions of higher learning is as legitimate in itself and as essential to national well-being as taxation for the support of the . . . army and navy and civil service'.[8] For Jones such commercialism was rooted in a thin and shallow individualism which disregarded the social roots to human nature.

For Jones the above attitudes also lay behind the typical British mistrust and scepticism of the intellectual and abstract thinker, particularly in politics, something Jones personally deplored. One fallacy which lay behind this British attitude was that abstract reflection bore little or no relation to *real* practice. For Jones, as noted in chapter two, such a distinction was vastly over-emphasized. All that the philosopher or abstract thinker does is to reflect upon what is. As he put it: 'philosophy is only the common consciousness seeking to do justice to all the facts and to think through them more persistently.'[9] Those who think that they live in a real world apart from theory, those who regard the philosopher with gentle contempt, are suffering from a deep misapprehension. As Jones argues: 'The man of the world turns a deaf ear to the theorist, quite unconscious that in rejecting the theories of his contemporaries he is victim of the theories of their predecessors.'[10] The practical mind is saturated with habitual theoretical nostrums. For Jones when the philosopher thinks, it is the traditions of a society become self-conscious. It is really 'society which criticizes itself in us'.[11] There is no way we can simply sidestep theory.

Jones's dislike of the categorial distinction between practice and abstract thought and his repudiation of the limited commercial mind in politics and education is also related to his irritation with the manners and habits of democratic politics in Britain. For Jones we should not confuse the mind of the people with electoral results and Parliamentary wrangling. Much of what goes on in elections is simply 'an unseemly scrabble' characterized by 'our blatant placards, our violent party Press, our excited public gatherings, by which we crowd the political education of the people into a few intemperate and heated weeks of vituperative controversies'.[12] He deplored the term 'masses' as an insult to citizenship,[13] and also, despite the inevitability of political parties, he was not particularly fond of their contestation. Parties, instead of acting as bearers of the common good, were often peopled with the ignorant and uneducated, acting as a focus and stimulation to passions and prejudice.[14]

For Jones, both ordinary citizens and politicians needed education in citizenship. Many working class people had 'a pathetic belief in those who pretend to lead them and profess to be educated'.[15] Only the best and most instructed minds, not the lowest, should participate in politics.[16] What was required for Jones was:

> a bulwark against error in the mind of the people themselves, to help them rise to such a level of intelligence and integrity that they cannot be exploited by specious argument, nor their will be corrupted by promises of class advantage. And that means then raising the level of the life of the people, and moralizing their politics.[17]

Jones looks here towards an active communally aware citizenship, a subject which we discussed in chapter five.

The call for the best minds in authority, wise leadership, moralizing institutions and so forth evinces a potentially deep-rooted élitism.[18] However Jones was not alone in such élitist beliefs. The fears and dangers of democracy, especially with a widening electorate, and the belief in wise leaders had been commonplace among conservative and classical liberal theorists throughout the second half of the nineteenth century. In fact neither party was really overtly committed to democracy even into the early twentieth century.[19] At the turn of the century even socialist groups, like the Fabians, overtly or covertly advocated élitist rule. Democracy had little charm or value for Sidney and Beatrice Webb.[20] The difference in Jones's case was that his élite was neither aristocratic, nor the most knowledgeable or technically able, but rather the most ethical. He was also, unlike some Fabians, not persuaded that party politics should be abandoned, for all its faults. Expert administrative autocracy had no appeal for him. His panacea tended to be a belief in what education (particularly in citizenship) could eventually achieve. The élitism was also tempered by his belief in the widening and extension of active citizenship to all. Education, particularly higher education, had a great civilizing mission.[21]

Jones argued that there was a clear need, though, for a science of society. This could not be a mechanistic science. Society is made by humans and constituted by their beliefs. There is no study of society which stands outside humans and observes them. There are no given social facts, no psychological instincts which cause political behaviour. Jones, for example, explicitly repudiates the psychologistic instinctual thesis of Graham Wallas's *Human Nature in Politics* (1908).[22]

To try to understand society it is necessary to comprehend the rational self-understandings of humans. Society, as Jones put it, 'is mind-made environment . . . the supreme outer condition of man's rational life'.[23] The science that Jones is thinking of here is therefore more hermeneutical, *Geisteswissenschaften* as opposed to *Naturwissenschaften*. To study society scientifically is therefore to study human nature and the ends of human life systematically. Such a study does provide some hope for the future. If projected social reforms and legislation could be rooted in such systematic social science then it would be premised on 'insight into the needs of man, a high opinion of human nature, strong trust in the good which is already working in the world and which has brought it thus far . . . these are the cardinal constituents of the reformers practical faith'.[24]

In sum, Jones's general stance in politics is a qualified optimism. He finds no perfection in the British or any other state. The character of the British people, their cultural, educational, political, democratic and economic awareness was lamentable. Both leaders and led, employers and employees, left much to be desired. However, he does see some hope in the growth and spread of enlightened education, ethical leadership and moralized institutions. A future science of society premised upon a clearer knowledge of human nature and society could provide the ballast for such a reform programme. It is against this background that we can now view Jones's reading of Edwardian political movements.

SOCIALISM

Despite his lifelong association and support of the Liberal Party Jones remarked in an article in 1910: 'If I were asked which of the political parties contains the largest proportion of able men, earnest in the pursuit of the ideal of a State . . . I should say, with little hesitation, that it is the Labour Party.'[25] Jones was not always so keen on organized labour representation. He advocated, on other occasions, that it would be in the interests of the working class if there were no labour candidates. However, in general, as we have seen, Jones attempted to avoid rigid dualities (such as liberal and socialist) in political, as well as metaphysical theory.[26]

Socialism as a movement was coming of age in Britain from the 1880s onwards. This was the period when the debates over individualism and collectivism took off. However, socialism as a European movement had a longer pedigree dating from the late 1820s in France and England.[27] Although some have attached the ideology of socialism to British movements like Chartism, trade unionism, Labourism and the co-operatives, it is straining the point to call all of these socialist, although undoubtedly by the final decades of the nineteenth century many of the surviving movements perceived socialism as the most acceptable vocabulary for discussing their aspirations.[28] The major preoccupations of these movements – parliamentary and suffrage reform, land reform and trade union rights – coincided with socialism.

Self-conscious socialism in the 1830s was associated primarily with what is now often called utopian socialism. Saint Simon, Charles Fourier and particularly Robert Owen were the most well known.[29] This form of socialism denoted a structured worked-out vision of a future society – Fourier's *Phalanstery*, Saint Simon's administered industrial society or Owen's New Harmony, in which humans would no longer be subject to the deprivations of capitalism and unjust rule and would become fulfilled and happy. This form of socialism declined in Britain considerably from the 1840s up to the late 1870s.[30] Marxian socialism, although having a dynamic impact in France and Germany over the 1870s and 1880s, had hardly any role to play in Britain until the 1920s. The early English Marxist group, the Social Democratic Federation (1884) (founded as the Democratic Federation in 1881), was relatively insignificant and always stood outside the mainstream socialist movement. It was led by an ex-Tory radical, H. M. Hyndman, an admirer of Disraeli and an enthusiatic imperialist, who was inspired by Gordon of Khartoum, stood for crushing the Boers in 1900, detested trade unions, and was personally repudiated as a reactionary by Marx and Engels. Only a very small proportion of socialist writers and political figures in Britain in the period 1880–1914 were Marxist inspired.[31]

The different perceptions of socialism in the 1880s and up to 1914 depended to some extent on the milieu of the author and the audience addressed. As one recent writer has put it: 'The history of socialism is the history of socialisms.'[32] The background to socialist ideas in the 1880s lay in a number of important figures and movements: the memories of Chartism; Ruskin, Carlyle and their critique of capitalism and its aesthetic and socially destructive aspect; Henry George and his idea of the single tax; Christian socialism in figures like Charles Kingsley; a radical use of Ricardo and the neoclassical economists (this became particularly characteristic of the Fabians); a more radical utilitarianism with roots in the later writings of J. S. Mill, particularly his work on political economy and *Chapters on Socialism*; Chamberlain's *Radical Programme* and the beginnings of the progressive liberalism in the 1880s; radicalized trade unions, and finally, Lib-Labism in the 1880s. All these and more influences constituted the backdrop to the growth of socialism. The most notable organizations from 1880–1914 were the Fabians, Independent Labour Party (ILP) and Guild Socialists. The grounds for the justification of socialism also varied considerably, moving through Christianity, utilitarianism, natural rights theory, neoclassical economics, Comtism and Kantian moral philosophy. The socialism which developed up to the 1900s was a hydra-headed creature.[33]

In terms of Jones's fellow Idealist thinkers, there was a recognizable community of views. However, they were often more concerned to score rhetorical points than to portray an accurate picture of the socialist movement. Firstly, Jones's perception of types of socialism was often limited to comments on 'true' and 'false' socialism. He refers in passing to a false socialism which is equivalent to 'rapine' that wishes to collectivize the economy and destroy all private property.[34] Jones does not put any names to this type and it is not quite clear to whom or what he is referring, although an intelligent guess would be Marxism. Secondly, he associates socialism with both collectivism and statism. In other words, socialism, whether true or false, is state socialism. This association of socialism with collectivism and liberalism with individualism was a common view from the 1880s. Paradoxically, Jones, Caird, Bosanquet and others were aware of William Morris's socialism, and none would have described him, or Belfort Bax the libertarian socialist, as statist or collectivist. This is also the case with Robert Owen. This point would be even more true of the Edwardian Guild Socialists, of whom Jones was well aware.[35]

Edward Caird adopts roughly the same view as Jones on socialism. He notes, like J. S. Mill in *Chapters on Socialism*, the existence of a form of utopian socialism, which he calls 'dogmatic socialism' and mentions Fourier and Owen.[36] However this socialism is kept distinct, as an older socialism, from a new socialism. In terms of this new, more 'ethical' socialism, Caird mentions Sidney Ball, the Fabian writer, although he cannot have been reading Sidney or Beatrice Webb at the time. In Caird, the Fabians (meaning Ball and possibly David Ritchie), appear as a more sensible version of the new socialism. Like Jones, Caird wanted to adapt this 'truer socialism' and to overcome its opposition to individualistic liberalism.

Certain of Jones's contemporaries, like William Wallace and Schäffle, had identified a powerful strain of scientific socialism, which in Schäffle's case focused socialism almost exclusively on Marxism.[37] Anyone who followed political events in Germany from the 1880s could not help but notice the impact of Marx. However, this was not taken up by Caird or Jones. On the other hand, another Idealist writer, J. S. MacKenzie, took Schäffle's discussion on board in preparing his book *An Introduction to Social Philosophy* (1890), but kept scientific socialism distinct from ethical socialism, admitting in the course of his discussion that 'socialism is a term of great elasticity of meaning, and it covers a variety of proposals which are widely different from one another'.[38] Bernard Bosanquet in a more sophisticated and, at the time, well-respected article referred to by MacKenzie and Jones – 'The Antithesis between Individualism and Socialism Philosophically Considered' (1899) – argued that the distinction must be between economic and moral socialism, as distinct from moral and economic individualism.[39]

We can see in many of the above writers an awareness of the diversity of socialisms. Scientific, economic, utopian, state and ethical socialisms are all discerned. These varying strands advocated both the disappearance of industrial capitalism and its improvement; regarded human nature as ready-made and also perfectly malleable; believed in the ethical potential of the state, but also condemned the state as corrupt and destructive. All these diverse and often contradictory beliefs, within the various socialisms, were present at the time of Jones's writing. With Jones, however, as with the majority of his contemporaries, 'state socialism' is his primary focus.

One of the major points of interest in many of the Idealists is that they tended to take the Fabians as a key point of reference for socialism in Britain. This was not always complimentary. Sometimes the Fabians were seen as exponents of a false mechanistic doctrine. The slight ambiguity found in these writers over Fabianism is due to the diversity of doctrine and belief found within Fabianism itself – a point that none of the above writers noticed explicitly. Usually the works referred to were the writings of Sidney and Beatrice Webb, G. B. Shaw's edition of *The Fabian Essays in Socialism* and some of the essays by Sidney Ball.[40]

For Jones there were clear problems with socialism. Socialism appeared to be connected to the development of democracy, and as we have already seen, democracy, for Jones, functions only if the best participate – 'Democracy was a most dangerous form of government in the hands of people who were not fit for it.'[41] Moral reform must precede economic or material reforms for socialism to succeed. Civic virtue or active ethical citizenship is the premise to any success. Jones advocated a form of moral egalitarianism, premised on citizenship, as a basis for any political or economic reforms. It should be noted, though, that Jones's worries concerning democracy were partly premised upon the fact that socialists, particularly Fabians *in toto*, were actually interested in extending democracy. This was, in fact, questionable.[42]

Another problem that Jones identifies is that many socialists equate socialism with egalitarian economic and material changes; in other words, to achieve socialism it is enough to redistribute wealth and implement welfare reforms.[43] The danger in this type of more materially orientated socialism is that individual moral character is neglected.[44] Welfare rights are met in the form of pensions, national insurance etc., and the active correlative moral duties of the citizen are totally neglected. This neglect of individual duty, in Jones's view, also led to neglect of self-help and individual freedom. The freedom for character development is a painful necessity. Socialism, however, tends, for Jones, 'to desire the profits of Individualism without its pains'.[45] Jones therefore contends that 'organic, civic or state methods can be employed advantageously only where the individual character is highly developed.'[46]

For Jones, the major danger of socialism, apart from the problems of mass democracy, loss of civic virtue and neglect of character, is working-class cupidity and the very use of 'class' as a social category.[47] The Labour Party and socialist movement for Jones 'are by aim and profession the representative of the interests of one class of citizens'; he continues that any class (working or aristocratic) which monopolizes the state taints 'the very spirit of citizenship'.[48] Jones does not even like the title of the Labour Party, since it immediately conjures up a vision of sectarianism. A party, for Jones, does not represent one class alone; it must represent the common good. Apart from publishing deeply critical articles on this theme, answered in one case by Ramsay MacDonald, Jones mentions the above point as the key reason why he does not join the Labour Party.[49] In a letter to Sidney Webb he writes:

> if I believed that by joining the Labour Party I could strengthen its power for good in the State, I should join it today and wear its label as a badge of honour. I want the working man . . . to be a good citizen . . . But, my dear Mr Webb, just here is what you will regard as my stone of stumbling. The Labour Party, as I understand it, is in the contradictory position of suspending and obscuring the well-being of the State as a whole, instead of placing it first and making the particular ends of labour the means of its attainment . . . Were I to join the Labour Party, the first and last service I should like to perform for it would be that of asking it to forget itself, cease to speak of 'class', especially of class intepreted in terms of economics . . . I love the working man too well to ask him to legislate primarily for himself.[50]

In fact, it is again far from clear that Jones is accurate in his reading of socialism. The early utopian writers, like Saint Simon and Owen, had no interest whatsoever in class or class warfare. This is even more true of Christian socialism. The Fabians also were often deeply élitist, illiberal and uninterested in class. Bernard Shaw and Ramsay MacDonald explicitly rejected class as a useful social category.[51] Because Jones preached this line to audiences throughout the country, particularly in Wales, and also to the peoples of Australia and America, one must assume that he was trying to persuade workers to vote, not on narrow interests, but for the common good.[52] In this respect he was arguing against the emotional and rhetorical appeal of the Labour Party to the working class.

Jones did have other criticisms of socialism, although the emphasis on class cupidity probably figures most prominently. Jones contended that occasionally socialists appear to favour public action on principle (rather as the individualist rejects it on principle).[53] Such principled advocacy of public ownership can lead *per se* to commercial inefficiency, waste and the destruction of individuality – 'if socialism is verily the extinction of all individual property, men would be reduced to things'.[54] Jones found such principled advocacy of public ownership both abhorrent and neglectful of the subtle pragmatic contours and demands of the economy. It was also premised upon a dogmatic dualism between public and private which Jones was again philosophically inclined to reject.

Finally, Jones, although never systematically pursuing a particular thinker, does make occasional critical remarks on the question of revolutionary movements. In fact the only groups advocating revolution at the time in Britain were the SDF and Socialist League, and these had a minority appeal within British socialism. Jones's argument against 'political revolution' is premised on a critical understanding of tradition. The 'good' is already present in embryo in the world of institutions. Genuine reform tries to bring this good forth. For Jones: 'It is an axiom of fruitful research and a postulate of real reform that their starting point shall be in things as they are'; Jones links this argument directly to Edmund Burke.[55] If we accept this argument then 'the less we shall trust in revolution'.[56] A revolution is by definition a hasty, often unthought, acceleration of evolution. It is worth noting here that Jones's position directly paralleled the evolutionary gradualism of both the Fabians and the German revisionist, Eduard Bernstein.

However the above criticisms did not lead Jones to abandon all socialism. There were fundamental and unavoidable truths in socialism. The one most important truth grasped by socialists is that humans are social creatures. Society is prior to the individual. Jones takes this as axiomatic, as we saw in chapter four, and thinks the assertion, by many individualistic liberals, of the contrary is equally an axiomatic error. All the individuals' ethical powers and freedoms are rooted in the community.[57] Socialists thus see the intrinsic organic character of society and are to be applauded for this.

Furthermore, socialists have no difficulty in relating freedom and rights to communal life. They are associated with a broader intellectual movement which has ascertained that freedom 'is no longer merely negative. It no longer sets the individual conscience against the universal order of the Church and the State. It is now divined that the State itself may be free, and the means of the freedom of its members.'[58] In consequence socialists are not afraid, like many individualist liberals, to moralize citizens. They are not afraid of extending taxation for the public good.[59] The state can broaden and extend the powers of the individual by increasing its activities. Jones contends, for example, that 'the Post Office managed by the State enlarges the capacities of the individual. I can use its utilities . . . You can't send a private messenger from John of Groats to Land's End for 1*d* . . . The State does not dispossess the individual of his property. It takes his money and returns it in increased utilities.'[60] Well-financed state education at all levels, pensions for the aged, school meals, and greater public utilities are all further examples of how the state can enhance the freedom of the individual. In all of these movements Jones notes:

> if we endeavour to forget 'names' and substitute the observation of actual facts for prophetic utterances regarding tendencies, we shall see, I believe, nothing worse nor better than an attempt to employ the organisation of the State and of the municipalities so as to place at the disposal of their members means for meeting their individual wants. These social means have been adopted little by little in the face of the most searching criticism.[61]

It is this form of socialism which carries our letters, provides defence, redistributes wealth where equitable, educates our children, lights our street and so forth.[62] This does not destroy or undermine rights of property, rather 'it is defending them by defining them a little more justly, which is their surest defence'.[63] We, as individuals, are not negated by public ownership policies, but rather become shareholders in a vast enterprise for the common good.[64] This sounds, in fact, remarkably like some statements on socialism by Sidgwick and Sidney Webb.[65] The point that Jones draws attention to is that: 'It is a significant fact that there is hardly any desire in England to take back an enterprise which has once been committed to the State or municipality.'[66] The right type of socialism would not weaken character, but in fact strengthen it by offering greater opportunities for self-development. Indeed, he asserts that: 'The obligations of parentage will not be loosened on the hearth of the respectable poor by any State regulations.'[67] Socialism, as collective action, is with us and has been accepted positively by many who know virtually nothing of the ideologies.

LIBERALISM

Jones's fundamental principles inclined him towards a belief in strong state activity and therefore a sympathy with socialism, a point to which we will return in chapter eight. This also led him (with other intellectuals) to a reassessment of liberalism in the period 1880–1914.[68] His particular stress was laid not so much on economic reform as on the ethical duties of citizens and the state. However, he was not alone in this. His ethical position was shared by many socialists and new liberals.[69]

The notion of individualism, which was used widely in political discussions of the period, was virtually synonymous over the 1880s and 1890s with liberalism, in the same way as collectivism was used as a popular synonym for socialism. The term individualism, like socialism, covered a broad spectrum of opinion. This makes precision difficult to achieve. When Jones discusses individualism, he does not overtly recognize that Bosanquet's ethical Hegelian individualism, Hobhouse's empiricized Kantian individualism, Sidgwick's moderate utilitarian individualism, Spencer's biological individualism, or Auberon Herbert's anarchic natural right individualism are distinct both in substance and social effect. Minimally, Sidgwick's moderate individualism was the norm. Spencer was regarded, by most Victorians, as too extreme. What was of key importance to Jones though was how to explain the changing character of liberalism and its relation to socialism in the period 1880–1914. Individualism was simply a word to denote a collection of views, which might be loosely termed classical liberalism, or any political position which pursues sectional interests to the detriment of the common good.

There are many forms of explanation of the changing character of British liberalism in the nineteenth century which can be found in recent literature, for example, those concentrating on socio-economic causation, in terms of the changing character of British industry; the growth of the mass electorate; the rising labour movement; the development of statistical social scientific information about the effects of industrialization, and so on. Since the 1970s a new wave of interpretations has arisen concentrating on the changing and complex character of the ideology of liberalism in the period 1880 to 1914.[70] Each of these areas incorporates an enormous body of material. Our focus will be on the ideological sphere.[71]

There are a number of interpretations of the relation between the old and new liberalism. One view, popular with some contemporary theorists, is that the classical liberalism was a clearly identifiable creed with an ahistorical continuity which was betrayed by the quasi-socialist new liberalism.[72] In this reading it is a misnomer to call the latter liberalism. It was really a form of socialism in disguise. However, the most popular line with historians, up to the 1970s, was that liberalism had two faces – individualist and collectivist. The new liberals, at the turn of the century, adapted liberalism to the needs of a new age and thus seismic shifts took place in the ideology.[73] In the last two decades this idea has come in for close and critical scrutiny. In consequence, two further interpretations have arisen. The first is that there was really no division at all between the classical and newer liberalisms. They were all part of a broad-church doctrine. There are two variations on this thesis: the first stresses the incoherence of this broad-church doctrine.[74] Gladstone, in this view, was the presiding deity over the radicals, classical economists, Nonconformists, Whigs, Liberal Unionists and Chamberlainite interventionists. Without Gladstone there would have been no unity. After his death liberalism inevitably went into a slow but irreversible decline. The second variation stresses the coherence of the broad-church doctrine.[75] The radical programme of Chamberlain, the policies of the National Liberal Federation and the new liberal policies of the early 1900s were incorporated into liberal theory and practice. In the 1900s even traditionalists like Campbell-Bannerman were, unselfconsciously, speaking in new liberal language without any sense of inconsistency.

The final view, which lies behind this present discussion, argues that the old was not simply reconciled to the new, but rather that this terminology obscures a profound and subtle dialectic at work within liberal thought. Core, but purely formal themes, were given substance in different contexts. They were worked and reworked. There was no seismic shift but rather a fluid development of interpretations around certain formal themes. Many of these themes were also in fact explored by other political movements. Classical liberal ideas were, for example, used by conservative theorists and politicians. In this context one can fully appreciate the comparative ease with which many liberals realigned themselves with conservatism and conservatives with liberalism, at the close of the nineteenth century. Also, it is clear that groups like the Liberty and Property Defence League (LPDL), which were basically propounding Spencerian ideas, had a large membership of conservatives, many of whom felt deeply disenchanted with the advent of Tory Democracy in their own party.[76] The major point, though, of this latter view is that the change in the character of liberalism was internal.

The above judgement, however, is not necessarily commensurable with that of the actual protagonists. Many Liberals in the 1880s and 1890s, like A. V. Dicey, W. H. Lecky, Henry Maine, Herbert Spencer and Henry Sidgwick, saw a break in the liberal tradition.[77] In their perception, there was a crisis of identity, which they identified with the growing 'socialistic' and 'collectivist' trends of liberalism. In 1882, Arnold Toynbee remarked, in a speech significantly titled 'Are Radicals Socialists?', that 'the gravest of [the] charges brought against Radicals is the charge of Socialism; a system which in the past they strained every nerve to oppose'.[78]

The turning-point for many was not so much the idea of Home Rule for Ireland (although this was the final straw for figures like A. V. Dicey) as the general legislative trends of the second Gladstone Administration (1880–85). In their perception a paternalistic path was being taken by liberalism which betrayed the classical liberal perspective. Acts like the Ground Game Act, Irish Land Act, Merchant Shipping Act and Employers Liability Act, were seen as manifest examples of this dangerous trend.

The present argument reads the crisis differently. Many of the concepts that were associated with the older liberalism were flexible and inchoate enough to be used by the more social liberals. At least the arguments used by the social liberals were often seen to be an extension of classical liberal principles. Furthermore, many of the classical liberal principles were inadequate as bench-marks for any orthodoxy, partly because the classical liberals themselves differed so markedly in their interpretations. The practical conclusion to this was that Liberals progressively found themselves enacting measures about which they felt increasingly uneasy. There were reasons, on principle, for supporting *and* criticizing legislation. The principles themselves were too flexible to be used as adequate measures of the extent of state activity.

Jones's particular reading of liberalism not only bears upon the earlier discussion of socialism, but also reflects this internal dialectic within liberalism. Jones saw undoubted benefits in the classical liberal persuasion in politics. It enshrined the central value of the individual person, and the rights to private property and liberty. Traditional liberalism allowed individuals the room to develop their characters, gave maximum space for self-help and thrift. It also enshrined concepts of limited government, the rule of law and the crucial role of the commercial market to create wealth.

However, for Jones, such values should not blind us to marked defects. For Jones individualism had an internal logic to it. The individualism embodied in the older liberalism, something Caird traced to writers like Godwin, Diderot and Rousseau, in fact found its most logically adequate expression in anarchism.[79] The older liberalism, in its more extreme votaries, was an inadequate half-way house to anarchy. Some in the LPDL appeared to concur with this. For example, Auberon Herbert favoured (unlike Herbert Spencer) a voluntary state and voluntary taxation. His compatriot Wordsworth Donisthorpe had strong sympathies with Tolstoyian anarchy. For Jones one dimension of individualism, and the negative freedom connected to it, 'obtained its boldest and most unrestrained expression in the French Revolution'.[80] Such individualism foolishly identified the good with something purely personal, whereas for Jones our good, as true individuals, is tied to the traditions and purposes of our society.[81]

Capitalist liberalism, also, when dealing with freedom identifies it with what Jones calls the 'pseudo-freedom of irrational caprice'.[82] Freedom or liberty is a fundamentally important value. Yet, developed freedom, for Jones, equates with moral activity. Much hangs here on what would be regarded as 'restraint'. For Jones, preventing humans from performing immoral or hurtful actions is, in itself, not a restraint. We should, he argues, not be able to 'make any bargains we please . . . We cannot employ women in pits . . . nor little children in factories'; he goes on: 'the liberty to do wrong is not a right, but the perversion of a right.'[83] For Jones all intelligent liberal capitalists and good citizens understand this.

Jones, therefore, envisaged a richer moralized individualism and developed view of liberty evolved out of an asocial, amoral, atomic individualism and negative conception of liberty. For Jones, 'it is the unmoralised community and the unsocialised individual which follow methods of resistance and social exclusion'.[84] In reality the individual and the state interpenetrate. The atomized individualism had no firm grasp of the social nature and destiny of individuality, imagining that private rights and freedoms were being undermined whenever the state acted. For Jones, individualism must either drift off into the absurdities and terrors of anarchy or develop and evolve through a richer and deeper grasp of its relation to the state.

For Jones, there is, consequently, no principled limit to state action; 'the limits', he says, 'are not to be fixed by any conception of the abstract antagonism of society and the individual: for each of these is true to itself precisely in the degree to which it is faithful to its opposite.'[85] Character, a popular term in the individualistic liberal vocabulary, is not something that, for Jones, can be separated from the environment or society. It is not automatically undermined by state action. Good character rather presupposes a good enabling state; the good state and good citizen go together.[86]

The upshot of an increasing stress, by some liberals, on the commercial mentality is socially damaging. In an article commenting upon his work in the Reconstruction Committee Jones remarked that he was 'sometimes startled by the distortion of the purely economic mind; how the Capitalist can see nothing except through the medium in which he is soaked'.[87] The exclusive focus of the commercial mind in education policy, social policy and the like can be deeply erroneous and destructive for both cultural and industrial development.

One point which should be mentioned here is that Jones did not feel that either Hegel, or many in the Hegelian tradition, got the commercial world right. In 1918 he wrote in a letter that he wanted 'above all to hit on the head the one big blunder of Hegel in the independence he gives to the economic world'.[88] He was outraged at the idea of the 'otherness' and alien quality of the economic world to ethics. This was again another example of false dualities and a neglect of the evolution of moral, political and economic thought and practice. He particularly disliked Bosanquet's notion of the economy as a world of 'claims and counter-claims'.[89] Many classical liberal economists made a rigid separation between the economy and politics. For such economists, individuals 'are supposed to be indifferent to each other, and no one is under obligations to any one else'.[90] Workmen and employers are thus indifferent to each other. Each makes amoral self-interested claims in the economic world. This is a form of exclusive individualism which he thinks Hegel and Bosanquet, amongst others, unwittingly accepted. It was a perspective that he thought he saw before him in employers, trade unions and the Labour Party.

What is fundamentally wrong here for Jones is simply that 'economic relations imply mutual trust . . . and a stability of will and purpose'.[91] Economics and the world of claims and counter-claims are premised upon a mutuality of accepted values, like trust, honesty, and keeping promises. In other words, Hegel's and Bosanquet's blunder was to separate ethics and economics. Ethical character is indifferent to its location. For Jones, any situation individuals find themselves in 'furnishes . . . the *opportunity* of doing right and wrong'.[92] If, argues Jones, this value consensus did not exist then even the economy and the world of claim and counter-claim would falter. It would be a world of anarchic solitude with no relations, which is, in part, the fallacy of 'thin individualism'. If once you encourage the separation of ethics from the economy then enormous social tensions, philistinism and greed rule the day. As Jones put it: 'business is all too often regulated greed.'[93] Jones adopts here a Ruskinian conception of wealth and commerce.[94] Jones links this critique of thin individualism of the economic world with the errors of finite individuality and the monistic absolute in Bosanquet's metaphysics. He comments: 'Mr Bosanquet ought therefore to have nothing to do with a world of exclusive wills, or with an Absolute which stands over against the finite . . . It is "beyond", "impossible", . . . and should be left to Herbert Spencer.'[95]

SYNDICALISM

For a comparatively short period up to 1914 a number of heavy industrial centres, like Clydeside, Sheffield and south Wales, experienced a period of severe social unrest.[96] Between 1911 and 1914 approximately 70 million working days had been lost through industrial action. There are a number of reasons cited by historians for the unrest. The period up to to 1914 saw a rise in inflation and fall in the price of real wages, especially between 1909 and 1913. Profits, rents and prices were slowly increasing but wages were not keeping pace. There was growing disenchantment not only with official Lib-Labism and the Independent Labour Party, but also with the leadership of the official trade unions. Further, the Trades Disputes Act had taken the pressure off trade union activism and given leeway for more radical elements.

There is considerable scholarly debate as to the impact in this period of syndicalism. Syndicalism (and by 1909 anarcho-syndicalism also) is essentially a form of revolutionary trade unionism (as distinct from ordinary reformist trade unionism). It was an exogenous import, mainly from France and North America. From France, Fernand Pelloutier and George Sorel, and from America, Daniel de Léon and Eugene Debs, are the most well-known figures.[97] During the period 1890 till the 1920s it had some influence on working-class movements in parts of Europe, Scandinavia, Latin America, North America and Australia. Some see syndicalism as a vital and important aspect of working-class radicalism, for example, in south Wales. In fact it is occasionally seen as the key explanation before 1914. However, there is a growing sense amongst a number of historians that it was more of an exotic import which has been vastly overrated, in fact some doubt that it had any really significant role at all. The unrest would have taken place without syndicalism, since it was rooted in different causes, for example, disaffection over wage levels.[98]

Revolutionary syndicalism stood outside the mainstream of the Second International and Marxism. It was essentially an anti-political and anti-statist movement concentrating 'on the revolutionary potential of working class economic organization, notably the trade union or industrial union'.[99] It claimed to have no faith in parliamentary or representative democracy. It rejected all forms of state organization, whether capitalist or socialist. In Britain the ILP, official unionism and social democratic liberalism were all treated with equal disdain.[100] The market economy was as objectionable as the centralized command economy and nationalized industries. Interestingly, their interpretation of new liberal welfare reforms in the 1906–14 period was deeply antagonistic. As one writer comments, the syndicalists saw such things as unemployment benefit and labour exchanges as 'designed to promote industrial efficiency and social discipline'.[101]

The principle economic actors for syndicalism were the working-class producer groups, not the consumers. Both the state and capitalism had to be destroyed by revolutionary 'direct action' by such producers. Violence was fully legitimate. George Sorel in his *Reflections on Violence* (1908) was to make much of this particular theme. The principle tool, apart from industrial sabotage, suggested by most syndicalists was the general strike. Unions were not only conceived of as the means to revolutionary direct action but also the nuclei for a future decentralized federal society. Although syndicalists tended to despise abstract theory and bourgeois intellectualism they none the less placed considerable emphasis on working-class self-education. This is something that can be seen in Pelloutier's *Bourse du Travail* in France and also in the Plebs League, Industrial Syndicalist Education League and Central Labour College in Britain.[102]

The entrance of syndicalism into Britain came initially around 1906 with the British Advocates of Industrial Unionism, reconstructed shortly afterwards into the Industrial Workers of Great Britain. The years 1907 and 1908 saw the setting up of the Industrial Union of Direct Actionists and the Industrial League. In south Wales the miners' lodges under the leadership of the South Wales Miners' Federation (SWMF) felt the impact of syndicalism through charismatic figures like Noah Ablett, Will Hay and Frank Hodges and educational groups like the Plebs League. However, the really dynamic figure of British syndicalism was Tom Mann who, after a visit to France, set up the Industrial Syndicalist Education League with an accompanying journal the *Industrial Syndicalist* in 1910. The syndicalist leaders of the SWMF formed their own Unofficial Reform Committee which in March 1911 produced what is regarded by some as the high-water mark of south Wales syndicalist literature, *The Miners' Next Step*, which preached many of the orthodox syndicalist ideas.[103]

Essentially syndicalism went through two phases: firstly, 1900–10 was a period of propaganda and discussion; 1910–14 was a period of action. Some commentators argue that the strikes and direct action of the period 1910–14 were different in character. They were more overtly aggressive and also more of a direct challenge to parliamentary rule.[104] The phase of unrest began in the south Wales coalfield in September 1910 and was followed in quick succession by stoppages in a number of industries. This unrest continued, on and off, in south Wales into the war period. With the British Navy so dependent on south Wales steam coal, the government kept a watching brief particularly on the miners. After 1917, in particular following the introduction of conscription, 'the valleys were seething again with class bitterness'.[105] Lloyd George appointed a Commission of Industrial Unrest to look into the matter of south Wales. The report drew an alarming picture of deteriorating conditions. Bad management practices were seen to be a root cause of tension which had in turn given rise to the 'messianic impact of "direct action" or syndicalist theories'.[106]

Jones had taken part in recruiting campaigns in Wales during the first years of the war.[107] He also sat on a number of committees and bodies concerned with Welsh affairs. Both Lloyd George and Tom Jones, his ex-pupil, considered that if anyone could provide theoretical opposition to syndicalism it was Henry Jones. In 1917, Tom Jones, in the prime minister's office, writing to the principal of Glasgow University and asking for Henry Jones's release from academic duties, wrote:

> The PM spoke to me this week on . . . the question of using Sir Henry Jones's special gifts in the best way during the war. As you know Sir Henry is serving on the Royal Welsh University Commission and on the Reconstruction Committee on Adult Education . . . You know something of the disturbed condition of the South Wales coalfield. The Miners' Federation is very largely in the hands of young men with extreme syndicalist views and they constantly threaten serious industrial upheaval. Those of us who heard Sir Henry during the recruiting campaign recognize that he has unusual gifts for dealing with this explosive material and the proposal is to ask him to give a long series of addresses during the next winter in the mining valleys.[108]

The substance of Jones's lectures form the basis of his book on citizenship.[109] In these lectures Jones did not want to get caught up in the internal bickerings of capital and labour. He thought, as we have seen, that both were equally at fault. He anticipated that the meetings would be civic events, and requested Tom Jones: 'As to the machinery, can you and Carson not make the meetings a civic and communal thing. Arrange that the Mayor take the Chair, that each of the political parties should have a place on the stage, and one or two of them speak, also the ministers, etc., invited. You know what I mean . . . Could a local committee then there be formed to carry on the agitation in the neighbouring villages?'[110]

His style was more extempore than formally structured. He took the theme of citizenship and developed it on the spot.[111] It is also difficult to gauge the impact of such lectures. If one reads the *Principles of Citizenship* it is hard not to conclude that much of the material must have gone over the heads of his lay audiences.[112] It is also questionable, firstly, as to whether syndicalism was having any widespread effect and secondly, whether any of his audience would have been syndicalist activitists.

The detail of his arguments has already been covered in the various chapters of this book. The basic gist of his claim is that citizenship cannot be dissociated from the state, and that the state is the guardian of the institutional setting in which the individual develops. The society, tradition and state form the substance of the individual nature. To deny one's citizenship or one's state was to deny one's humanity. Any contention that humans can do away with the state, civil society or even a controlled market economy was seen by Jones as absurd. Our destiny is to live and evolve in states. One weakness in Jones's position here is his neglect of groups, which were central to both syndicalists and guild socialists. Like Bosanquet, he had an interest in the guild socialists, but as Hetherington comments: 'he disliked the intensity with which they laboured the notion of class consciousness. Nevertheless, he believed that some of their practical suggestions for the control of industrial life were entirely consistent with his own very different political theory.'[113] However, apart from his discussions of the role of the family, Jones never really met head on the role, nature and character of group life within the state, as developed, for example, by pluralist writers. His fulmination, on the grounds of equal citizenship, against class analysis did not bode well for his attitude to groups. Groups, also, could be seen to intervene in the general pattern of citizenship.

DUALISM OVERCOME?

Jones's resolution to the diversity of political doctrine was to appeal to the device of identity in difference and the overcoming of dualism. His analysis of the problem of the individual and society is a classic example of his identity in difference method: 'We know that the public good will not be obtained by separating man from man, securing each unit in a charmed circle of personal rights . . . We must find a place for the individual within the social organism.'[114] The reality of the situation is that the individual cannot do without society. The very nature of individuality implies society. This does not entail that individuality is lost; rather both are preserved in a deeper and richer unity. States and individuals, for Jones, 'are ultimately nothing but different manifestations of one self-revealing spirit, – the spirit of *man*'.[115]

Jones deploys a similar argument on a number of disputed issues. Freedom is often seen as a negative principle of opposition to public authority and order. However, for Jones, in reality there is no opposition: 'the State itself is free, and the means of the freedom of its members.'[116] As argued earlier, the opposition between character and environment is another false distinction. The substance of character, as unique and private, is formed out of the social environment. Further, the state 'can provide the means for the development of a character... [in fact] the prime and paramount business of the State *is* to provide the means'.[117]

The above attempts to overcome dualisms also inform his analysis of socialism and individualistic liberalism. L. T. Hobhouse pointed out in his book *Democracy and Reaction*, a work that Jones reviewed and criticized extensively in two articles, that the older liberalism had done considerable service. The newer social liberalism 'appears not as an infringement of the two distinctive ideals of the older Liberalism "Liberty and Equality". It appears rather as a necessary means to their fulfilment. It comes not to destroy but to fulfil.'[118] Jones uses virtually the same argument. His view is that liberalism is neither superseded by socialism, nor has two faces, but rather that the dualism and separation between the two is misleading. He attempts thus to show the inner evolving unity of the two ideologies.[119] True socialism and true liberal individualism are therefore not opposed. The coming of socialism, says Jones, may justly be described as the coming of individualism. Private and public enterprise grow together.[120] The truth for Jones is that 'the individual gains by that which strengthens the State, and the State by that which increases the efficiency of the individual'.[121]

Such an idea of social liberalism or liberal socialism was in fact fairly widespread among intellectuals up to 1914. The ILP programme and most of the Fabian ideas shared, consciously or not, exactly the same ethos.[122] Essentially liberalism has had two important responses from socialism. Some socialists argue that socialism comes to bury liberalism once and for all. Leninism represents probably the clearest example of this. The second view, under which rubric we can place Jones and Hobhouse, is that socialism builds upon the best of liberalism.[123]

One example that Jones discusses in some depth, and which serves to clarify the above points, centres on the concept of property. Private property is valued by most citizens and it appears, *prima facie*, to be deeply exclusive. Communal property negates this value. Physical property simply cannot be shared. It resists commonality. For many (and Jones again here is thinking of state socialism), this is the great stumbling-block to socialism. Public ownership and nationalization are seen in this negative light by many liberals.

Jones, however, reflects upon this issue with the eyes of philosophical Idealism which resist all hard materiality and rigid separations of objects. Private property is premised upon a crude assumption of self and not-self, subject and object. For Jones, property is more than mere possession. It is a right. Possession *per se* does not entail owning. Property requires more than just a private will to possess. Something becomes mine, but, more precisely, mine by right and right implies recognition. A right is something, in fact, that '*ought* to be recognized' and other wills in the organized setting of a society recognize and respect my appropriation. Thus my private property is not something gained or acquired *through* my privacy, rather my possession and private use are granted by society (or more precisely the organized will of society – the state). Private property is a reality which must be respected but we must realize its point of origin and justification.[124]

Both socialists and individualist liberals, in their different ways, embody an aspect of the truth of property. Private property is an ethical fact, but its essence 'is that it is the result of an act whereby society endows its individual members with rights against itself'.[125] On the other hand, individualists are right to insist that private property is unconditionally necessary to the individual and state. Unless its privacy and necessity were recognized by the state it would not function as a liberating force.

In one reading, Jones's stress on the ethical dimension of politics makes his views appear somewhat anachronistic, especially in the context of twentieth-century history. The moralism and religiosity often make the contemporary reader uncomfortable. However, the problem of ethics, communal values and citizenship is not without relevance to contemporary political issues. A decade of market-orientated individualism has given rise in Britain in the 1990s, once again, to a call for active civic virtue and the yearning for some form of communal consensus. The comparatively recent communitarian critique of liberalism and the espousal by some of Civic Republican beliefs partakes of the same general intellectual ethos as that of Jones. Jones's stress on the intrinsic ideological compatibility of certain types of liberalism and socialism is, to say the least, prescient and resonates with some of the developments of post-1945 ideological thinking.

In conclusion, as we have seen, Jones was not over-optimistic concerning British political life at that time. The cultural and political level of the British people was seen as depressingly philistine and commercially orientated. Politicians and the general public, employers and employees, tended towards cupidity and self-interest. Jones, however, looked optimistically toward a future where the fundamental truths of both socialism and liberalism would be realized. The dualism of collectivism and individualism had to be overcome. Individualism needed to develop or evolve within the richer framework of an ethical state. Such an overcoming would be an 'identity in difference'. For Jones individuality implies society. Individuality is not lost but preserved and sanctified in the higher unity of the state. In fact, both state and individual were viewed as different manifestations of the one self-revealing spirit. True socialism and true individualism were not therefore opposed. As Jones liked to assert, the coming of socialism was also the coming of individualism. Having reviewed Jones's thoughts on domestic Edwardian politics, we move on in the next chapters to consider the international dimension of Jones's political thought. Most political thinkers of the late Edwardian period had to adjust themselves and their theories to international events. The cataclysmic event of the First World War and imperialism demanded comprehensive explanation. For Idealists, like Jones, the issue of the war was particularly acute. Having his philosophical roots so deep in German philosophy he felt doubly sensitive to the issue of statism and international aggression.

CHAPTER SEVEN

NATIONS AND THE IMPERIALISM OF MORAL IDEALS

We have seen how, for Jones, the state is an ethical organism through which the self-consciousness of a people is expressed, and by means of which freedom is attained. Through citizenship of the state we at once fulfil ourselves and promote the common good. The state is an educational institution which, when acting in accordance with its true purpose, that is, to secure the conditions conducive to the development of the individual's capacities, both strengthens itself and extends its own activities, while at the same time increasing individual freedom by releasing the potential that might otherwise be stultified by poverty and social deprivation. For Jones the state is a coherent organism held together by the ethical relations which saturate it. It is therefore viewed as the 'Kingdom of God on Earth', through which, and by means of which, Spirit progressively, and more adequately, reveals itself in the individual and social actions of its citizens. This whole perspective raises a considerable number of questions in international politics. The questions of national identity, imperialism and war could not be avoided, and all had to be addressed in some way or other by any thinker who purported to espouse a political philosophy.

During the course of the nineteenth century the Kantian principle of self-determination as the criterion of moral agency became the guiding principle of liberalism. It combined with the nationalist aspirations awoken by the French Revolution and the Napoleonic Wars, and sustained in the realm of ideas by such thinkers as Fichte, Herder and Schleiermacher. Eventually it became translated into the criterion of national integrity impelling each self-respecting nation to liberate itself from alien oppressors, and aspire to create a state coincident with itself, and through which national self-determination could be expressed.[1] The United Kingdom of Great Britain and Ireland comprised four peoples asserting their distinctive national identities, demanding, with differing degrees of intensity, varying levels of political self-determination or autonomy. Jones felt that he had to reconcile these political demands with the broader conception of the British nation and its relation to Greater Britain or the Empire.

While acknowledging that iniquities had been perpetrated, British Idealists argued that there was no incompatibility between identifying oneself with a particular nation within the United Kingdom, while at the same time expressing patriotic sentiments for the British state. Indeed, the collective consciousness, of which the British state is an expression, incorporates the lesser organisms within itself, and through it they express themselves. Among these thinkers there was a good deal of soul-searching concerning the question of imperialism. Every one of the Idealists condemned outright any justification of imperialism on economic grounds which entailed the exploitation of the lower races by the mother country. Conversely, almost all could accept the view that there is something noble in the enterprise of spreading civilization to the inferior peoples of the world, namely with the intention of preparing them for self-government and full participation in the higher cultural and spiritual attainments of Europe. Such missionary zeal was more enthusiastically expressed by some than by others. However, it was usually acknowledged that the Empire was a fact and, whatever one thought of the way it was acquired, Great Britain now had a moral responsibility to protect the natives from private profiteers by means of responsible government, encouraging self-government where possible, while acting for the common good of the colonies and Empire as a whole.[2]

The aim of this chapter is to identify and discern Jones's ideas on the status and integrity of nations, and their relations to Empire and imperialism. It will be concluded that a number of the Idealists, including Jones, deplored the economic and social imperialism against which Hobhouse and Hobson reacted so vociferously. In fact Idealist principles inclined the British Hegelians to a grander and more noble understanding of the Empire which is derived from Burke and which stresses the responsibilities of the mother country to the Empire, and to which Hobhouse and Hobson themselves were not averse.

THE CHARACTER OF THE NATION

Questions of nationalism and patriotism were liable to elicit extremely emotive responses towards the end of the nineteenth century because of the apparently positive and negative forces they unleashed. On the one hand the aspiration for self-determination was laudable, but on the other the conflicts which such aspirations generated, and the frequent disregard of the integrity of other nations by those asserting their own will and destiny, were a cause for deep concern. Such concern was voiced by the Idealists. A. C. Bradley attributed the political unrest and war which had bedevilled Europe since 1815 largely to the 'sentiment of nationality' which was passionate to the point of becoming 'almost a religious faith'.[3] T. H. Green believed that 'national vanity' masquerading under the name of patriotism had proved to be 'a more serious disturber of peace than dynastic ambition'.[4] Nevertheless, nationalism showed no signs of abating and had to be acknowledged and incorporated into any serious political theory.

Idealists, on the whole, emphasized the positive virtues of nationalism. Hetherington and Muirhead contended that it is only when a state becomes a nation that it achieves from its citizens the personal devotion which is the foundation of its community. The state signifies the political frontiers, whereas a nation's boundaries are characterized by a 'common sentiment'.[5] Similarly, Bosanquet, who believed that universal moral principles emanate from and are represented by the higher nationalities, was well aware that patriotism, or what we would call today nationalism, was 'a source of brainless and often fraudulent clamour, or at best a dangerous fanaticism'.[6] He was nevertheless convinced that there was a form of patriotism which could be harnessed to the service of the good life, and which was grounded in one's blood-ties, in the heritage of land and customs for which there is a common affection, and in one's shared 'power and means of acting upon the world – language, ideas, modes of life, social habits'.[7] In other words, this understanding of patriotism for Bosanquet was indicative of both a common experience and tolerance of diversities. The institutions which are accepted, and to which the people are subject, are only capable of working because of the common experience upon which they are predicated. This form of positive patriotism is expressed in our sentimental attachments to our homeland and loyalty to its institutions.[8]

D. G. Ritchie was rather more contemptuous than other Idealists about the claims of nations to the right of self-determination and autonomy. Nations, he argued, are only metaphorically organisms, or persons, and we should not be blinded by the laudatory connotations of such words as national freedom and independence. Such ideas may be voiced in the name of the most reactionary of causes.[9] Nations, he suggested, exist for the benefit of people and not people for the benefit of nations.[10] Their emergence, or absorption, into a larger social unity may be either for the betterment, or to the detriment, of the people affected.[11] If a nation fails in its purpose of improving the condition of those people to whom it is the focus of their sentiment, then 'it has no absolute moral right to block the onward movement of human progress'.[12]

As a Welshman, Jones participated in and contributed to the political life of the Principality. While working in Scotland he retained his keen interest in Welsh affairs and periodically abandoned his voluntary exile to intervene actively. It is therefore hardly surprising that Jones had strong views on the issues of national identity and nationalism. On the question of the unity of a social organism we saw earlier how Jones frequently deferred to Burke's view of an enduring moral partnership between the living, the dead, and the yet to be born. For Burke, a nation exhibits a distinct identity, having prescriptions, prejudices and customs which are characteristically its own. A nation combines individuals into a whole; making a unity out of diversity, and constituting an entity which is more than the sum of its parts. The nation has a spirit which is its vitality. A nation is 'a moral essence, not a geographical arrangement', and there can be no more terrible a revolution to a nation which is proud and great than a change in its national spirit.[13]

For Henry Jones the fundamental axiom of the social sciences is that a nation, like a state, has a moral and spiritual existence: it is a living organism which evolves, like the individual, through the development of its own self-consciousness. It lives upon assumptions, and is guided by principles, the truth and efficiency of which are often taken for granted.[14] The nation has a character, or personality, which constitutes its distinctiveness, and 'which gradually reveals itself in the events that are its deeds'.[15] It has, like the individual, habits of mind, a moral disposition and political convictions. The liberty which it enjoys cannot be conferred by another nation because moral freedom has to be won through the self-conscious efforts of the people,[16] and it is better that each nation express its own character and assert its particular claims than to be a semblance of another.

Wales, for Jones, and many of his fellow Welshmen, was one such distinct, but not independent, nation which had struggled against, and overcome, all attempts to subvert her character. It bore the burden of an English religious establishment, yet its own Nonconformity flourished; suffered the yoke of an alien aristocracy, and had its laws imposed by a foreign legislature whose administration of justice was conducted in a foreign tongue. Yet, despite being overshadowed by the English nation, Wales had maintained its distinctive personality, mental disposition, moral temperament and religion, but above all, and in contrast to Ireland and Scotland, its language thrived and grew stronger in adversity. In all of the principal respects which distinguish the unique characters of nations, with the exception of hatred and antagonism, Jones tells us, 'Wales is to-day as different from England as it is from France'.[17]

Modern political life, in Jones's view, began in Wales in 1868.[18] This, of course, was the date after which the Liberal Party began to gain ascendancy in the Principality and a new wave of nationalism found expression through educational, religious and land questions, as well as in poetry and literature, and the proliferation of Welsh-language publications. It was great causes, Jones believed, which enabled a nation to develop its moral integrity and win its freedom, but Scotland, which he loved dearly, was unfortunate in lacking a good grievance in terms of which to press its claims for Home Rule.[19] Wales was more fortunate in this respect having, in addition to the educational issues, the passionate cries for disestablishment of the Church and land reform.

We have already discussed Jones's views on education, but their specific bearing on Welsh nationalism needs to be added at this point. The Welsh language, he thought, had been and would continue to be kept alive by well-established national institutions other than the schools, namely the religious services, and religious education classes, held for people of all age groups, in the medium of Welsh, in the local chapels. Among the great teachers with whom he was acquainted, Jones ranked Robert Hughes, an elder in 'the little church in Llangernyw'.[20] Similarly, the eistedfoddau made a significant contribution to sustaining Welsh as a living language. The love of poetry, prose and musical competitions indicated to Jones 'that the Welsh seem to have inherited the literary side of the olympic games'.[21] On the other hand, although he thought that the schools should do all they could to promote the Welsh language it should be an optional class subject, and not a substitute for English. Bright children deficient in English, if adventurous enough to broaden their ambitions and compete against others in the United Kingdom, would find themselves at a considerable disadvantage.[22]

Modern Wales, Jones believed, was a religious nation and its politics had been inspired by its religious character. For Jones, the disestablishment of the Church and the land question were inextricably linked as the manifestations of an alien Establishment, constituted by a landlord class allied with the Church of England clergy, who together were insensitive to the needs and aspirations of the ordinary people. Apart from the Welsh being forced to maintain a clergy which they did not want, and suffer the iniquities of the annual renewal of leases which were to the detriment of most tenant farmers, such institutions, 'just because they are alien, limit the development of a people, make demands on it which it cannot recognise as duties, and thereby instigate the strongest spirits of such a people to assert their freedom by force, more or less disguised'.[23]

The Dissenters and the Establishment, in Jones's view, represented the liberal and conservative forces in Wales. The former stood for progress, and the latter, through its inertia, for spiritual and social stagnation. It was through the Liberal Party that Jones believed Wales would win some degree of autonomy to deal with its own problems, unimpeded by a legislature too preoccupied with the affairs of the Empire and the Irish problem to pay due regard to the legitimate grievances of Wales. Even though he thought that that Party had put the loyalty of Wales to liberalism under great strain, he was convinced, as late as 1911, that Lloyd George was committed to Home Rule for Wales, or at least devolution of decision-making authority in its own affairs.[24]

Although Jones believed that it is a characteristic of every living organism 'that the ultimate determining element is to be found within itself, and not in its surroundings',[25] he was not a Welsh separatist, and did not see Welsh patriotism as incompatible with loyalty to Great Britain, or to the Empire. Such apparent inconsistencies were by no means unusual among Welsh nationalists. Thomas Edward Ellis combined his vision of Future Wales, or the 'Wales that is to be' (*Cymru Fydd*), which emphasized the total immersion of the people in their cultural, social and religious heritage, with an admiration for Cecil Rhodes and the idea of an Empire in which Wales was to take its rightful place.[26] The Empire, Jones contended, is not English, and Welshmen would do well to bear in mind the greatness of that imperial entity which Wales had a hand in building.[27] Wales, for Jones, 'is a partner in all the privileges and responsibilities of the Empire',[28] and what it asks of Westminster is 'room *to live within that Empire its own life*'.[29]

IMPERIALISM

British attitudes towards imperialism have followed a tangled path since the American War of Independence. J. H. Muirhead, writing at the height of the second Boer War, identified four distinguishable phases through which British attitudes to imperialism had travelled. The first was that of enthusiasm, followed by indifference, which then developed into outright hostility to the Empire, and finally became transformed into a passionate and consuming jingoism,[30] which was epitomized in the South African War.

This characterization is, of course, schematic and does a disservice to the facts. As Gallagher and Robinson have argued, any analysis of imperialism needs to take into account 'informal' as well 'formal' expansionism. The mid-Victorian period of indifference and hostility witnessed, paradoxically, large-scale acquisitions. However, the period of enthusiasm for Empire, which is supposed to date from 1880, and which the proponents of the economic theory of imperialism, like Hobson, Hobhouse and Lenin, saw as a period of annexation constituting a break with previous policy (because of the decline of free trade, the desire to protect foreign investments, and the conversion of statesmen to the necessity of territorial expansion), was characterized by no such absolute break. The scramble for Africa was merely the last, and perhaps the least significant of the informal and formal acquisitions made throughout the century.[31] Nevertheless, the South African War of 1899–1902 did serve to focus the various and diverse discussions of imperialism and polarized politicians and intellectuals into the pro-Government and pro-Boer camps. This polarization has for most historians obscured the subtle, and quite significant, differences in the attitudes towards Empire in general exhibited by opponents of the war. This point needs to be explored further in order to locate Jones precisely in the contemporaneous debates.

In 1895 Cecil Rhodes made the observation that social discontent and the possibility of civil war erupting in industrial Britain could be averted by a commitment to imperialism.[32] This so-called 'Social Imperialism', justified on the grounds that the financial gains made abroad could be used to fund expensive social welfare reforms at home, and thus minimize class antagonism by identifying the national interest with the common interest, was embraced in various forms by all shades of political opinion. The form which dominated was that of Joseph Chamberlain and his followers who linked social imperialism to Tariff Reform and a system of imperial preferences. The majority of the parliamentary Liberal Party opposed Chamberlain's policies and condemned the conduct of the war. On the other hand, there were Liberal Imperialists, led by Rosebery, who gave qualified support to Chamberlain's Boer policy. They established the Liberal League in 1902 with Rosebery as its president. H. H. Asquith, R. B. Haldane and Sir Edward Grey acted as principal spokesmen. Henry Campbell-Bannerman, and Henry Jones's compatriot, David Lloyd George, represented the vast majority of the parliamentary Liberal Party in condemning Liberal Imperialism. The Liberal Imperialists based their social reform policies on the principle of Free Trade. It was in fact the domestic issues associated with this social policy, and opposition to Tariff Reform, which helped to unite the party in its 1906–14 social reform programme, combined with a less overtly pronounced imperial policy. Many Fabians also officially espoused support for social imperialism, but wavered on the question of whether it would be most expedient to support the Tariff Reformers or the Free Traders.

The issue which clearly differentiated Liberal social imperialism and Chamberlain's social imperialism was the actual source of the revenue for financing social reform. For the Free Traders the answer was by increasing taxation on the profits derived directly and indirectly from imperial ventures, whereas for the supporters of Tariff Reform the revenue would be raised from the increased charges on commodities, and would be borne by the populace in general, more secure in its employment and better paid because of the policies of protection and imperial preferences.[33]

The Liberal opponents of social imperialism, like Hobson and Hobhouse, saw in the Boer War all of the insidious manifestations of the Unionist Government's imperial policy. They sought to sever the connection between social reform and imperialism by suggesting that the purported benefits were illusory. Hobson believed that the conspiracy of financial interests was insidiously influencing government policy in the direction of militaristic imperial expansionism. Far from reaping a surplus for social reform, such a policy was actually diverting resources away from servicing welfare needs and channelling them into expensive, and domestically debilitating, foreign adventures. Meanwhile it relied upon the irrational jingoism of the mob, the roots of which lay deep in social psychology. The mob could be manipulated by the press and popular culture to placate potentially hostile reactions.[34] For our purposes, however, the ideas of Leonard Hobhouse are of more significance because they provide a direct link with the views of Henry Jones.

In 1899 Hobhouse argued that in the years since 1895 liberalism had become as extinct as socialism. The humanistic and social questions which collectivists aspired to address had gradually become subordinate to, and supplanted by, questions of imperial expansionism and external relations. He argued that:

> The conditions of labour, the working day, the living wage, the provision for the aged and the sick, the education of the young, are, as Mr Chamberlain would tell us, after all, merely parochial matters. The real function of a Government, as we know on the same authority, is to act as a commercial traveller for the businessmen of the nation, and tout for concessions at the court of dying nations.[35]

In his *Democracy and Reaction* Hobhouse drew upon and expanded many of his earlier criticisms of social imperialism. He argued that liberalism in embracing socialistic principles had cleared the way for imperialism by jettisoning all but the Free Trade aspect of the school of Cobden. For Hobhouse such a policy was integrally related to the principles of non-interference, peaceful foreign relations, arms reduction, tight control of government expenditure; and at home popular government, and for the colonies self-determination.[36] Collectivism, in rejecting *laissez faire* at home, also abandoned non-intervention abroad. The new positive role of the state in domestic affairs was translated into external affairs.[37] The new militaristic imperialism of the post-1870s, he suggests, is based not on a noble sense of national duty, but on 'racial supremacy and material force', which has consumed the national resources which could have been used 'to improve the condition of the people'.[38] This aggressive imperialism is a reaction against the central principles of both liberalism and democracy, and in subverting them abroad, they are surreptitiously undermined at home. Liberalism stands for self-government and autonomy, whereas imperialism stands for subordination and ascendancy. Democratic imperialism, Hobhouse argues, is simply a contradiction because the former espouses self-determination, whereas the latter practices the imposition of government by one people upon another.[39] He contends that:

> Neither the state of war which conquest presupposes, nor the despotic government, military or civil, which conquest brings, are compatible with vigorous, free political life and growth in the democracy which undertakes them. They are a violation of its principles, and a violation which reacts on its character.[40]

Furthermore, Hobhouse puts forward an argument which he was later to expand in response to the Great War.[41] He argued that philosophical Idealism, the dominant philosophy of the day, had paved the way for the reaction against the principles of liberty and self-determination, and in its exalted view of the state encouraged jingoism, militarism and imperialism at the expense of humanitarian, or universal, ideals of morality.[42]

Most Idealists, irrespective of whether they aligned themselves with the pro-Boers, condemned the aggressive imperialism of which Hobhouse was so critical. It is true that Ritchie, the early Fabian, was rather less condemnatory than others. He attributed pro-Boer sentiment to the propaganda of Afrikaners and journalistic sensationalism, and thought that the very nature of the British Empire was being misunderstood.[43] It is as inevitable, he believed, that 'vigorous and enterprising white races should overflow into other lands as it is that water should run down hill',[44] but this placed a responsibility upon governments to ensure that their citizens were regulated by proper authority and not by the charter of a trading company.

On the other hand, Henry Jones, who aligned himself with Liberal Imperialists, and who was an active member of the Liberal League, applauded many of Hobhouse's criticisms, suggesting that they were a reasonably accurate account of the political climate immediately prior to, and during the Boer War. He dissented from Hobhouse in believing that such circumstances could not be generalized as indicative of a more long-term and persistent reaction in, and degradation of, the British people and their political principles.[45] Jones read the manuscript of *Democracy and Reaction* for Macmillan in June 1904, while Balfour's Conservative Government was in power, and although he thought its one-sidedness and shrill tone might with profit be modified, he nevertheless strongly recommended its publication. The main arguments of the book, he thought, were based on a sound political philosophy, detracted from only by 'the immeasured character of the condemnation of certain recent acts of the Government'. Jones went on to suggest that if Hobhouse had to condemn the Boer War 'it might be *done better* if he did not allow the philosopher to turn into a prophet, with flaming eyes and flying hair'. Nevertheless, he suggests that Hobhouse's 'warning is timely and good', and that 'the *passion* in it is quite right, but it requires to be made to walk quite soberly'.[46] When Jones came to write a fuller assessment of the book in 1907, a change of government had occurred, which for him indicated in the very least that the people, in voting for the Campbell-Bannerman Liberal Government in 1905, could not have been quite as endemically corrupt as Hobhouse had prophesied, nor were the prospects of social reform now quite as bleak.[47] Jones argued that there would be no accounting for the defeat of the previous government, nor for the evident impatience with the present government, especially with regard to social justice, if the people had become insensitive, and unconcerned about matters of right and wrong.[48]

From his evolutionary perspective Jones emphasized that the period through which Britain was passing was a transitionary one. Moral progress entailed the struggle against evil, which was manifest in all of the forms which Hobhouse claimed. However, such pessimism had to be balanced against the goals towards which society was moving, and the guiding hand of the spiritual principle which in its various guises gave direction to the movement. Britain was not without sin nor, on the other hand, without virtue, and it was the latter upon which the hope for a better life rested. Contrary to Hobhouse's view, for Jones, the people were not 'deaf to the cries of the wronged and oppressed, whether within or without its gates'.[49]

Hobhouse claimed that British Idealism contributed to the reaction against liberty and self-determination by elevating the state to sacred heights and by placing its absolutist claims above humanitarian considerations, and thus encouraging an insensitivity towards other nations. However, almost without exception, the British Idealists, who purportedly subscribed to the above philosophy, in fact wholeheartedly condemned the type of imperialism which Hobhouse himself deplored. Conversely, and somewhat ironically, he condoned the sort of imperialism of which the British Idealists approved. We have to be careful not to confuse condemnation of particular incidents like the Jameson Raid or episodes like the Boer War with condemnation of imperialism *per se*. Indeed, Herbert Samuel makes a similar point when he says: 'one need not have been a friend of aggression to approve the war, nor a disbeliever in empire in order to think it unjust.'[50]

Jones and Muirhead, for example, admirably illustrate the above contention. During the debate over fiscal reform Jones argued that it was a gross error to suggest that business, and more particularly international business, was exempt from moral constraints, or somehow operated according to a different code of ethics. No sphere of life, or occupational calling, he argued, had an inherent ethical content. The station one occupies allows of the opportunity to do right and wrong, and it may be used well, or ill. The moral character of a profession is completely derived from the way in which its activities are discharged by the individuals engaged in it.[51] As a people the British were acting as if considerations of morality were irrelevant to, or of marginal significance in, securing material prosperity. In Jones's view there had been a preoccupation with statistics, and economic causes and effects, as if the problem was purely material. As a result the terms in which the problem was diagnosed determined the character of the remedy, that is, one in which human qualities are largely irrelevant. Both the Tariff Reformers and Free Traders, disposed towards and experienced in the arena of industrial competition, had 'treated the state as if it were a business concern and nothing more',[52] confining their own thoughts and those of the people to the issues of commercial methods. In consequence, both sides of the debate had magnified the importance of the methods out of proportion to their significance, and had coloured the national perspective with these thoughts. In this respect the way in which imperial relations were viewed was grossly distorted. Imperial Britain was viewed as a fiscal unit, 'the wooden idol of our times',[53] whose unity consisted in economic ties. This fiscal unit was related to others in a world of competition and conflict, and advantage was gained only at the expense of one's competitors. Jones contends that even though the Empire was acknowledged as resting on the dual foundation of a unity of sentiment, which tariff preferences were expected to strengthen, and sound business practice,

> the unity of sentiment is thought of comparatively little moment, as if it were feeble and fragile as well as intangible; while all the emphasis is thrown upon the material bond, if bond it be. And, of course, the obligations of the citizens to the Empire must suffer in consequence; for the meaning of patriotism depends upon the conception we have formed of our country, and if the latter is superficial the former will be shallow.[54]

The importance of reforming methods of international trading could not be denied, and for his part he believed that artificial impediments to free trade would diminish the living standards of the poor and widen the gulf between the classes, leading to greater social discontent, as well as making more difficult relations with the Empire and foreign nations. The ultimate destiny of the nation and its Empire, however, lay not in fiscal reform, but in moral improvement. Jones concurs with Green and Bosanquet in believing that improvements in the international sphere have to emanate from the domestic sphere, and are premised upon the improvement of moral sentiments, rather than the mere reform of political institutions. The political institutions are a reflection of the will of the people, and the moral integrity of the former depends upon the moral improvement of the latter.[55] Economic protectionism, for Jones, contributed to moral degradation because it encouraged sectionalism and selfishness, and linked one's politics too closely to commerce. The lobbying of industrial interests would distract the political leaders of the nation from considerations of the common good in offering greater opportunities for economic and political corruption. The indirect moral and political consequences of converting Parliament into an arena for pressing the conflicting claims of industrial trusts and combines were, for Jones, simply deplorable.[56] It was, then, the viewing of the Empire as a fiscal unit, to the detriment of giving full acknowledgement to the bonds of sentiment, which Jones deplored, and he thought that the introduction of a system of tariffs and preferences would further undermine the moral foundation upon which that sentiment was based. Jones argues that:

> To change our open into restricted markets, to set up barriers against the free interchange of utilities so far as that lies in our power, to adopt methods of antagonism to other nations, to endanger our own larger patriotism by making our colonies an unwelcome burden to our citizens at home, to lay aside a powerful instrument of amity and goodwill amongst the peoples of the earth, and all for the sake of a limited and still more doubtful material gain, is a wrong against humanity which we ought not to have been invited to commit. And we shall not commit it. We shall not turn back upon the methods that have made our Empire great, nor shall we weaken the moral foundations on which alone it can securely rest.[57]

Nothing should be allowed to debase the bond of sentiment which Free Trade promoted, and any commercial practice which did, whether in the name of Free Trade or Tariff Reform, deserved to be condemned unequivocally.

The Boer War, for Jones, while undeniably reflecting elements of brutality and economic greed, was at the same time a war to restore freedom to a conquered people and strengthen the moral bond of the

Empire. It was at once the outcome of 'blatant imperialism' and reckless greed which would always remain a stain on the national character, but at the same time it exhibited the elements of a 'far-sighted imperialism' in the magnanimous efforts of British statesmen to remove some of its pernicious effects.[58] Imperialism, for Jones, always exhibited something of this contrast between the sharp practices of businessmen, whose exploitation of native peoples was 'deep and nauseous',[59] and whose trade had 'been as cruel as the ancient sword',[60] and the more noble efforts of British statesmen and their representatives in mitigating the evils in the name of higher ideals. It was the struggle towards such ideals which showed that the nation and the Empire were slowly progressing.

This was a theme to which Jones returned during the First World War. He wanted to remind the British that their own inglorious past should temper the tendency to attribute all the blame for the war to German aggression. Britain had to accept some blame itself. Jones argued that the 'lands of the heathen' were acquired neither by religious conversion nor for the sake of the ideals of civilization. Acquisition and conquest followed trade, and rarely in our business dealings with the 'lower races', were our actions honourable. He argued that: 'We have been as ruthless and we have been as ready to plead "the rights of a higher civilization over a lower", as the German people are to-day.'[61] Our circumstances are mitigated only by the fact that we are evolving towards a higher ethical ideal and learning to respect the rights of those peoples over whom we exercise authority.[62]

Muirhead was not as vociferous in his opposition to the Boer War as he would like to have been. Joseph Chamberlain, who founded Birmingham University, in which Muirhead was a professor, was also its conscientious chancellor. Muirhead did not hesitate, however, to express his opinions privately. He believed, like many others who opposed Chamberlain's policy, that there was a growing current of opinion among Dutch residents in the Orange Free State, Cape Colony, and the Transvaal in favour of widespread reforms. It would only be a matter of a few years before Kruger left the scene, and with him the resistance to such reforms. It therefore seemed to many that it was imprudent of the British Government to risk a South African war, which could escalate into a European conflict. However one looked at the war, it appeared to be designed to destroy the independence of a people who were of the same race as the British.[63]

In his article 'What Imperialism Means', Muirhead suggests that 'the present war has come with a sword into our midst'.[64] But he declines to enter into a discussion about events in South Africa, and addresses instead the broader questions of the meaning of imperialism. He concludes that irrespective of how Great Britain came to acquire its Empire, the circumstances themselves imposed responsibilities which could not be repudiated. To disown the obligations of Empire, Muirhead argues, 'would be a crime outweighing all we have committed in creating it'.[65] Rule of some kind is necessary, and trade may be consequent upon it, but neither should be the motive for discharging the obligations of Empire.

Muirhead, like Jones, stresses the moral, or spiritual foundation of the Empire necessary to promote the unity of sentiment which binds together the whole. This was a vision of Empire which other Idealists like Bosanquet, Haldane, Watson, Hetherington, and, to a lesser extent, Ritchie shared. What, then, are its essential elements? First, there is an explicit ranking of races, or nations, according to their degree of civilization, and it is acknowledged that different forms of government are necessary to suit the various circumstances. Secondly, whatever form of government it might be, it must always be government for the people, even if it is not by the people. It goes without saying that rule must always be in accordance with law, and that crude notions like might is right, state necessity, or the reason of state, can never justify the exercise of arbitrary government, or the substitution of will for law, in our relations with the colonies and dependencies. The ultimate aim of Empire must always be to educate the people to a level whereby they can exercise a greater degree of self-rule and autonomy, with a view to letting them walk alone.

These principles were in part eloquently articulated by Burke, whose larger vision of the Empire, as more than a trading partnership in calico and tobacco, stood as a monument for the Idealist imperialists to emulate. For Burke no abstract principles could determine the ideal form of government applicable in all times and for all circumstances. Government is an eminently practical matter, and must conform to the circumstances, and to the people over whom it is exercised. He says, for instance, 'I never was wild enough to conceive, that one method would serve for the whole; that the natives of Hindostan and those of Virginia could be ordered in the same manner.'[66] No form of government could work effectively without due respect for local customs and traditions, and it was because of Warren Hastings's blatant disregard for such matters that Burke so vehemently took him to task.

Jones essentially follows the same path as Burke. For Jones the nation has a personality, which may, of course, not yet be fully developed, but it must always be treated as an end in itself, and never as a means. Respect for the personalities of distant nations and the acknowledgement of their rights and freedoms are what the loyalty of the Empire are built upon.[67] Great Britain was slow to learn this lesson. In its dealings with primitive peoples, however, Jones claims that Britain had been more tolerant of their local customs and ineptitudes than any other imperial power,[68] and had tried as best it could to encourage the development of every glimmer of good in the local habits, customs and beliefs. No creed or institution is crushed, and no ritual insulted that shows reverence for what is morally upright. This was confirmed for Jones by the example of his own son who was an assistant commissioner in Burma, and who, in his administration of the local people, worked through their system of patriarchy. Only in this way could the good of both the mother country and the natives be promoted.[69]

Although the British people were shamefully ignorant of their colonies, he believed that they were learning, and that the Empire was gradually getting nearer to becoming 'a really healthy organism'.[70] Its health, in Jones's view, could not be promoted by such shallow inducements as trade preferences, and if its unity depended upon the filaments of a cash-nexus, the unity was already lost. Nevertheless, although governments utilize the traditional forms of authority, the unity of the Empire actually springs from the fact that the powers which dominate in the councils, industry and commerce are the descendants of the British forms. They often have the same character of mind, having been heir to the same spiritual, moral and religious traditions, as well as sharing common aspirations and destinies.[71]

There is no doubt that like Burke in his attitude to America, Jones was of the opinion that the predominantly white colonies, like Australia, New Zealand and Canada, had a privileged status in the Empire because of the higher degree of civilization they expressed as a result of their more direct relation to the mother country. This, of course, was a common enough attitude among the British, and the white colonists themselves. Indeed, the white colonies were often seen as laboratories for social experiment from which Great Britain itself could learn. In Australia the free trade colony of New South Wales, for example, could be compared with the adjacent protectionist colony of Victoria to reach 'objective' conclusions about the relative merits of the different commercial practices.[72] W. Pember Reeves, a member of the pro-imperialist dining club, the Coeffecients, whose number included R. B. Haldane and the Webbs, expressed the view of the white colonists admirably. Reeves was New Zealand born and sent by its government to London to act as Agent General. He later became the Director of the London School of Economics. Reeves thought that the white colonies had a great deal to teach the Home Country,[73] but was under no illusions about the inglorious past of Britain's expansionism. He nevertheless, like Burke, Jones and Muirhead, believed that whatever one thought about the acquisition of the Empire, and whether it was a financial burden or asset, no one could deny the 'weighty responsibilities and exacting duties which the ownership of her great empire imposes upon Britain'.[74]

Furthermore, whatever may divide the British in their attitudes to the Empire, Pember Reeves thought, like Jones, that the views of the pro-Boers provided a useful corrective to the common misconceptions. Reeves believed that there was one division about which Britons could be united, and that is that 'the White Colonies are justly the subjects of national pride', and worthy to be called 'daughter nations',[75] whose loyalty had grown as their liberty increased.

For Jones, such integrity of character exhibited by the white colonists could justify policies which excluded other races from entering their shores. In an address at Adelaide University, on his 1908 visit to Australia, Jones sympathized with that country's objection to the influx of coloured races, not because of the colour of their skin which had a beauty in its own right, but because there was uncertainty about 'the kind of character which a mixture of races was likely to produce'.[76]

On the second set of elements of the noble vision of Empire, Burke was adamant that whatever the form of government, it had a duty to rule in the interest of the people with whose welfare it was entrusted. With reference to India, Burke argued that the East India Company was 'a state in the disguise of a merchant',[77] having derived many of its powers by various charters from the Mogul Empire. Had the Mogul Empire retained its strength and vigour, the East India Company 'would have been bound under that responsibility to observe the laws, usages, and customs of the natives, and to pursue their benefit in all things'.[78] When Great Britain tacitly acceded to the arrangement and subsequently used it to its advantage, it became the guarantor of those duties conferred upon the East India Company, and bound itself to preserve the rights, laws and liberties of the Indian people which its natural sovereign was obliged to uphold had he been in a position to do so.

In Burke's view the Imperial legislature is the superintendent of the subordinate governments of the Empire. It derives its strength from a relaxation of authority in its remote regions, allowing relative autonomy in matters which do not undermine its rule. The various co-ordinate legislatures look for guidance, peace, justice and assistance from the centre, and as long as they are equal to the tasks with which they are endowed the Imperial legislature should not be unduly intrusive.[79] However, in those cases where arbitrary government usurps the rule of law, and where the interests of the people are neglected, the British Government should spare no effort in bringing the culprits to justice, and restoring a legitimate government.[80] Furthermore, to resort to force to retain those colonies whose love of liberty and national spirit is equal to that of the mother country must always be a mistake, and conciliation rather than confrontation is to be preferred. He argues that 'we have no sort of *experience* in favour of force as an instrument in the rule of our colonies'.[81] Force is no solution because it has to be repeatedly applied. A nation which has constantly to be conquered by the Imperialist ruler can hardly be said to be governed.

Jones shared many of these concerns with Burke. Jones argued that the responsibility of guiding and guarding people of lower civilizations is 'to govern for the sake of the governed' and in this respect, 'government *for* the people is worth having even when it cannot be, as yet, government *by* the people'.[82] The analogy Jones invokes to reinforce his view is that of the mother whose concern is always for the welfare of the child. In Australia, for example, he told the people of Adelaide that he hoped 'the mother country, with her many children hanging to her skirts, will be like most mothers – glad if her sons surpass their parents'.[83] John Watson, another of Caird's gifted pupils, similarly held a noble view of Empire, and stressed that there should always be a genuine intention on the part of Great Britain to develop institutions which are best able to give expression to the will of the people.[84] Muirhead and Hetherington, like Jones, acknowledged that we cannot pretend that anywhere as near the same degree of vigilance had been exercised in protecting the rights of indigenous peoples as for the security and material benefits of the civilized whites. They suggested, however, that states must adopt a more honourable attitude to the less developed races, and in regulating the relations between the civilized and uncivilized, the interests of the latter should predominate.[85]

Government in the interests of the people, which for Idealists necessarily excluded arbitrary rule and promoted the elimination of force, was not sufficient in itself and had to be motivated by a magnanimous ideal. This ultimate aim, as Jones expressed it, was to educate the native peoples to a level where they were capable of self-government, and of pursuing their own highest good.[86] 'There is no other people in the world', Jones contends, 'which of deliberate purpose has sought to foster the spirit and to teach the uses of political freedom to races which probably had never known them, while all the time it was aware that it was rendering its own rule obsolete.'[87] Such a process, however, does not entail the imposition of an alien civilization upon another ill-equipped to receive it, but instead to encourage the good which lies in their own customs and traditions. There can be no firmer foundation of the unity of the Empire than the attainment of liberty by its member nations.[88] In this respect Jones is emphasizing the general point to which all Idealists subscribed, that is, that freedom is not a gift that can be given by one individual to another, or by one nation to another. It is an attainment achieved by means of a long moral struggle, and the best that one country can do for another is to secure and sustain the conditions by which it may by its own endeavours win freedom.[89]

In a different context, however, and with an uncharacteristic note of scepticism and pessimism, he expresses doubt about the wisdom and possibility of success of such an enterprise in the face of peoples who 'can hardly be taught to rule except as despots, or to obey except as slaves'. He goes on to suggest that in modern times there has been 'no more interesting spectacle, or more doubtful enterprise, than this of inoculating these Eastern peoples with the spirit of the West'.[90] A people which does not profess and practice its principles, and instead is forced by circumstances to deny or suppress them, is enslaved. It is the moral force of a people which determines its future, and this force emanates from its self-awareness of freedom. Jones argues that 'a slave in spirit, so far as he is a slave, can have no virtues; for his acts are not his own, but the product obtained through him as means, by the power that uses him'.[91]

Muirhead does not minimize the difficulties of preparing a people for self-rule, but nevertheless believes that this must be the aim of the ruling power. Lack of success so far, he believed, was a result of too little effort being made to understand the people who received the education. There can be no genuine education when the ideas that are imparted 'stand in no organic connection with the ideas already there'.[92] Watson, too, thinking that he finds justification in Green for holding such a view, suggests that the only legitimate defence of rule by a higher over a lower people is the raising of the latter to the level of the former, and 'unless the civilised people acts from this principle, its rule can only be regarded as an unjustifiable tyranny'.[93]

What has been suggested, then, in this chapter, is that many Idealists, and in particular Jones, condemned the sort of imperialism against which Hobhouse and Hobson reacted, and that their principles disposed them to a higher, or nobler, moral conception of Empire which was more in keeping with Burke's grand vision than with the justifications of social imperialism espoused in their own day.

On the other hand, liberals like Morley, Hobson and Hobhouse, who were critical of many aspects of Idealism, sympathized with the grander conception of Empire which Idealists like Jones, Muirhead and Watson espoused. If we take Hobhouse as an example, we can see that he acknowledges that many of the ideals of the older conception of Imperialism were laudable, but is dismayed by the fact that reality was so distant from the ideal. He says that 'if Imperialism means a high sense of the honour of the Empire and of its duties to subject races, then we cannot have too much Imperialism'.[94] The new Imperialism, he suggests, contains nothing of the 'ennobled sense of national responsibility.'[95] The view of the older liberalism was that the colonies freely entered into an informal union with Great Britain, and that the dependencies which had fallen to its care were to be ruled by government, both conscientious and tolerant.[96] The colonial Empire, he believed, in so far as its members develop self-government, is compatible with democracy.[97] Liberalism, although opposed to the 'Imperial idea as it is ordinarily presented', is not hostile to the Empire and its possibilities, nor 'to the sentiment of unity pervading the white population'.[98] The colonial Empire, founded on the principle of self-government, is largely the legacy of old liberalism, and its members, for the most part progressive in their politics, are the natural allies of British liberals. For Hobhouse the issue of ruling the 'inferior races' of the dependencies is a rather more delicate matter. He contended that we cannot be sure whether they possess the mental and moral capability to exercise self-government, or participate in a self-governing state. The safest way to proceed, Hobhouse suggests, is to support whatever means may be necessary to protect them from physical and moral harm, especially in their relations with white men. Ideally, it would be best to leave them alone altogether until whites can better rule themselves.

Hobhouse, then, is not as hostile to that type of Imperialism which we have attributed to Henry Jones, as one might at first have thought. The main line of difference between their views is that Hobhouse is assessing the ideal in terms of the actual performance, whereas Jones is assessing the performance in terms of the ideal. The former sees the ideal perverted and subverted by the circumstances, while the latter sees the circumstances, despite all their faults, embodying the ideal. Having examined the issues of nationalism and the 'nobler imperialism' in Jones's thought we turn, in the final chapter, to the question of German philosophy and the morality of states. Jones, like most of the Idealists during the First World War, encountered the problem of explaining his adherence to German thought and state theory in a very antagonistic intellectual environment. The last chapter will refocus and reflect again on many of the themes already touched upon in previous chapters.

CHAPTER EIGHT

'GERMAN PHILOSOPHY' AND THE MORALITY OF STATES

The First World War had long been anticipated by Idealists, not least because as well-seasoned travellers of Germany, and keen observers of changing trends in German philosophy, they were well aware of the rise of aggressive nationalism and the cult of militarism which pervaded the country. Although the British Idealists condemned German aggression and lay the blame firmly at her door for precipitating the war, they nevertheless invited reproach because of their ostensible, or at least perceived, reverence for the state and the apparent subordination of the individual to its interests. Even though many of them were less collectivist than their critics, the semi-mystical language in terms of which they expressed their theories was sometimes impenetrable and could not help but generate confusion and misunderstanding when opponents tried to draw out the practical consequences.

Many commentators who tried to explain Germany's aggressive militarism attributed blame to her philosophers, often indicting Kant, Fichte and Hegel for formulating doctrines which became accentuated and exaggerated by later thinkers like Schopenhauer, Nietzche, Treitschke and Stirner. By implication, and also by explicit reference, the same criticisms were directed at the British Idealists who were self-confessed Kantians and Hegelians. It was Haldane and Bosanquet who felt the brunt of direct criticism. However, other Idealists like Muirhead responded by arguing that those philosophers who came after Hegel and reacted against him perverted all that was good in German philosophy. It was they who were to blame for its degeneration and insidious influence. Other Idealists, like Watson, who agreed that a perverted course had been charted after Hegel, nevertheless wanted to question any direct link between political philosophy and practical politics.

For the Idealists, as one would expect, the state was the principal actor in international relations. Its dealings with other states were believed to be qualitatively different from the imperial relations in which the state was dealing, for the most part, with peoples of a 'lower level of civilization' whose collective wills were not expressed in the organic unity of the person of the modern state. On the question of the relations between the higher ethical organisms, the British Idealists also exhibited differences over the degree to which they saw the self-conscious moral community (which the state encompassed) having any counterpart in the international sphere. Their views on this issue had a bearing upon their conclusions as to whether the state had the same or similar moral duties in its relations with other states as the individuals had within a state.

When one looks carefully at their arguments differences emerge over the conditions necessary for moral action. More importantly they disagree about whether those conditions actually prevail in the contemporaneous international situation, and thus over whether states can act morally towards each other in the current circumstances. There is, nevertheless, a considerable degree of consensus concerning the causes of war and the prospects of achieving a long-term unity between states conducive to a lasting peace. The evolution of ethics within the state was also possible between states. Following Kant, and with varying degrees of optimism, they contend that a world federation of states, beginning on a small scale, is both desirable and possible. In this respect, the civilizing mission of imperialism, about which we spoke in the previous chapter, has the added justification of promoting the attainment of republican or democratic forms of government, which Kant believed to be a prerequisite to the success of a pacific federation of states. The establishment of the League of Nations was indeed a step towards such a unity for many Idealists, while others doubted any immediate prospect of success in the absence of an international community spirit.

The purpose of this chapter is to articulate the terms of reference surrounding these issues and to locate the contribution of Henry Jones in the context of Hobhouse's criticisms of the metaphysical theory of the state and its British adherents. Once again we will find that Jones is much closer to Hobhouse than the latter would want to admit.

MILITARISM AND THE GERMAN MIND

We have already seen that for Jones the state is an ethical organism with a distinctive personality. He argues further, however, that we cannot attribute an ethical character to the state 'except on the assumption that it is a Person'.[1] The personification of the state is, of course, a commonplace in political philosophy enabling the attribution of a will and deliberative rational and responsible agency to the collective entity. Hegel, as we saw in chapter four, for example, viewed the state as an organism which contained within itself the internal relations of its own substance. The state while being in contact with states external to itself is both self-determining and self-sufficing. Hegel speaks of it as both a person and an individual. Like a person, the state has individuality only in its awareness of being distinct from others, and in entering into relations with them.[2]

This endowment of personality and will upon the state lost much of its subtlety and ethical nuances in the work of later German historians and philosophers who used the theory to justify German militarism and the spread of Germany's higher civilization by means of force. This is less pronounced in J. K. Bluntschli than in Heinrich von Treitschke, the former of whom argued that 'history ascribes to the state a personality which, having spirit and body, possesses and manifests a will of its own'.[3] For him the personality of the state is masculine, in that it consciously rules itself and acts freely in its external affairs.[4] Treitschke took the theory to greater extremes, arguing that the personality of the state is both legal and historico-moral, and that its will, far from being fictitious, 'is the most real of all'.[5] War is its 'essential function' and maintaining its power 'a task of incomparable grandeur'.[6] The fact that this aspect of the state had long been misunderstood and little theorized was for Treitschke 'proof of how effeminate the science of government had become in civilian hands'.[7] The state, he argues, is a higher moral will and the individual has no right to oppose it even if in his opinion it is acting immorally. As a member of his state the individual must 'have courage to take its errors upon him'.[8] Treitschke wishes to emphasize, however, that even though the state is a physical power, it is also a co-operative institution in the education of mankind which is disposed to see advantage in taking its place among the community of states by affording a degree of respect to its neighbours.[9]

The temperate elements in Treitschke, such as they are, become totally suppressed, and the more crudely realist and militarist elements become accentuated in one of the most infamous exponents of Germany's civilizing mission, General Friedrich von Bernhardi. What had been in Hegel a polite dismissal of Kant's project for perpetual peace on the grounds that it would lead to the internal stagnation of the state, became a contemptuous condemnation in the writings of Treitschke and Bernhardi.[10] Furthermore Bernhardi contended that it was both the right and duty of the state to make war. Drawing upon naturalistic evolutionary theory, he argues that in Nature the struggle for existence is the foundation of 'all healthy development', and the principles underlying such progress are equally applicable to intra-social, and extra-social advancement. Self-sacrifice is unnatural and self-assertion the true activity of the state which entails more than mere self-defence in the positive satisfaction of ensuring the safety and development of its own citizens.[11] Arbitration treaties, he contends, are impediments 'on the natural laws of development' because 'with the cessation of the unrestricted competition whose ultimate appeal is to arms, all real progress would soon be checked, and a moral and intellectual stagnation would ensue which must end in degeneration'.[12]

Such theories as these with their strong emphasis upon the subordination of the individual to the will of the state precipitated a hostile reaction in Anglophone philosophers of all philosophical persuasions, including the British Idealists themselves. The British Idealists naturally wished to dissociate themselves from the later German philosophy, arguing that it was a gross perversion of the theories of Kant, Fichte and Hegel. Hegel, they wished to impress upon their audiences, unlike the later militaristic philosophies, wished to ground the authority of the state upon will and not on force.[13] There were, of course, Idealists who did think that some of the earlier German philosophers should bear partial responsibility for the implications of their ideas. W. R. Sorley, for example, argued that the modern German theory of the state was not the invention of Treitschke. The centrality of power in the idea of the state, its use as the measure of *Kultur*, and the duty of the omnicompetent state to maximize its power are, Sorley suggests, all to be found in Fichte's political philosophy.[14]

In addition, J. S. MacKenzie and Ernest Barker both absolve Kant of blame, but implicate Hegel in the responsibility for later events because of his insistence upon the self-sufficient and independent state. MacKenzie argues that the theory which Hegel 'whispered prepared the way for that which Treitschke proclaimed from the housetop'.[15] Barker was much more forthright in his condemnation, arguing that 'Hegel expresses that sense of the absolute finality of the state which made Frederic seize Silesia in spite of an international guarantee of the integrity of the Austrian dominions, and impelled him to carry Prussia further and further along the paths of militarism'.[16] Many other philosophers less committed to Idealism saw the egotism and militarism manifest in the later philosophy nascent and endemic in the earlier. Among the vast literature attributing blame for German aggressiveness to the earlier philosophers the books by George Santayana, John Dewey and L. T. Hobhouse are the most substantive.

Santayana, while not attributing the war to German philosophy, claimed that the philosophers of that country shared and justified the excessive egotism characteristic of the actions of the modern German nation. Egotism is that perversion of thought which asserts that one's being and power emanates from within, and upholds the omnipotence of will and logic, contesting that the mind and conscience should be constrained or controlled only by the mind and conscience itself. It is, he claims, a transcendental theory in which the will is absolute, and in which the ego imagines its own world. Egotism is for the Germans a 'new religion' which 'dominates the judgment and conduct of the nation'.[17] Notwithstanding evidence to the contrary Santayana discerns the seeds of German egotism in Kant, Fichte and Hegel, and its full flowering in Nietzsche, after finding incomplete and distorted elements of it in Goethe, Schopenhauer and Stirner.[18]

Dewey's indictment of German philosophy rests on the contention that the aggressiveness manifest in Germany's self-styled historical civilizing mission is attributable not to Nietzsche, but to Kant, whose distinction between the phenomenal and noumenal worlds is the germinal idea from which all else follows. The phenomenal world is the outer domain of causal necessity and science, while the noumenal world is the inner realm of freedom and moral action, that is, the former is 'physical and necessary', and the latter is 'ideal and free.' Irrespective of their autonomy the inner has primacy over the latter.[19] Even though the former cannot intrude into the latter, it is the character of morality to bring about the realization of free rational action in the sensible world. Moral obligation cannot arise from causal necessity, or the pressure of physical circumstances. Duty is an *a priori* categorical imperative – a self-imposed law capable of transforming the world of sense into a condition which conforms with universal reason. In ennobling and almost sanctifying the performance of one's duty, but without giving it a content, Kant created a void which could be filled with a content by his successors.[20] For Kant the state has a moral basis and purpose in that the law of reason, and not natural sociability, impels its creation. However, the state cannot itself coerce a moral motive in that it is external to the autonomous realm of morality. This apparent anomaly, Dewey tells us, 'almost calls for a theory which shall make the state the supreme moral entity'.[21] Fichte and Hegel give substance to the moral void which Kant has left by means of a progressively greater shift away from cosmopolitanism to an assertive nationalism, and the deification of the state which they identified with a moral mission constituting the concrete duty of its citizens. In other words, when the political circumstances required a universal military commitment, Fichte and Hegel provided the justification by associating duty with obedience to the state.

In Dewey's view Hegel 'is the greatest realist known to philosophy. He might be called a Brutalist'.[22] In his doctrine the state has greater objective reality than nature in that it is Absolute Spirit realized in consciousness, and it is only as a member of a state that the individual realises his objective existence in truth and morality. Hegel saw the state as an organized individual organically growing in history. History itself was the Absolute evolving from one National Individual to another. The justification of war, Dewey contends, follows inevitably from such a nationalistic doctrine. For Hegel, he claims, 'war is the most effective preacher of the vanity of all merely finite interests; it puts an end to that selfish egoism of the individual by which he would claim his life and property as his own or as his family's'.[23] Dewey contends that Bernhardi's appeal to both Kant and Hegel, rather than to Nietzche, in exhorting Germans to spread their noble civilization by means of military force throughout the world, is testimony to the fact that the philosophy which supports German militarism is no modern aberration and was rooted firmly in the earlier writers.

Many Idealists had been convinced for a long time that Germany would have no compunction about attacking Britain and was capable of launching an all-out offensive which it might sustain for up to ten years. Jones and Haldane, for example, concurred with these views but continued to project a spirit of friendliness towards Germany in the hope that it might avert war. Jones believed that his own expressions may have been misinterpreted to mean that he 'believed Germany was herself friendly and had no hostile intentions'.[24] When the war came he had no reservations about condemning German aggression, but he also wanted to press home the point that the mistakes made by, and the self-interestedness of, all the nations, from which Britain could not be absolved, could not totally acquit them of all responsibility for the war.[25]

The Germans, Jones believed, had become victims of a one-sided creed which posited state individualism and egotism in its relations with other states, and which it was putting to the test in the war. In so far as they are half-truths they cannot be left out of any serious moral and social theory,[26] but because individualism and egotism are one-sided and thus 'misleading errors' the purposes they contrive fail to succeed. Such one-sided errors conjure up their opposites and demand to be reconciled and harmonized with them. Jones argues that 'the world resists being shredded into parts, and persistently maintains its concrete totality'.[27] Germany over a long period of time had devoted her thought to the development of the natural sciences, applying the results to economic and military uses.[28] The people convinced themselves that they were at the zenith of their national strength, and the epitome of the highest level of civilization yet attained.[29] The responsibility for the war must rest mainly with them in that it 'was premeditated, planned in detail by its rulers, eagerly desired by its military and triumphantly entered upon by the whole nation.'[30] Its actions are far worse than those impelled by a barbaric desire for slaughter and plunder, or the ignorant neglect or disregard of civilization's rights, because 'it is the *reasoned* belief in terrritorial brigandage and in the methods of barbarism provided they are employed by and for the sake of the German nation'.[31]

Unlike Dewey and Santayana, Jones contends that it is not to Idealism we must look for the origin of such developments, but to the turning away from Idealism towards materialism. With the advance of the sciences and territorial conquests industrial and commercial interests made things of the spirit of secondary value.[32] It is true that Hegel did not condemn war as an absolute evil, or a contingent irrationality. It was ethically necessary in preventing internal corruption and stagnation, but he did not regard war as a good. Although he greatly elevated the national state and had no hesitation about supplying it with ample arms, he had no one state in mind, and saw them all having to give good account of themselves before the court of the World Spirit. Unlike the present generation of Germans Hegel did not subject 'life to mechanism, or the spiritual to the material'.[33] The spiritual and cosmopolitan Idealism of Lessing, Kant, Goethe, Fichte and Hegel had been perverted by substituting a material self-assertion satisfying the particular interests of specific states, for that spiritual striving, or self-assertion, which Hegel spoke of satisfying.[34]

There was no necessary connection in the anti-German Idealism literature between the condemnation of what was called the Prussian theory of the state and the theories of the British Idealists. Dewey, for instance, suggests that only in Germany was Idealism 'both indigenous and widely applied'.[35] While F. C. S. Schiller makes the observation that:

> The large and influential section of our rulers which was educated at Balliol by T. H. Green and his followers has been for years indoctrinating us with the same theory without any terrible effects. So may not the verdict of history on the Great War ultimately be that philosophic ideas had as little to do with it as with other wars?[36]

On the other hand theorists like L. T. Hobhouse, J. A. Hobson and G. D. H. Cole argued that the manifestation of the Prussian theory of the state in British Idealism constituted a serious threat to individual liberty, and acted as an obstacle to the development of a genuine international morality, and the establishment of co-operative international institutions. Let us first address the question of the threat of the Absolute State to individual liberty.

Hobhouse wishes to refute the claim of many British Idealists that modern German philosophy represents a falling away from the Idealism of Hegel.[37] Bismarckian German militarism, he claims, in agreement with William Clark, is a product of Hegelian philosophy, which is the progenitor of all things reactionary in the nineteenth century.[38] In identifying freedom with obedience to law, merging the personality of the individual with the state and elevating the state to the highest form of association,[39] Hegel formulated the doctrine which substituted the rights of the state for those of the individual, and instead of conceiving the state as the servant of humanity, saw it as an end in itself.[40] This was the 'wicked doctrine', Hobhouse contends, of which 'the visible and tangible outcome' was the bombing of London.[41] Hobhouse is not satisfied with deprecating Hegel, but wishes also to bring into disrepute his British followers. With the aberrant exception of Green, Hobhouse accuses them of holding the genuinely Hegelian 'doctrine of the state as an incarnation of the Absolute, a super-personality which absorbs the real living personality of men and women'.[42]

J. A. Hobson, fearing that individual liberties were being eroded by the demands of a war-time state, warned of the dangers of the Prussian theory and of those British intellectuals who espoused versions of it. Prussianism, Hobson argues, consists in the state exercising absolute control over the individual wills of its citizens. He contends: 'The State has imposed itself as a super-personality upon the individual citizen, who is taught and compelled to regard himself, his activity, and his very will, as mere instruments of this higher personality.'[43] He specifically cites Henry Jones as an exponent of 'the pure milk of Prussianism' which he substantiates with reference to a speech Jones made in Bangor in connection with his work for the Parliamentary Recruitment Committee. Jones is reported to have said 'that the state had a right to compel, provided it stood for its own welfare . . . It owned us, we belonged to it. We derived the very substance of our soul from the organized community in which we lived and which we called the State.'[44] In opposition to this theory Hobson argues that the British state rests on the principles of free will and the right of an individual to appeal to his own conscience and choose his own good even if that entailed refusing to make private sacrifices for the public good.

THE MORALITY OF STATES

Hobhouse, Hobson and Cole all argue that the emphasis which the Idealists give to the state as the ultimate form of association disguises and detracts from the fact that we have obligations and duties in the context of, and express ourselves through, a multiplicity of associations which may on occasions have a stronger moral pull for us. The emphasis upon the state as a person subsumes the individual personality to the will of the state, which is not as it ought to be viewed. It is not the means to the ends of its individual members, but an end in itself. Hobhouse and Cole specifically take Bosanquet as their target,[45] whereas Hobson focuses upon Jones. Hobson argues that the state is only an instrument, or aspect, of society: 'What Sir H. Jones calls "the substance of our soul" is only to a very limited extent furnished by the political organization of the state, as distinguished from the many other modes in which society moulds and educates us.'[46]

Jones's defence of Bosanquet against Hobhouse equally constitutes an answer to Hobson's criticisms. Jones argues that Bosanquet did not view the state as it is usually conceived, that is, as a series of institutions correlative with the government and its agencies, but instead, 'as a rule it means all that we mean when we speak of "our country" '.[47] Nor did Jones believe that the state, whatever its nature, could override the moral consciences of its individual citizens. As moral agents neither the state nor the individual can delegate responsibility for judging what is right and wrong, and it is the obligation and privilege of the moral entity that wills to make such judgements. It is unwarranted to assume that the state has unlimited rights over the individual, any more than to assume that individuals have permanent rights over other individuals. The most meagre individual can challenge the state on a matter of right because it is the *cause* which makes the act sacred, not the enormity of the will.[48] 'Very lowly and humble men and women', Jones argues, 'who stand for some causes have rights that are superior to the most powerful of all states, when it stands merely for itself.'[49] The state just because it exists has no ultimate right to the obedience of its citizens, nor does it have the right, nor ultimately the power, to continue to exist if it denies or deviates from its proper nature, that is, the promotion of the good in the life of each of its citizens. The state which lacks the requisite moral demeanour and persistently does wrong has no absolute value in itself and has no ultimate right to exist. Thus a state which calls upon its citizens to fight in a war it has declared 'must not be judged on the mere assumption that it has a right to exist'.[50] The judgement of whether such a war is just is a matter, as moral agents, for both the state and the individual. It is the duty of every individual to make a judgement on its justness and act accordingly: 'If he is convinced that the war is wrong, it is his duty to refuse to fight.'[51] It is conceivable that it may even be the person's duty to fight against his or her own state. It cannot, however, be the duty of a citizen to take no stance on the question of right and wrong. The pacifist in time of war is simply asserting a moral principle which is inapplicable in the circumstances. The good person has to confront the present conditions and determine his, or her, duty in relation to them.

Jones, then, is certainly not arguing for an unconditional and unlimited sovereignty in the sense that the rights of the state can be constrained only by its own power. Such a claim reduces citizens to slaves, and it is this conception of the state to which critics claim Germany subscribes in theory and practice. This unlimited sovereignty which is at variance with democracy assumes lawlessness, capriciousness and the assertion of the right of the state to do what it pleases. Unlimited sovereignty conceived in this way and attributed to the Prussian conception of the state is in fact meaningless and impotent. There are constraints upon its character as a moral individual, and in this respect 'a good and wise state cannot have too much liberty or power or sovereignty, nor an evil and foolish one too little'.[52]

As we have already seen, for Jones the state and the individual do not stand in an external relation to each other. The state fulfilling its purpose as a state empowers its citizens concurrently with the extension of its own powers. The so-called interference in the organizations, or personalities, of those groups and activities which it encompasses is not to dominate, subdue or abolish them, but to remove those hindrances which retard moral progress, and to facilitate the will to moralize the relations as they stand. The moral world only exists in being willed, and the state must assist the removal of impediments to the exercise of such a will, and ensure the availability of the external conditions conducive to moral action. The organization of the affairs of individuals into collective personalities like the economic system always carries the danger that the individuals themselves may be systematized into conforming with the machinery of its volition, which constitutes an invasion of the personality of the citizen. It is the purpose of the state as an enabling and educative moral will to circumvent this lack of respect for individuality by promoting conditions favourable to the good life. Every mode of association must be transformed into a moral institution, and each occupation the expression of a freely chosen way of life through which the citizen can direct his, or her, devoted energies.[53]

The sovereignty of the state, then, is unlimited only in so far as the state is true to its purpose. It may do *anything* that contributes to the good life of its citizens, but no more; and the citizen may ask *anything* of the state which facilitates that same good life, always cognizant of the fact that 'the good life is a common good, the well-being at once of the individual citizen and of the state'.[54] Contrary to what Hobson implies, Jones's state absolutism is not unconditional, nor does the state in any narrow sense provide the substance of the individual's soul, because the state actually encompasses all those 'many other modes' which mould and educate us. The state is, for Jones, correlative with the social environment, in conjunction with which individuals build and perfect their characters.

The allegation that the Idealist conception of the state is a serious threat to liberty is, then, vehemently denied by Jones who, as we have seen throughout this book, saw individual liberties being enhanced rather than decreased by the extension of the power of the state intent on fulfilling its true purpose. However the question remains concerning the claim that the Idealist theory of the state inhibits the development of international morality, and co-operative international institutions.

Critics of the Idealist conception of the state, irrespective of what the Idealists themselves wished to include within it, took the ideas of organic unity and personality to be indicative of exclusivity. Cole, for example, argues that even if the state is taken to incorporate all the functional institutions within its sphere, making the obligations to it inclusive of those to other associations, the theory fails to account for associations which are international or cosmopolitan in nature. Our obligations to these cannot be encompassed by the national state.[55] Hobhouse believes that the fashionable theory which had in some quarters become an 'academic orthodoxy', actually 'sets the state above moral criticism, constitutes war a necessary incident in its existence, contemns humanity, and repudiates a Federation or League of Nations'.[56]

If the state is conceived as a moral agent, which the critics did not wish to deny, the question arises concerning the degree to which its actions are subject to the same moral principles as those which govern the individual citizen. Hobhouse, opposing what he believed to be the implications of the metaphysical theory of the state, argued that the state is only one form of organization in the broader society of mankind which has been conceived to fulfil purposes which have sometimes clashed, but at the same time have settled down to exhibit a relative stability. The stability is constantly subject to the pressure of change and the established order has no immutable permanence.[57] The state is one of the means through which a community expresses its life, and the positive or collectivist view of its function is that of an agent of civilization whose associated values of progress and social justice are not the preserve of, and cannot be confined to, the limits of one nation. If peace, harmony and justice are qualities necessary to the internal functioning of the state, then surely they are applicable to relations between states. External relations must reflect and react upon internal relations, 'and the negation of a principle in one relation must affect its authority in others'.[58] The state belongs to and must abide by the laws and interests of the much broader community of civilized nations.[59]

The moral law which governs conduct between states, Hobhouse argues, does not imply the existence of a sovereign authority to enforce it. Law is complied with, and has force and authority, in primitive communities where no sovereign or courts are evident to enforce obedience. There are two respects in which the nations of Western Europe resemble primitive societies: they have no acknowledged sovereign, but nevertheless share many moral and religious traditions which constrain their activities.[60] Even if the existence and enforcement of law is predicated upon the establishment of a sovereign authority, it would not affect the question of international morality because 'moral rights and duties are founded on relations between man and man, and are therefore applicable to all humanity'.[61] To deny the basis of international ethics is to deny the foundation of civilized ethics in general. As far as Hobhouse is concerned, there is 'no distinction in principle capable of any logical justification between individual and national ethics'.[62] It is important to note that Hobhouse is not basing the international community of which he speaks upon the idea of cosmopolitanism. He acknowledges the state system as it stands, and claims that states are an integral, although imperfect and partial, expression of the values which constitute the foundation of the community of civilized nations.[63]

The First World War undermined Hobhouse's confidence in the possibility of improved moral relations between states in the international system as it was then constituted. He believed that while there could be no guarantee of lasting peace, a world federal state was the only hope of salvation. Like Hobson, he did not believe that such a federation could be achieved other than by means of building upon the small beginnings already implicit in the European configurations of power.[64] Hobhouse thought that a first step towards European union could be taken by a federation of the allied nations who through such co-operation would become accustomed 'to a broader outlook, to the duty of subjecting their egoistic impulses to a common good, to the cultivation of the Parliamentary habit in international affairs'.[65]

To what extent, then, are Hobhouse's views at variance with those of the British adherents to 'genuine Hegelianism'[66] in general, and to Henry Jones in particular? In answering this question it is necessary to distinguish between the explanations the Idealists gave of international relations as they stood, and as they might yet become. In this respect, they did not all have the same conception of the relation of philosophy to political practice. Hegel and Bosanquet, the philosophers that Hobhouse most vehemently attacks, saw the task of philosophy as the analysis of the given in experience. Therefore it was not their business to portray the ideal state in its relations with other ideal states, but the state and its significance in the condition in which it then stood.[67] This is also the view to which Bradley and Watson subscribed.[68] Hobhouse, of course, was a crusading philosopher and polemicist who thought by exposing the weaknesses in current political and social conditions he could point the way to their future improvement. On this issue Jones was nearer to Hobhouse than to Hegel and Bosanquet. No one, not even Green or Caird, propagated the practical implications of Idealism 'with a more daring abandonment and passion and a more genuine enthusiasm than Jones'.[69] A practical purpose, Jones maintained, does not diminish a philosopher's thinking 'provided always that the purpose be broad enough and he makes the universe an accomplice in his plot'.[70] Furthermore, our philosophical ideas have an impact on the world. Jones argues that: 'Ideas have hands and feet. We live to carry them out. A wrong theory of state and of its relations to its citizens or to other states is bound in the long run to tell upon its practice.'[71] This, Jones acknowledges, is in direct contrast to the views of Bosanquet and Bradley whose denials of the direct relevance of moral philosophy to moral practice made his 'blood boil'. They simply confused generalizations which are vacuous, with principles like those we find in science, which are central to every fact and permeate every action. It is our conceptions of the good, whether right or wrong, which guide and inspire our deeds. Speaking of the death of his own son in the war, Jones rhetorically asks: 'And what has sanctified the death of my own boy, the most tender lover of animals that I have ever seen, as he poured death upon his fellow mortals from his machine gun, till he fell himself and "God took him", took him whether to be alive or dead? What did this except his knowledge of the good?'[72]

It is true to say that some of the things which many of the Idealists say about the place of war in contemporary international relations appear shocking and brutal when severed from their broader theories. Hegel, as we have already suggested, saw war as an ethical necessity for the internal health of the state, and externally its individuality could only be established and maintained in its struggles with other states. The state is an organic, organized whole within which morality flourishes and private persons are under the jurisdiction of a court which can by its power give effect to what is right. States differ from private persons in that they are completely autonomous and their relations are non-moral. Because there is no power that can decide what is right in principle and enforce it we can in international relations never get beyond the belief that right ought to prevail. States in their relations with each other do not constitute a moral community expressing a general will. They stand in relation to each other as particular wills looking to their own and not a common interest. When conflicts arise between the particular wills and cannot be placated there is no alternative but to settle the dispute by war.[73]

Ritchie, Watson, Bradley and Bosanquet all to a certain extent agree with Hegel in maintaining that morality depends upon the existence of a general will, and a properly constituted authority exercising legitimate force to defend and uphold the way of life a community has developed. Bradley and Bosanquet, for example, maintain that for humanity to be a genuine organic whole individuals must be conscious of it. In other words there has to be a general will representing a communal mind. Nothing more existed at present, they suggested, than a 'mere reciprocal influence', or 'external convention', which fell far short of a social organism.[74] Such international agreements as there are have as their basis individual wills which ultimately determine their own welfare. Bosanquet contends that 'agreements are of no use *per se*; it is the power and will to keep agreements that are the point'.[75] Ritchie and Bosanquet, following Hegel, are of the opinion that states as they currently stand in their relation to each other are in the equivalent of a state of nature in which the resort to war remains the ultimate court of appeal when serious disputes arise.[76] Ritchie argues that 'war is a harsh form of dialectic, a rough means of solving hard problems; but war or the genuine threat of war, is often the only way',[77] and in its own way it 'has ever been the great maker of nations'.[78]

Green's views, of which Hobhouse approves, seem to stand in sharp contrast to those just adumbrated. For Green war can never be morally justifiable however widely one wants to dissipate responsibility. The end aimed for by resort to war indicates a defect or failure in the previous actions of states which prevented that same end being achieved by peaceful means. War is a consequence of sin, and far from being just, it is itself a sin. One may be exempted from a share of the guilt if it can truly be pleaded that war was the only means whereby the social conditions required for moral development could be preserved, and in fact such a motive is very rare, and does not in any case 'make the wrong-doing involved in war any less so'.[79] D. A. Routh argues with plausibility that for Green a general will of humanity did exist in a rudimentary form and provided the basis of an ethical code in terms of which to judge the conduct of states in their international relations. Green did not think that such a code was in any way complete, but wished to deny Hegel's claim that it was *a priori* impossible.[80]

This apparent contrast between Green and other British Idealists, which Hobhouse himself wished to exploit, is in fact largely illusory. Bosanquet and Watson, for example, like Green denied Hegel's claim that war was endemic in an international states system. It is internal defects of the organization of the state, caused by the moral shortcomings of the people or of the rulers, which give rise to conflicts. Improvements in international relations, they all agree, can only be precipitated by improving the internal organization of society which requires the moralization of the people and institutions which are a reflection of their own character.[81] Bosanquet, for example, calls war 'the great type of irrationality in history', and the 'crowning stupidity' of human relations.[82] In fact he claims 'that the normal relation of states is co-operative'.[83] Bosanquet did not wish to deny that states have a moral responsibility, he merely wished to affirm that its moral responsibilities are different from those of the individual person. The state has the responsibility of organizing the moral organism and sustaining the conditions for the good life of its citizens, while it is the responsibility of the citizen to take advantage of the opportunities provided to fulfil himself, or herself, within the organized system of rights and duties which the state sustains. Individuals have to acknowledge that in the absence of a universal general will the value we attribute to humanitarianism, whether in terms of culture or civility towards fellow human beings, is developed, learnt and imparted within the social and ethical fabric of the great civilized nations. It is the nation which is at once the source of the ideal of humanity itself, and our main instrument for contributing to it. For Bosanquet patriotism and humanitarianism are not opposed. The state in so far as it lives up to its function of promoting the good life is the representative and sustainer of the ideals and values indicative of the highest achievements that humanity has yet attained. The state has a responsibility to defend these ideals and values against states who would destroy them. This is quite a different theory from that which equates your own and your state's view of the moral world with immediate interests.[84] Bosanquet maintains: 'As the individual must ultimately follow his conscience to the end, so the state, if it is to be morally responsible, must follow its own. It is the guardian of moral interests and must follow its duty.'[85]

Jones, like the British Idealists in general, and for that matter like Hobhouse and Hobson, did not attempt to minimize the extent to which morality played such an insignificant part in contemporary relations among states. International morality, Jones argues, is little better than economic morality. The relation is one of 'competitive strain', as it is currently understood, and without an element of honesty the economic system would collapse. But it is for the most part a prudential honesty calculating the benefits and costs of right or wrong conduct.[86] The *laissez-faire* individual egoism which dominated the ethical thinking about relations between citizens in the middle of the nineteenth century, and which had been discredited in theory and legislative practice, still prevailed in inter-state relations.[87] '*International ethics*', Jones suggests, 'measured . . . in any recognized and ordinary moral terms, are crude, confused, uncertain and extraordinarily feeble.'[88] Each state interprets its own good in naturalistic and materialistic terms: it is a good which is exclusive as opposed to the moral good which is common. The economic sphere is one of struggle and it is under the auspices of the state that this struggle can be controlled. Knowing that war does not pay is therefore unlikely to lead to universal peace or disarmament: some nations, like men within states, would use the methods of force and fraud to satisfy their own greed. The exclusivity in terms of which states think is an illusion because it at once implies inclusiveness. The state as a moral person lives in the world, acts through it, and realizes itself in relation to other states. The problems of international relations are moral problems, and it is the failure of morality which gives rise to the appeal to physical force. Morality is not something which is fixed and final, standing above the circumstances to which it is applied. As we have already seen it is an evolutionary process whose existence depends upon being willed.[89]

Jones vehemently denies that the state stands above the moral law. Like Green he believes that even though current state behaviour may sometimes indicate otherwise, the unity of mankind is no mere metaphorical expression. The moral world is not bifurcated: it is one and the same evolving system, and its principles are as applicable to states as they are to individual human beings. The state's obligations and duties may differ in degree, but not in kind from those of the individual citizen.[90] The individual and the state, in so far as they fulfil their moral obligations, cannot be at odds with humanity, whose good is higher and whose rights are superior to those of the state.[91] Jones contends that 'both the state and the individual are in truth in the service of humanity, and they are loyal to their own good in the degree to which they are faithful to its well-being'.[92] Jones, then, in agreement with Bosanquet, is suggesting that there is no contradiction between patriotism and humanitarianism. The state is, in fact, the vehicle through which we make our contributions to humanity. It is 'the highest moral being in the world, harmonising, however imperfectly wider and more various forms of good than any other'.[93] For the individual the state most frequently represents the 'moral Absolute', and for this reason its good can rarely be postponed. Jones argues that it is only in so far as the state serves a higher authority, that of righteousness, that the state can lay claim to our own services.[94]

The fact that as moral persons all states have fundamental rights makes them in the most important respects all equal, and it is on account of confusing the possession of such rights with the armed capacity to enforce them that international relations stands in such a sorry predicament. Like Green, Bosanquet and many other British philosophical Idealists, Jones believes that only with the advent of an improved moral consciousness in the internal organizations of the state can we expect improvements in external relations.[95] In defending Idealism against Hobhouse's charge that it is conservative and reactionary, both in internal and external affairs, Jones maintains that Idealism 'is the most radical of all social and political theories. For while preserving present institutions, and civic and international relations, *it would moralise them*'.[96] Elsewhere Jones contends that: 'The world will not be at peace until it deserves peace; that is, until it has extruded the motives of self-assertion and felt the attraction of wider ends even than those of the nation.'[97]

The First World War was for Jones a battle between two conflicting conceptions of the state. On the one hand was the view that the state exclusively embodied force, and shunned higher loyalties, while on the other hand stood the view that the state is the 'trustee for a moralized and universal will'.[98] This, however, did not make the war right: every war that has ever been fought is wrong. That, however, does not mean that we can never find ourselves in the paradoxical or contradictory position of having a duty to wage war; a war which nevertheless cannot be right. In Jones's view the circumstances of the First World War impressed upon Britain a duty to fight which the people discharged with honour, rectitude and a clear conscience. No necessity of circumstance, however, or sense of pressing duty can convert what is wrong into a right, and the tragedy of the predicament is that deeds of violence are perpetrated in the name of duty which can never be anything other than what they are. War suspends morality and its only justification is on the ground of inevitability, but the inevitableness of an action is no moral justification. In fact it is the contrary. Morality depends upon the free choice of an end believed to be good, but inevitability renders choice inoperative. Because of the interdependency of circumstances and the impossibility of attributing absolute beginnings or turning-points to history, no nation in Europe could be totally absolved of the blame of making war inevitable: 'On the contrary, it has taken all the nations of Europe in the past to make the war inevitable, and it will take them all in the future to make it impossible.'[99]

The British Idealists, in so far as they followed Green rather than Hegel in believing that war is a consequence of the internal deficiencies of states, saw no logical barrier to the development of international co-operation. Hegel, of course, did not believe that relations between states were completely unconstrained. Among the Europeans he thought that customary relations had developed which served to regulate international relations. Such modifications were possible because of the common principles which lay at the foundation of their customs, law and civilization.[100] A state system, however, was the necessary corollary of Hegel's political theory.[101] The British Idealists, however, saw this common European *Sittlichkeit* as the foundation of a universal morality which it was hoped, with varying degrees of confidence, would lead to the establishment of institutions sustained by the will for a genuine pacific federation of states.

Haldane, Ritchie and Bosanquet, for example, did not think that the integrative organizing process of mankind ceases with the state. Bosanquet and Haldane argued that the absence of a determinate system of international law with a sovereign authority to enforce what is right need not imply that there is an absence of moral relations. The sharing of a common *Sittlichkeit*, which Haldane defines as 'the system of habitual or customary conduct, ethical rather than legal, which embraces all those obligations of the citizen, which it is "bad form" or "not the thing" to disregard',[102] is the fundamental prerequisite to greater international co-operation. It is a morality of conscience with no legal compulsion implied. They all maintain that there is nothing inherent in the nature of nationality that would preclude the development of common ideals strong enough to develop a general will capable of making the cohesive power of the ideals a sufficiently 'reliable sanction' for the obligation of states to each other.[103] Bosanquet was initially sceptical about the effectiveness of leagues or federations, and saw them as purely *de facto* resting on no firm spirit of community, and having a tendency to generate rival counter-leagues.[104] He later came to be a firm supporter of the League of Nations and thought it the 'hope and refuge of mankind',[105] but was under no illusions about its success depending upon the extension of *Sittlichkeit* to all the nations concerned. Furthermore, Ritchie contended that the invention of representative government and federalism held out the possibility of substituting for war more peaceful methods of conflict resolution. An international court, if it is to be effective, must be the organ of a federation with a federal armed force to prevent rebellion. Ritchie argues that: 'It need not be thought that the soldier will ever become useless on this earth, although his duties may be more and more assimilated to those of the policeman.'[106]

Jones, like most of the British Idealists, was convinced of the necessity for a genuine League of Nations, but warned that it must be much more than an administrative instrument tied to the principles that already characterized international relations. The will on the part of so many nations to constitute a league of peace was only significant if it went beyond the establishment of regulations for limiting the size of the armed forces and the production of armaments, and the institution of judicial procedures for settling disputes. While these are important implements for the improvement of relations, a league of peace must be indicative of a transformation in mental attitudes. The old way of individualism with its associated pursuance of exclusive goods, which at best periodically constrained nations not to cause injury to one another, must give way to a mutual caring for the well-being of one another.[107]

In 1909 Jones was arguing that the time must come when the long-suffering peoples of the different nations will themselves inaugurate a diplomacy greater than that of the diplomats and institute a form of arbitration other than that of violence. The changed outward circumstances of the world, that is a greater economic interdependence, would, he thought, lead to a recognition 'of mutual responsibility in other matters'.[108] These are ideas which he pursued further in 1918 when he was prevailed upon to write a pamphlet for the League of Nations Union and in his address on the 'Privileges and Obligations of Citizenship'. Jones argues that the Kantian principle of treating every person as an end, and never as a means must come to prevail in international affairs: 'All nations alike, whether they be civilised or savage, must be objects of respect and reverence to one another – sacred as they stand, and inviolable in virtue of their "personality".'[109]

How did Jones envisage that the will towards lasting peace would be actualized? He was under no misapprehension about the obstacles that would have to be overcome. He argued that while there are many transnational cultural and scientific communities which transcend state and national boundaries, the narrow ambitions of organized Capital and Labour, whose personal or class advantage precluded them from asking questions about the good of other nations, have found such boundaries to be obstacles to the wider view of the common good. The issues surrounding 'Reconstruction', Jones argues, are almost exclusively concerned with economic well-being, while the question of moral reconstruction pales into insignificance. There are no signs of the weapons of economic warfare being abandoned in favour of reconstructing the industrial and economic world on a more humane model like that of the family.[110] If a lasting peace is to be secured, then it is the people themselves who must demand of their government that the moral issues of 'Reconstruction' be addressed. The forces which inspire a lasting peace must emanate from within the nation.

We have already seen the importance which Jones lays upon the educational system in this respect. As a condition of freedom it must be less enslaved by economic interests and more directed to the building of moral character by means of the practical demonstration, both at school and in all other aspects of life, that the moral will extracts from every station it occupies, and every event which touches it, '*the highest value that is implicit in them*'.[111] Furthermore, he advocates the establishment of a League of Learning initially between the universities of the United States and Great Britain, to which professors as well as humble school teachers would all belong as members of the same profession embarked upon the project of the spiritual care of mankind. While material things on the whole tend to be exclusive, the things of the spirit are universal and can be shared, not with loss, but with profit. Knowledge is power and therefore a League of Learning, far from being impotent, is more powerful than any other union. Jones maintains: 'I entertain a strong faith in the value and power of learning, especially of learning in this domain of the humanities. And I believe the world would gain if the devotees of learning more consciously leagued themselves together, and more deliberately exercised their influence on the practical affairs of the nation.'[112]

In addition, the Christian Church with its cosmopolitan responsibility for the common good of mankind must take the lead in elevating the consciousness of citizens to the recognition of the oneness of the world, and of our mutual responsibility for each other. Each church should have at its altar a petition for its congregation to sign demonstrating the resolve and will to form a genuine League of Peace which would impel the plenipotentiaries of peace to follow the moral will of the people.[113] Of further assistance in applying pressure upon governments Jones believed that the press had an imperative responsibility both for promoting the ideals of citizenship and of internationalism. In a series of lectures delivered in 1913 Jones maintains:

> It seems to me that amongst the organic filaments which make modern society with its multitudinous life into one whole, we must reckon the journalistic press. Without it civilized society, except on rare occasions, would for all practical purposes be disintegrated once more into petty parochial units, and we should have never felt the throb of the larger citizenship. It is owing to you, in great part, that our people is one people and our Empire one Empire. Nay, you bind nation to nation, and involve the fate of one in the fate of all the others. There is no isolation any more, and the scale of every human has changed. If there is war it is like a fire in the heart of a great city; no one knows where the conflagration will stop.[114]

In 1918 he maintains his faith in the role of the press by arguing that like the Church the press would find the problems associated with the establishment of a League of Nations a most worthy theme, and that it should open the columns of its newspapers to a free discussion of opinions on how such a league might be achieved. In this respect, the press, usually distrustful of experts, may at least on this occasion adorn itself with the apparel of 'reticent modesty'.[115]

The establishment of a League of Nations would not, for either Jones or Bosanquet, entail transferring the state's moral responsibility to a higher authority which exercises its conscience on the behalf of its members. No moral beings, including states, can divest themselves of the moral duty of choosing what is right. A state, like an individual, may consult with its associates on matters regarding its duty, and may, indeed, try to emulate the good examples it finds in the world, but the choices it has to make cannot be delegated. Jones suggests: 'There is a certain isolation and sacredness of soul in this matter of morality. We can send no proxies to meet duty or death.'[116] In other words Jones, like Bosanquet, is suggesting that the success of a League of Nations rests not upon the authority vested in its institutions, but upon the moral will without which those institutions would be but hollow shells.

In summary, then, we may conclude that the fashionable Hegelianism which Hobhouse viewed as so sinister in its implications for British liberties and the development of humanitarianism, was not at all denying the role of individual conscience in questioning the morality of the state, nor was it denying the possibility and desirability of war ceasing to be the means by which disputes between nations were resolved. Contrary to Hegel, they believed for the most part that war was not endemic in a system of sovereign states, but the consequence of the extent to which each failed to be a state. In so far as it fulfilled its proper function as a state, that is the promotion of the good life, it at once enhanced the conditions of its own citizens, and was the bearer and protector of the highest principles of humanitarianism. Like Hobhouse himself, they all believed that current moral attitudes and practices would have to become transformed before one could view with optimism the possibility of a League of Nations securing a lasting peace.

CONCLUSION

This book has been an attempt to reconstruct Henry Jones's thought. Instead of reconstructing his ideas in isolation we have tried to use Jones as a catalyst and guide to explore the various philosophical, religious, political and scientific debates in Britain at the close of the nineteenth and beginning of the twentieth century. This has allowed us to investigate his ideas in a broader intellectual context. It has also allowed Jones's ideas to resonate within their intellectual environment in a richer and more satisfying manner. It is not our intention in this conclusion to reiterate the arguments of the previous eight chapters, but instead to highlight some of the salient features which characterize the whole of Jones's philosophical quest for the principles of political and social life.

The most important facet of Jones's thought is the complex and indissoluble link between his philosophical and political thought. It is impossible to understand his social and political thought without grasping the metaphysics which underpins it. The idea of citizenship has throughout this book been one of the central themes permeating all of the controversies into which Jones entered. A citizen, for Jones, is not just a legal category or body of economic or social entitlements. It is an ethical and metaphysical state of mind or being. Each citizen's life is determined by what Jones called 'colligating hypotheses', which dominate the whole pattern of thought and practice. The breadth of experience and the character of a person are dependent upon such hypotheses. The histories of individuals, societies, states and mankind in general are determined by the nature of these fundamental hypotheses. True citizenship, for Jones, is therefore viewed as an integrative experience whereby the self has become a focus of reason and colligating hypotheses. Such hypotheses bring into play the deep traditions and operative memory of society. Citizenship is therefore a state of mind where the individual has evolved to a level of self-consciousness and ethical awareness broad and inclusive enough to review his or her own life, the community and its history.

For Jones the fundamental metaphysical premise of such a broad and inclusive vision is the hypothesis that the universe is one coherent unified system. It is the differentiations which stand in need of explanation not the unity. All human understanding is seen to be conditional upon the working out and testing of hypotheses until such time as they cease to account for significant elements in experience, which nevertheless demand incorporation if the whole is to be understood adequately. All previous philosophies have taken as their starting-point the dualism between the mind and its objects. In their attempts to account for our knowledge of the world they have unsuccessfully tried to overcome this dualism. Even Kant who took the revolutionary step of wondering whether we could dispense with the demand that ideas must correspond to things, and assume instead that things must correspond to thought, nevertheless failed to reconcile 'thought' and 'things'. Ultimately, things in themselves were unable to reveal their true reality in thought. For Jones, the great Copernican revolution in philosophy was self-consciously completed by Hegel when he identified what Richard Norman has called the dilemma of epistemology.[1] The epistemologist has to presuppose what he, or she, sets out to prove. The examination of the forms of knowledge and their relation to reality with a view to declaring which are genuine and which are not requires a criterion of true knowledge in advance of the enquiry which is supposed to establish it.

Instead of trying to reconcile differences, Hegel assumes a unity whose differentiations have to be accounted for. Philosophy must start by conceiving reality as Absolute self-consciousness, or Spirit, which knows itself in and through all things. Ideas are not obstacles between the thinking intelligence and the world of reality, but that very reality expressing itself in the individual thinker who in the process of thinking makes it his own. Hegel is concerned neither with thoughts disengaged from the thinker, nor with worlds of ideas which are abstract. Instead he wishes to understand the process of thinking itself as the self-realization of Spirit, or God, within reality. In this respect, the subjective and the objective are not a dualism separated by a world of ideas, but are the differentiations of the one all-encompassing unity. As far as Jones was concerned, Hegel had given the definitive statement of the fundamental philosophical and metaphysical principles. All that needed to be done was to put the hypotheses to the test by applying them to every aspect of social and political life.

Jones consistently maintained that the Hegelian hypothesis of unity must be the starting-point for all genuine thinking and philosophizing. This is the only broad and inclusive vision which is intellectually adequate. The idea of a totality, or unity in diversity, does not deny the differences. This unity is what the Idealists called an 'identity in difference'. In adhering to the hypothesis of unity there is simply a refusal to rest content with abstract dualisms of any kind. We have seen throughout this book the consistent application of this principle by Jones to every problem he confronts in metaphysics, religion, politics and science. The unity which transcends the opposites, like that between 'individualism' and 'socialism', is not a third category which abolishes the opposites, but one of the opposites itself which includes within itself some of the crucial elements of the correlative opposing category. Thus socialism, or increased state intervention, undertaken in the right spirit, actually enhances individualism, in that it extends the capacities of the individual to benefit from common enterprises.

For Jones, the unity of experience, in which Spirit knows and reveals itself, does not come into existence once and for all, but develops gradually and continues to do so in the face of many trials and impediments. However, all branches of knowledge, between which there could be no absolute distinctions, converged upon the idea of 'evolution', in order to conceptualize and understand the unity of the natural and spiritual world. For Jones, evolution implies that very 'identity in difference' which the idea of the spiritual unity of the universe demands. The process of the development of freedom and reason in human character and true citizenship is an evolutionary progression. Evolution, for Jones, if understood correctly, does not level human beings down to the naturalism of their ancestors. In rationalizing our ancestors we actually level upwards. This does not entail that nature is made intelligent; conversely, it means instead that 'nature' is intelligible and mutually implicated with 'human beings', the one being inseparable from the other. On Jones's understanding of evolution, there could be no distinction between the natural and ethical processes. Spirit and nature are *one* in the development of rational consciousness towards the attainment of freedom of the will.

Freedom is the fundamental postulate of morality and the aim of all human existence. The attainment of this freedom should lead to the moralization of all relations both within states and between them. Within a state true freedom is coincidental with genuine citizenship.

No theory of evolution, then, which gave any credence to determinism could be acceptable, because of its implications for undermining the very possibility of morality. Yet, for Jones, neither our inherited capacities, nor the environment at whose breast we are suckled, can determine the character of our existence. Our capacities can only attain their true potential in conjunction with the environment. But the environment offers the opportunities which can never be realized if our capacities cannot make them their own. Environment and heredity, in Jones's view, cannot be opposed because their relationship is one of mutual inclusion. There is no diminution of the one as a result of the growth of the other. The greater our inherited capacities, the greater are the possibilities of identifying opportunities in the social environment and acting upon them.

The principles of 'unity' and 'moral or spiritual evolution' informed every question which Jones addressed. Anything that was not a unity was for him an artificial abstraction and therefore must be the result of an inadequate understanding. Because theory and practice are so integrally related for Jones, wrong conceptions of the world have adverse implications for the way we act. Good citizenship and freedom are dependent upon the right 'colligating ideas'. Therefore it is imperative that we do not allow language, and particularly metaphorical language, to cloud the issues. Furthermore, anything which diminishes individual responsibility is a constraint upon freedom, not the negative freedom of doing anything we want, but the positive freedom of doing what is right, and must therefore diminish our opportunities and even capacities for moral action.

On these principles, when applied directly to practical politics, only a political party which stressed the common good, and not any particular class interest, could be said to be in harmony with the nature of things, that is, the principle of the spiritual unity of the universe. In this sense, the grounds for Jones's unease with the Labour Party are, at root, metaphysical. In addition, only a party which used the instruments of the state to develop moral capacities, without diminishing individual responsibility, could be said to have (in Jones's favourite phrase) 'the universe at its back'. Such a political party or group would have the capability of conceiving great purposes and carrying them out and would attract the support of all genuine citizens. Jones's political views here are focused on a new social liberalism.

For Jones the development of freedom depends upon knowledge. Knowledge is freedom to act in the world and a condition of moral development. Every child born into poverty and without the opportunities for acquiring knowledge is potentially both intellectually and morally stultified. It is therefore the responsibility of the state, broadly and narrowly conceived, to provide for the education of every child, irrespective of birth, to enable that person to share in the full benefits of citizenship. A political party, then, in Jones's view, should not shy away from using the state to its fullest effect. There was, for Jones, as we have seen, *no* limit to the power of the state in relation to the individual, as long as it was faithful to its purpose, namely, the promotion of the good life of its citizens. Contrary to Hobson's criticism of Jones, this did not imply an arbitrary absolutism, which subordinated the will of the individual to the will of the state. No moral person could be absolved of the responsibility for making moral judgements. Therefore if the state deviated from its proper purpose it was the duty of the individual to oppose it.

Jones's theory of political obligation is unlike that of modern contract theorists, like Rawls, Nozick and Gauthier. Any hypothesis which places the individual outside the state is inconceivable. Like Hegel, Jones believes that to understand political obligation in terms of a contract between individuals, or between individuals and the state, is simply a misconception of the character of the moral relations which constitute the ethical unity of the state and its citizens. Obligation is not based upon self-interest, but upon the self-awareness or self-consciousness of belonging to a higher unity which is the expression of the real will of the citizens who comprise the state. In other words, the state for Jones, as for Hegel, is an expression of a higher unity than civil association. Civil association represents an aggregation of individual self-interest as characteristic of liberal market theory. In this respect Jones's understanding of citizenship is not confined to civil, economic, or social entitlements. Jones is looking for a common ethical identity among citizens. Citizenship is therefore understood as a higher level of association expressive of the common good.

Jones's nearest analogue in modern political philosophy is Michael Oakeshott, who is himself an Idealist. Oakeshott rejects the prevalent predilection, to which contract theory is particularly prone, of conceiving the state as an enterprise association with substantive ends whose laws are instrumental in achieving those ends. The citizens of such an association stand in a transactional relation and are united by a common purpose. Enterprise association is equivalent to Hegel's civil association. The proper understanding of the state, Oakeshott contends, is as a moral association whose laws are non-instrumental and which imposes obligations without assigning the performance of specified actions to designated people for the attainment of particular substantive ends. The rule of law is for Oakeshott a mode of moral association which specifies the procedural conditions to which individuals freely subscribe in choosing to perform their own substantive actions in pursuit of their own ends.[2] This, for Oakeshott, is civil association, which is clearly equivalent to what Hegel and Jones meant by the state. Where Jones differs from Oakeshott is in attributing to the state a much more positive role in promoting the material and spiritual well-being of its citizens.

Finally, the conception of the state as a 'moral person'[3] necessarily entailed the moralization of its relations with other states, and in relation to primitive peoples, the responsibility for educating them to a higher moral level in preparation for self-rule. A reformed Liberal Party, for all its faults, receptive to the voice of the people, expressed through the churches and a responsible press, was for Jones the nearest to fulfilling all these demands, and the most capable of attaining their realization uncorrupted.

If there is one sentiment which characterizes the whole of Jones's work it is eternal optimism. Even in the most adverse circumstances, including his own personal suffering, he could always see an ideal *on the way* to realization. Pure citizenship was not a remote utopia but rather an immanent process of spiritual and moral evolution in society. We have made it plain that he was by no means ignorant of the depravity and squalor which marred the lives of many late Victorians, and he was not blind to the considerable moral failings of individual entrepreneurs, or of the economic system in general. Nevertheless, because evolution taught him always to level upwards, he was capable of seeing the ideal, however faint the glimmer, in the most adverse circumstances. What for Hobhouse was always tainted with despair, for Jones would have some redeeming features which held out hope for moral progress.

APPENDIX

JEAN HUNT (NÉE JONES) REMEMBERS HER FATHER'S FATHER, SIR HENRY JONES

My Taid Jones died in 1922 when I was seven. Taid, pronounced to rhyme with 'tide', is the north Welsh word for grandfather. For some years after his death, old men would put their hands ponderously on my small shoulders and say to other old men, 'This is a granddaughter of the late Sir Henry Jones.' Then they would all stare down at me, shake their heads, and say gloomily, 'Well, Well!'

It was all so different from my memories of merry, laughing Taid that at last I asked my father, 'What did Taid Jones do? Was it something shocking?' Amid parental consternation I was at once set to read Sir Hector Hetherington's *Life and Letters of Sir Henry Jones.* I then understood that my grandfather had meant a lot to the Welsh nation, and the gloom of the old men on beholding me must have been caused merely by disappointment that national figures can have such ordinary descendants.

The revelation that Taid Jones was so very much a son of Wales came as a shock to me, as I had seen him only in his house in Argyll. I associated him with Scotland and my gentle Ayrshire grannie, his adored wife. In his sixties, he was the dominant man in my childhood, my father himself being overseas for most of the first seven years of my life. My brother and I spent six months of every year with him and grannie until he died.

At the time of his centenary celebration a hundred years after his birth, people used to say to me, 'Of course, you wouldn't remember your grandfather.' Not remember Taid! It would be a strange child who could ever forget so vital a relation, quite apart from the fact that he had a tremendous rapport with children.

See him, then, through the eyes of a child.

You always knew when Taid Jones was in the house. Doors would blow open, things would smash, everyone rushed about. You might be suddenly whisked up on a manly shoulder, and a great rich voice below the silky white curls, on to which you clung like mad, would boom forth a bellow of song. I can still see the check pattern in his slippers when I remember my rides on his feet; and I can see the leather patches on the elbows of his old jacket, for to the end of his life he kept up his habit of changing his coat in the house. I was just eye-level with those elbows when I used to stand by the piano watching his supple fingers on the keys. He enjoyed teaching action songs to my brother and me. From the age of two my brother had a clear, true little treble and must have been a joy to teach. One song I especially liked was about 'a wee, wee man, in a wee, wee house' who made shoes. 'With a tiny awl he bores a hole, and the hammers buzz and blow.' I always sang 'awl' as 'oar', because we had a boat on the edge of the kyle at the bottom of the garden, and I knew about oars, but not about awls. Taid taught us sol-fa and we were too young to read so learnt the words by ear. It is only now that I realize the word must have been 'awl', also that the shoemaker theme had special significance for Taid.

I can be forgiven for thinking of Taid as a Scot. He used words as Scottish as any used by my grannie. We were 'the bairns', I was the 'wee wifie' and 'crying' was 'greeting'. Yet I am told he never lost his Welsh and even tried to teach it to his wife. But she never forgave him for telling her on their honeymoon in north Wales that 'Good morning' was 'Cau dy geg' ('Shut your mouth.').

We adored him, but at the same time we were always on our toes for alarms. One vivid memory I have is of hiding behind his legs, which towered above me in fishing waders at the edge of an Argyll loch, while he argued with my mother and aunts. They were saying I was too young to go in the rowing boat alone with him. He was roaring, 'Havers, women! She's never too young to learn to sit still,' and popped me into the boat. We rowed away triumphant.

After that, I often went with him fishing on Loch Fyne or Loch Ascog. He always told me, 'Mind you sit still, or we'll have all those women after us.' Once he threw a fish into my lap because I kept worrying him to 'let me love the poor fish'. When I failed even to hold the slippery thing, and it jumped overboard, Taid said, 'Let that be a lesson to you. Never, never try to love a cold fish!'

Taid had a fairy who told him everything about us. After breakfast, before he settled at his desk, or after lunch, or when the spirit moved him, he would go into the study to talk to Fairy. The study was out of bounds, so my brother and I would stand in the lobby under the portraits of three metaphysicians, whom I always thought hideous compared with my handsome grandfather. Taid would leave the door open and stand where we could see him, looking up into the sunshine that streamed down the Kyles of Bute and into his south-facing study window. Somewhere in the beam of sunshine, Fairy was flying about, or sitting up on the picture rail. Sometimes, Taid told us, she perched on his little bust of Socrates.

The conversation was one-sided, with pauses for Fairy's replies, which of course sounded to us like dead silence. 'And do you mean to say,' Taid would boom, raising his face to the ceiling, 'that he said THAT to his mother?' or 'What? She wouldn't eat her dinner? She just wouldn't? What do you advise, Fairy? Oh dear. No sweets. No sweets at all?'

But on the good days, there were sweets. The fairy always put them in the same place – in the flower border under the study window. Taid would hang out, his pen rakishly behind his ear, and watch us hunting. 'Isn't she KIND!' he would murmur. When I think of those golden days, the sun was always shining and the flower bed always blue with forget-me-nots. Yet a terrible war was being waged, and Taid had three sons as hostages to fortune.

My grandfather tried very hard to fill the gap left by our father's absence overseas. He and my brother used to have great games of 'shinty' in the lobby of Noddfa, his house in Argyll. Once my brother, then aged about three, borrowed one of his grandfather's stiff cuffs and put it round his neck 'to look like Taid'. He wore this cuff even with his pyjamas until my mother begged her father-in-law to devise some means of persuading him to take it off. Taid hit on the bright idea of winning the shinty matches, and then suggesting that the 'stiff old cuff' was preventing my brother from lowering his chin. The 'collar' was discarded, and my brother won every match from then on.

But the writer of *Idealism as a Practical Creed* did not believe in being *too* soft. One day he said to me, 'Come into the greenhouse and we'll play a trick on your brother.' To him he said, 'Come and I'll show you a fairy horse.' The small boy's enquiring face peeped round the greenhouse door, and Taid picked up something wrapped in a duster and flung it at the little freckled face. My brother yelled as the fairy horse fell on its feet and dashed on to the grass where it curled up as a ball. It was a hedgehog, the first we had ever seen. It became a great pet in the garden.

I well remember the day when my brother, who had inherited his Taid's red hair along with much of the rebel spirit that goes with it, told me he was going into the forbidden study 'to see what Taid did in there'. I stood petrified in the lobby while the small figure marched in, carrying a paint-brush and an egg cup full of water.

'Out!' said an astonished and interrupted Taid at his desk. My brother advanced three steps. 'Out' shouted Taid again. But this time my brother threw the egg cup in his grandfather's face and ran. Clinging to each other in the lobby, expecting Nemesis, we were amazed to hear roars of laughter coming from within.

One of my grandfather's pleasures, after a bout of work at his desk, was to emerge on to the porch and 'throw his voice over to Bute'. This habit was all very well except when we as babies were having our naps on each side of the porch, and woke shrieking in fright in our prams at the enormous yodel a yard above us. Our mother would rush out despairing, and Taid would slink back to his study, in disgrace again with his womenfolk for having forgotten us.

I must have been about six when I realized that Taid's face hurt him. He was walking my brother and me to the village along the shore road in the teeth of an east wind. My brother was dawdling on an upturned boat and Taid turned his back to the wind to call him on. As he did so he took his handkerchief from his cheek, and I saw a deep, dark red wound. I remember putting my hand in his, because I felt his suffering. He was to die of cancer of the mouth within the year, and was at that time, in spite of mortal pain, delivering the last of his *Gifford Lectures* in Glasgow.

My last memory of all is of a day in February when I was not allowed upstairs. I wandered through the silent house and into the empty study. I stood at the window looking down the garden to where the driving winter rain swept down the sea from Inchmarnock. I recall the deserted chair, the shiny, tidy desk, the idle pens. In the flower-bed under the window the first snowdrops were pushing up; but Fairy would never put sweets there again. I said goodbye to her for ever. But I remember her, when I remember my Taid.

NOTES

NOTES TO CHAPTER ONE (pp. 1–21)

[1]In a letter to Andrew Seth, dated 3 August 1883, Henry Jones says: 'Muirhead is hankering too much after philosophy to go in for classics, and I am not quite *unconcerned* about him. I am not sure how far he is right. If you, Ker and Muirhead were side by side there would be a trio that would not let scientific or any other bigotry trample the humanitarian powers under foot. But Muirhead, I am afraid, will not go in.' TJC, Class U, vol. ii, fol. 20, NLW. It was Muirhead who undertook to complete the biography of Caird which Jones felt unable to complete because of pressures of work and progressive illness. See Jones and Muirhead, *LPEC*. Manuscript materials relating to this project are deposited in University of Glasgow Library (UGL), MS Gen 1475.

[2]Seth received a sizeable bequest on condition that he adopted the name Pringle Pattison, and henceforth became known as A. Seth Pringle Pattison. See his *The Balfour Lectures on Realism*, edited with a *Memoir of the Author* by G. F. Barbour (Edinburgh and London, Blackwood, 1933), 84. J. S. MacKenzie succeeded Seth in the chair at Cardiff and was in turn succeeded by one of Henry Jones's students, Hector Hetherington.

[3]See *The Dictionary of National Biography 1961–1970* (Oxford, Oxford University Press, 1981), 510–12.

[4]It was MacCallum who, as Dean of the Faculty of Arts, was responsible for Henry Jones's lecture tour of Australia in 1908.

[5]See, for examples, Jones, *OM*; H. J. W. Hetherington, *The Life and Letters of Sir Henry Jones* (London, Hodder & Stoughton, 1924); Thomas Jones, 'Shoemaker's Son to University Professor', *John O'London's Weekly*, 11 March 1922, 751; Thomas Jones, *A Theme with Variations* (Newtown, Gregynog, 1933), 85–113; J. H. Muirhead, 'Sir Henry Jones 1852–1922', *Proceedings of the British Academy*, X (1921–23), 552–62; H. J. W. Hetherington, 'Jones, Sir Henry (1852–1922)', *Dictionary of National Biography 1922–1930* (London, Oxford University Press, 1937), 458–60; H. W. Morris-Jones, 'The Life and Philosophy of Sir Henry Jones', and H. D. Lewis, 'Y Ffydd Sy'n Ymofyn' in *Henry Jones 1852–1922* (Cardiff, University of Wales Press, 1953), 5–17 and 18–32 respectively; H. W. Morris-Jones, 'Syniadau Gwleidyddol Syr Henry Jones', *Efrydiau Athronyddol*, XVI (1953), 1–9.

[6]The house 'Y Cwm' is preserved as a memorial to the life of Henry Jones.

[7]Letter from Jim Jones, Henry's son, to Thomas Jones dated 3 April 1921. TJC, Class U, vol. i, fol. 120. Also see Hetherington, *Life and Letters*, 18.

[8]Morris-Jones, 'Life and Philosophy', 5.

[9]Henry Jones to Cadwaladr Davies dated 23 October 1880. TJC, Class U, vol. ii, fol. 6/5. The recipient of the letter used the example of Henry Jones in evidence before Lord Aberdare's Commission into Higher Education in Wales, which recommended the establishment of a university college in north and south Wales. Report of the Commission on Welsh Higher Education, 1881, question 2731, 126.

[10]Letter from Henry Jones to Andrew Seth dated 30 October 1882. TJC, Class U, vol. ii, fol. 25/2.

[11]Or, to put it in the words of Revd J. Dyfnallt Owen, relations 'weren't very brotherly'. An address on 'Syr Henry Jones' (in Welsh), J. Dyfnallt Owen MSS and papers, NLW, no date, 23. Also see J. Gwynn Williams, *The University College of North Wales: Foundations 1884–1927* (Cardiff, University of Wales Press, 1985), 34–5.

[12]See letter from Henry Jones to Andrew Seth, dated 11 March, 1894; and Seth Pringle-Pattison, *Balfour Lectures on Realism*, 41.

[13]Jones, *OM*, 171; and, the address in J. Dyfnallt Owen MSS, NLW, 24.

[14]Harry R. Reichel, 'Sir Henry Jones', TJC, Class U, vol. iv, fol. 122. The first part of this sketch is reproduced in Hetherington, *Life and Letters*, 37–8; also see Williams, *University College of North Wales*, 60–4.

[15]Report of a lecture, 'The Making of Character' delivered in Adelaide University, *Adelaide Register*, 18 August 1908, and *Adelaide Advertiser*, 18 August 1908. Cf. Jones, *PC*, 70.

[16]See Jones's own account of this episode in *OM*, 179–82; Williams, *University College of North Wales*, 184–5.

[17]Tom Jones, *Theme with Variations*, 108–9. Tom Jones is here referring to the reasons which Henry Jones gave in *The Welsh Leader*, 3 March 1904.

[18]Letter to Cadwaladr Davies, 26 June 1892. TJC, Class U, vol. ii, fol. 64.

[19]See, for example, Jones's comment that Donaldson's 'vacillation has nearly done for us this time. But I don't want the kind old man to suffer for it'. Letter to Munro-Ferguson, undated, probably mid-1893. TJC, Class U, vol. ii, fol. 67/4.

[20]Letter to Munro-Ferguson, 17 June 1894. TJC, Class U, vol. ii, fol. 79/2.

[21]Jones, *BPRT*; Henry Jones, 'The Nature and Aims of Philosophy', *Mind*, NS II (1893), 160–73; Henry Jones, 'Idealism and Epistemology', *Mind*, NS II (1893), 289–306 and 457–72; and, Henry Jones, *PL*.

[22]Letter from Caird to Miss Mary Sarah Talbot, 7 May 1890. Printed in *LPEC*, 168.

[23]Letter from Caird to Miss Talbot, 22 August 1892. Printed in *LPEC*, 183.

[24]Letter from Jones to Monro-Ferguson, 17 June 1894. TJC, Class U, vol. ii, fol. 79/2.

[25]Ibid., 7 July 1894, fol. 80. Also see Jones's account in *OM*, 217–22.

[26]Letter to Mrs Maclehose, 9 July 1894. TJC, Class U, vol. ii, fol. 81. In some letters from D. G. Ritchie to Gilbert Murray the question of the Glasgow

appointment is discussed. It appears to have been of great interest, and the subject of much gossip. Ritchie himself was a candidate and was aware that the competition was between Jones and MacCunn, with Watson as the Cairds' second choice should Jones appear unlikely to win. Ritchie was Jones's successor at St Andrews. See papers of Gilbert Murray, MS 3, fols 80–3; 88–9; 176–7; 180–1; 191–2; 196–207; and 215, BLO.

[27]See Henry Jones's letter to Thomas Jones, 10 January 1912. TJC, Class U, vol. i, fol. 7/2; letters to Gilbert Murray, 8 January 1912 and Harry Reichel, 11 January 1912 in Hetherington, *Life and Letters*, 222–3. See Thomas Jones's account in *A Theme with Variations*, 110. The latter of the awards Henry Jones accepted in the hope that the addition of his name to the list would not devalue the honour for others who had received it. Letter from Henry Jones to David Lloyd George, 18 December 1912. TJC, Class U, vol. i, fol. 132.

[28]Jones, *OM*, 142 and 160.

[29]Henry Jones, 'The Higher Learning in its bearing upon National Life in Wales': an address delivered 28 June 1895 (Bangor, University College of North Wales, 1895), 10.

[30]Henry Jones, 'The Idealism of Jesus', *Hibbert Journal* supplement for 1909, 81–106.

[31]Letter from Henry Jones to Revd G. MacNaughton, 26 March 1909. TJC, Class U, vol. ii, fol. 169. Printed in Hetherington, *Life and Letters*, 215–16.

[32]Jones, *BPRT*, 329.

[33]See, for example, T. H. Green, *Works*, ed. R. L. Nettleship (London, Longmans, 1888), vol. III, p. 225.

[34]Jones, *BPRT*, 341.

[35]Jones, *FE*. Of Jones's completion of this book, while suffering the effects of advanced mouth cancer, it was said, 'the sustained gallantry of his defiance of pain and death in this his last tragic battle bordered on the miraculous. If, inevitably, the body was at length conquered, the spirit was as surely conqueror'. Quoted by Morris-Jones, 'The Life and Philosophy of Sir Henry Jones', 8.

[36]Letter from Henry Jones to Erie Evans, 4 May 1905. Dr Griffith Evans Papers, No. 446. NLW.

[37]'An Apostle of Ideas', *Sydney Morning Herald*, 11 July 1908; Reichel, 'Sir Henry Jones', fol. 122; Thomas Jones, 'Shoemaker's Son', 751; Muirhead, 'Sir Henry Jones', 553; J. H. Muirhead, *Reflections by a Journeyman in Philosophy* (London, Allen & Unwin, 1942), 72; Metz, *A Hundred Years of British Philosophy*, 302. Also see Hetherington, *Life and Letters*, 78–9; and David Phillips, *Athroniaeth Syr Henry Jones* (Dolgellau, Evans, 1922), 1.

[38]Thomas Jones, *Theme With Variations*, 102.

[39]Agnes Saville, 'The Late Sir Henry Jones', a letter printed in *John O'London's Weekly*, 8 April 1922.

[40]Metz, *Hundred Years of British Philosophy*, 302.

[41]See, for example, the letters from Henry Jones to Reichel, 14 October, 18 October and 11 December 1915. TJC, Class U, vol. iii, fols. 8, 9 and 23. In

reference to the meetings Jones says: 'I would like, were it possible, for meetings to have the high seriousness which religious meetings have, and the influence of religious leaders let loose. Surely this war is a Jähad if ever there is one.' Letter of 18 October.

[42]Henry Jones, *The Philosophy of Martineau* (London, Macmillan, 1905), 33.

[43]P.H.W., 'Philosophers of the Spirit', *The Inquirer*, 25 November 1905, 749.

[44]Elzevir (Walter Murdoch), *Melbourne Argus*, 25 July 1908, 6. In addition to lecturing in Sydney, Jones spoke in Brisbane, Newcastle, Wollongong, Melbourne and Adelaide.

[45]Elzevir (Walter Murdoch), *Melbourne Argus*, 30 May 1908, 6.

[46]'The Visit of Professor Jones', *Sydney Morning Herald*, 7 August 1908, 6.

[47]'The Making of Character', *Adelaide Register*, 15 August 1908. Cf. Thomas Jones's description of Henry Jones's presence: 'his eyes were so full of light that you felt sure they could belong to no ordinary person. When one thinks of him in the hey-day of his powers it is in terms of heat and light – flaming, radiant, passionate, inspiring.' Thomas Jones, *Theme With Variations*, 101.

[48]See Hetherington, *Life and Letters*, 43.

[49]C. C. J. Webb, *A Study of Religious Thought in England from 1850* (Oxford, Clarendon Press, 1933), 101–2.

[50]Jones, *WFSR*, 77 and 197.

[51]Jones, *IPC*, 12–13.

[52]Letter from Henry Jones to Lord Haldane, 2 June 1921. NLS, MS 5915, fols. 35 and 36. In a similar vein Jones wrote to his son, H. H. Jones, 'I have far too little respect for the ordinary run of professional philosophers, nor have I taken enough trouble to follow what younger men have had to say. I don't want any philosophy or poetry except the very best and I want it stored for a while like port wine.' Dated 25 July 1921, TJC, Class U, vol iii, fol. 228/2.

[53]Henry Jones, 'The Social Organism' in *Essays in Philosophical Criticism*, ed. Andrew Seth and R. B. Haldane (London, Longmans Green, 1883), 187–213.

[54]'The Growth of Freedom', *Sydney Morning Herald*, 15 July 1908, 8.

[55]Jones and Muirhead, *LPEC*, 36.

[56]Edward Caird, 'The Problem of Philosophy at the Present Time', *Journal of Speculative Philosophy*, January 1882, 28.

[57]Jones, *PL*, xiii; Jones, introduction to P. Janet and G. Seailles, A *History of the Problems of Philosophy*, p.xii. This, in essence, is the criticism he makes of Hobhouse's accusations against idealism.

[58]G. W. F. Hegel, *The Phenomenology of Spirit*, tr. A.V. Miller (Oxford, Oxford University Press, 1977).

[59]Jones, 'Aims of Philosophy', 162.

[60]Jones, 'Social Organism', 209.

[61]For the published views, to be discussed in chapter six, see Jones 'The University of Wales: the line of its growth', an address delivered at Cardiff, 3 October 1905 (Bangor, Jarvis and Foster, 1905), 10; Jones, *WFSR*, 134 and 298; Henry Jones, 'The Corruption of the Citizenship of the Working Man', *Hibbert*

Journal, 10 (1911–12), 154–78; and Henry Jones, *Dinasyddiaeth Bur* (Pure Citizenship) (Caernarfon, Gwmni y Cyhoeddwyr Cymreig (CFF), Swyddfa 'Cymru', 1911), 23 and 26.

[62]Letter dated 6 April 1910. TJC, Class U, vol.ii, fol. 175/2. Cf. 'If "Labour Party" meant the party of the industrious against the idlers, I could join it myself; but it means Labour versus Capital, or *Man* against *Master*.' Letter to Lloyd Thomas, 9 April 1910. TJC, Class U, vol. ii, fol. 176.

[63]Letter from Henry Jones to Sidney Webb, 29 March 1918. TJC, Class U, vol. i, fol. 45.

[64]Jones, *SR*. Reprinted in *WFSR*, 305.

[65]Appointed April, 1916. Reported February, 1918.

[66]Letter dated 15 December 1916. TJC, Class U, vol. i, fol. 18.

[67]Jones, *WFSR*, p. x.

[68]Henry Jones, 'The Function of the University in the State' (Aberystwyth, University College of Wales, 1905), 14. Also see Hiral Haldar, *Neo-Hegelianism* (London, Heath Cranton, 1927), 360–1.

[69]Jones, *PC*, 117.

[70]Letter from H. Reichel to Henry Jones dated 23 July 1910. TJC, Class U, vol. ii, fol. 182.

[71]See Jones, *OM*, 177–91.

[72]See Third Report of the Royal Commission on *The Working of the Elementary Education Acts, England and Wales with Appendices*, 1887, 320–30.

[73]Jones and Douglas, *SE*.

[74]Henry Jones, 'The University of Wales' (Bangor, Jarvis and Foster, 1905). Also see, Reichel, 'Sir Henry Jones', fol. 122; and, Hetherington, *Life and Letters*, 38–40. A dispute that has re-emerged with the recommendations of Sir Goronwy Daniel's University of Wales Working Party, 1989.

[75]See Henry Jones, draft unpublished chapter of *Old Memories*, TJC, Class U, vol. iv, fols. 146/l – 146/7, and 147–51. Also see Hetherington, *Life and Letters*, 87–92.

[76]See ns. 80–8 below.

[77]Henry Jones, 'A League of Learning', Rice Institute Studies, VI (Houston, Rice Institute, 1919); and *Report of the British Educational Mission* (Manchester, Morris and Yeaman, 1919). The authors were J. Joly, Henry Jones, Henry A. Miers (Chairman), A. E. Shipely, Caroline F. E. Spurgeon, E. M. Walker.

[78]Henry Jones, printed letter to William George (in Welsh) dated 15 August 1919, 3–8. TJC, class D, vol. iii; and 'Cenadwri Syr Henry Jones – Angen Uno'r Eglwysi a'r Colegau – Cyfnod Anodd Protestaniaeth', *Yr Herald Cymraeg*, August 1919; printed letter and list of provisional committee of which Jones is listed as a member, dated 14 August 1919. The aim of the scheme was to supplement, and not to supplant, the good work of the WEA and YMCA. In a letter to Lloyd George, Jones says that the 'scheme had two distinct purposes. (1) The churches should back in every way they can the organization of the WEA or YMCA wherever they find it, (2) where these do not exist, it must start its own'. Dated 13

September 1919. Also see Lloyd George to Henry Jones, 6 October 1919. All these items, including the letter to William George are deposited in National Library of Wales, NLW 16350D.

[79]'Child and Home', *Sydney Morning Herald*, 9 July 1908.

[80]Nor at this time did Perth in Western Australia.

[81]Jones, 'The Function of the University in the State', 15.

[82]'Metaphors that Mislead', *Melbourne Argus*, 11 August 1908; and 'Metaphors that Mislead', *Melbourne Age*, 11 August 1908.

[83]'A University for Queensland', *Brisbane Courier*, 4 August 1908.

[84]Hetherington, *Life and Letters*, 130.

[85]'The Business of a University', *Adelaide Advertiser*, 15 August 1908; 'The Making of Character', *Adelaide Register*, 15 August 1908, and *Adelaide Advertiser*, 15 August 1908. Cf. Jones, 'The Function of the University', 12.

[86]Reported in 'Professor Jones on Australia's Future', *Adelaide Register*, 12 August 1908.

[87]'The Individual and the State', *Melbourne Age*, 12 August 1908; and, 'The Making of Character', *Adelaide Register*, 15 August 1908.

NOTES TO CHAPTER TWO (pp. 22–47)

[1]See, for example, Phillips, *Athroniaeth Syr Henry Jones* 1–2.

[2]Jones's published work does not contain any really systematic analysis of philosophers like Mill or Bentham. However, in the full notes taken by Tom Jones from Henry Jones's lectures in Glasgow, there is clear evidence of extensive, full and detailed expositions and criticisms of Greek, seventeenth, eighteenth and nineteenth-century philosophy.

[3]For example, in a letter to A. C. Bradley, after the publication of *PC*, he commented: 'Most of the critics have been kind. I only saw one which was not, – and it was signed BR – a little thing, calling my ideas mid-Victorian etc., probably written by Bertrand Russell, and therefore does not matter,' 29th May 1919. TJC, Class U, vol iii.

[4]In a letter to A. C. Bradley Jones says: 'Your brother I value. I think both he and Bosanquet are bigger men by far than the men some folk cackle about, than Bergson or Croce, etc.; and your brother is the bigger of the two, and the biggest *known to me* since Hegel', Hetherington, *Life and Letters*, 264

[5]In his lectures in Glasgow he does give a full exposition and critique of Alexander's *Moral Order and Progress*, TJN, vol. 11, 64ff.

[6]He does however remark in a letter that he had been pushing Dewey for the Gifford Lectures: 'I was pushing Dewey, the best of the American philosophers . . . and never dreamt of their turning round to me', 31 December 1919, TJC, Class U, vol iii.

[7]See Sanford Schwartz, *The Matrix of Modernism: Pound, Eliot and Early Twentieth Century Thought* (New Jersey, Princeton University Press, 1985). In his Honours lectures in Glasgow, Jones occasionally mentions Nietzche and

Schopenhauer in passing, but never in a substantive manner. Despite his antipathy to Bergson's philosophy, in one of his regular reports to Macmillan publishers, Jones warmly and fulsomely recommends Bergson's *Creative Evolution* for translation and publication. He says in his report 'In France no thinker can compare with him . . . On the whole I am inclined to think that Bergson's work will be more and more in evidence in the discussion of philosophic questions during the coming years', MA 3rd series, Col Mcc 11, 1905–11, 25 March 1908.

[8]J. W. Scott, *Syndicalism and Philosophical Realism* (London, Black, 1919). The work is devoted to Jones.

[9]Jones, 'Aims of Philosophy', 162. In his Glasgow lectures he describes philosophy as 'the rational account of [the] growing experience of mankind', TJN (Hons), Lecture 2, 19.

[10]Jones, 'Idealism and Epistemology', I, 305.

[11]Jones, *IPC*, 59.

[12]Jones compares this process of recovering the lost unity at the micro individual level with the macro level of the growth of civilization. Philosophical maturation, recovering unity through a diversity of rich experience, is paralleled to the growth of a civilized culture, see 'Aims of Philosophy', 172.

[13]Review of Josiah Royce, *The World and the Individual*, in *Hibbert Journal*, 1, 1902–3, 132. On Green and the teaching of philosophy in Oxford, see W. G. Addison, 'Academic Reform at Balliol 1854–1882, T. H. Green and Benjamin Jowett', *Church Quarterly Review*, January 1952.

[14]Jones, 'The Moral Life', 5.

[15]Jones, *BPRT*, 168–9.

[16]Jones, *BPRT*, 314. This is quite a common view among the Idealists and continued to hold sway with the new generation of whom R. G. Collingwood and Michael Oakeshott are the most notable exponents. see R. G. Collingwood, *An Essay on Philosophical Method* (Oxford, Clarendon Press, 1977), 11, 100, 161, 163–4, 168 and 205; and M. Oakeshott, *On Human Conduct* (Oxford, Clarendon Press, 1975), vii, 1 and 9–10.

[17]Jones, 'Aims of Philosophy', 164.

[18]Jones, *BPRT*, 33. For Jones self-consciousness 'means that man's substance turns back upon itself in being aware of itself and of its laws', TJN, vol 11, 4.

[19]Jones, 'Aims of Philosophy', 171.

[20]Jones, *IPC*, n.1, 296. This particular issue of absolute postulates will be returned to in the section on 'Metaphysics'.

[21]Jones, *PL*, 351.

[22]Jones, *BPRT*, 174.

[23]Ibid., 175. In his Glasgow lectures he remarked that ordinary science 'treats natural objects as if they had no ontological relation to thought. But relation to thought is one of the qualities of all objects. There is no matter that is crass and dead and alien to thought', TJN, vol. i, 29 November 1897, 65.

[24]Jones, 'Idealism and Epistemology', 1, 303.

[25]Jones comments in his Glasgow lectures 'it has seemed to me that [the] present age has been somewhat facile in its adoption of [the] view that experience is altogether of the finite. It has acquiesed too easily in [the] notion that [the] object of Religion must at best be unknowable if not also unreal and that the attempt of Kant to reach ultimate truth . . . must be vain', TJN (Hons) 12 November. The theological point will be examined in the next chapter. However there are also implications for this Kantian view on the realm of aesthetics, where 'taste', rather than reason, becomes the arbiter of beauty. This particular argument subsequently led to a number of difficulties within the aesthetic realm. This problem becomes the starting-point for Hans Georg Gadamer's study *Truth and Method*, tr. W. Glen-Doepel (London, Sheed and Ward, 1979).

[26]Jones, *BPRT*, 265.

[27]Jones, 'Idealism and Epistemology', 1, 304. This point will be looked at under the section 'Epistemology and Ontology'.

[28]Jones, *BPRT*, 201; 'Philosophical Landmarks', 200. Croce's philosophy of the spirit gives an extensive elaboration of this process. Collingwood's theory of the philosophical concept may be viewed as an extension of Croce's ideas, see B. Croce, *Logic as the Science of the Pure Concept*, tr. Douglas Ainslie (London, Macmillan, 1917) and Collingwood, *Essay on Philosophical Method*.

[29]Jones, *BPRT*, 20.

[30]The issue of evolution will be looked at in chapter 4.

[31]Jones, *BPRT*, 29. In his lectures Jones notes: 'systems of philosophy may be said to fail but that is not a complete history. Each in turn becomes an element in a complete system of the process from system to system', TJN, Vol. i, 67.

[32]Jones, *IPC*, 70. For Hegel on history see *Lectures on the Philosophy of World History: Introduction: Reason in History*, tr. H. B. Nisbet (Cambridge, Cambridge University Press, 1975). Jones's comments on India reveal some of the weakness of applying such a teleological pattern to history.

[33]Jones, *IPC*, 79.

[34]Ibid., 80.

[35]Ibid., 76–7. Jones also follows the fortunes of the Roman world in the same sections. The whole passage is a summary pastiche of sections of Hegel's *Phenomenology of Spirit*.

[36]Jones, 'Aims of Philosophy', 173.

[37]Jones, *BPRT*, 174.

[38]Jones, 'Social Organism', 187. This reading again reflects Hegel's judgements on the French Revolution. Such optimism concerning the growth of philosophy might have been reasonable in the 1880s and 1890s, but even by the turn of the century Jones must have been aware of its frailty. The revival of Kantianism and British Empiricism and the growth of Phenomenology, before the First World War, are difficult to reconcile with Jones's speculative and optimistic history.

[39]Jones, 'Social Organism', 195.

[40]Jones, *IPC*, 47–8.

[41]This distinction parallels the use of critical tradition by Gadamer in his *Truth and Method.*

[42]Jones, 'Idealism and Politics', II, 743.

[43]Ibid., 749.

[44]Jones, 'Idealism and Epistemology', I, 292.

[45]Lindsay, 'The Idealism of Caird and Jones', *Journal of Philosophical Studies,* 1 (1926), 175.

[46]Jones, *PL,* 47.

[47]Jones, 'Idealism and Epistemology', II, 469.

[48]Jones, *FE,* 169–70. In one of his honours lectures, underlined by Tom Jones, the following comment is made: '*If I seek proof I seek it in a system*', TJN (Hons), December 1899, 45.

[49]Ibid., 70

[50]Jones, *BPRT,* 314. Jones comments on traditions: 'what we call intuitions are really truths which have been obtained by a process which has been forgotten.' Pure intuitions, for Jones, are strictly impossible, TJN, vol. i, 59.

[51]Ibid., 176.

[52]Ibid., 281.

[53]See, for example, Hermann Lotze, *Microcosmus: An Essay Concerning Man and His Relation to the World,* tr. E. Hamilton and E. E. Constance Jones, vol. i (New York, Books for Libraries Press, 1971: 1st publ. 1885), Book V, chs I–V.

[54]Jones, *PL,* 343.

[55]Ibid., 359. There is an interesting interchange of letters in the early 1890s between Jones and Bradley focusing upon questions concerning Lotze on thought and reality, amongst other topics. Bradley comments in his letter: 'Is Thought to be discursive or what more? I do not see that on a matter like comparison, say of Caesar and Napoleon, you will satisfy Lotze that you are meeting his argument. Yes or No? he would say. Is this movement a movement of the Reality or not? For myself I should attempt to say both Yes and No. I do not know whether you would say "Yes" simply.' In part of Jones's reply he remarks that 'I have tried .... to show that his [Lotze] doctrine of thought forces him to treat it as reality. In volume II [which was never written] I shall try to show that his doctrine of reality forces him to treat it as thought'. Jones goes on later: 'I have no special love for the term "Thought" but so long as we use it, I think we should be sure that it is not a logical abstraction like Lotze. *His* thought is not pleasant or painful; mine always is – mostly painful. His thought goes on without the help of reality and is engaged *upon* reality. My thought is never really mine', TJC, Class U, Vol. iii, 76–82; also Hetherington, *Life and Letters,* 186–90.

[56]Jones, *FE,* 112.

[57]Ibid., 111–12. For a vigorous defence of the link between theory and practice see letter from Jones to Henry Hadow, 14 July 1918, TJC, Class U, Vol. iii. Also Hetherington, *Life and Letters,* 248.

[58]Ibid., 110–11. Although Jones was dismissive of Croce he is at one with him on this point. Croce argued, for example, that theory and practice cannot be

separated. They are 'a duality that is unity and a unity that is duality', B. Croce, *Philosophy of the Practical: Economic and Ethic*, tr. Douglas Ainslie (London, Harrap, 1921), 12. Despite his philosophical disagreement, Jones does recommend Croce's work to Macmillan publishers, remarking 'I believe that Croce has suffered in this country through the shortcomings of his translator', MA, vol. MCMII, 1911–21, 29 June 1913.

[59]Jones, *BPRT*, 23.

[60]Ibid., 24. For Jones 'Men are to a very large extent ruled behind their backs unconsciously', TJN, vol. i, 6.

[61]Ibid.

[62]Ibid., 41

[63]Jones, 'The Moral Life', 6.

[64]Jones, Introduction, *Problems of Philosophy*, ix.

[65]Jones, 'Idealism and Epistemology', I, 469.

[66]Jones, 'Aims of Philosophy', 161–5.

[67]The origin of this term derives from the nineteenth-century philosopher Whewell, see essay by W. H. Walsh, 'Colligatory Concepts in History' in Patrick Gardner (ed.), *The Philosophy of History* (Oxford, Oxford University Press, 1974), 133.

[68]Jones, Introduction, *History of Philosophy*, xii.

[69]Jones, *FE*, 95. For Jones 'presuppositions [are] as natural as our skin and as difficult to escape', TJN, vol. II, 3.

[70]Jones, 'Immortality of the Soul', 32.

[71]Jones, *FE*, 93.

[72]Jones, 'Aims of Philosophy', 164.

[73]Jones, 'Immortality of the Soul', 46.

[74]Jones, *IPC*, 296.

[75]See R. G. Collingwood, *An Essay on Metaphysics* (Oxford, Clarendon Press, 1940), 21–33.

[76]R. G. Collingwood, *Speculum Mentis* (Oxford, Clarendon Press, 1924), 74. Jones warmly recommended Collingwood's *Truth and Contradiction* to Macmillan, see MA, vol. MCIII, 1911–21, 4 March 1918. Published in R. G. Collingwood, *Essays in Political Philosophy*, ed. D. Boucher (Oxford, Clarendon Press, 1989).

[77]Jones, *BPRT*, 169.

[78]Collingwood, *Essay on Metaphysics*, 47.

[79]Jones, 'Idealism and Politics', II, 751.

[80]Jones, *BPRT*, 32.

[81]Jones, *FE*, 82–3.

[82]Ibid. This point may be likened to what Thomas Kuhn was later to call a paradigm shift, see T. S. Kuhn, *The Structure of Scientific Revolutions* (Chicago, University of Chicago Press, 1970), 111–35. Bernard Bosanquet appears to be saying something similar when he argues: 'the history of thought shows certain leaps or breaks in culture; when the human mind seems to open its eyes afresh on a new platform, from which new point of view all its adjustments have to be remade

and its perceptions re-analysed', Bernard Bosanquet, *The Philosophical Theory of the State* (London, Macmillan, 1965), 77. In another sense we should not be overly surprised by Kuhn's affinities with Jones and Bosanquet. Recent philosophers, like Richard Rorty, have drawn attention to Kuhn's 'incidental "idealism"', Rorty, *Philosophy as the Mirror of Nature* (Oxford, Blackwell, 1980), 325. Barry Barnes denies the imputation of idealism to Kuhn. *T.S. Kuhn and Social Science* (London, Macmillan, 1982), 9 and 70. For a refutation of Barnes's claim see D. Boucher, *Texts in Context: Revisionist Methods for Studying the History of Ideas* (Dordrecht, Nijhoff, 1985), 158.

[83]Jones, *FE*, 82. The usage of the term *conjecture* directly parallels Karl Popper. However it is virtually certain that there is no intellectual debt here on Popper's part.

[84]Jones, 'Immortality of the Soul', 31.

[85]Jones, *FE*, 67.

[86]Jones's pleasure in such argument appeared to irritate his old teacher Edward Caird. He remarked to Jones in a letter: 'Can't you philosophise without "fechting"? Is Donnybrook essential to the beatific vision? Ask your wife what she thinks of this', Caird to Jones, 28 August 1893, in Jones and Muirhead, *LPEC*, 191. Donnybrook, it is said, was an Irish fair where men, carrying their cudgeons, asked others to come and tread on their coat tails. See also Caird's comments on Seth's and Jones's arguments on 2 June and 12 July 1893 in *LPEC*, 188–9. It is often argued that Jones's early writings, on Lotze and in *Mind*, are probably his best, see, for example, C. A. Campbell, 'Philosophy', in *Fortuna Domus* (Glasgow, Maclehose, 1952), 118–19.

[87]Jones, 'Idealism and Epistemology', II, 470.

[88]Ibid., I, 301.

[89]Jones, *PL*, 48. Caird also noticed the parallel between Bradley and Lotze, see Caird's letter to Jones, 28 August 1893, in Jones and Muirhead, *LPEC*, 191.

[90]Jones, *PL*, 40–1.

[91]On the history and origins of epistemology, see Rorty, *Philosophy and the Mirror of Nature*, 132–5.

[92]A. Seth Pringle Pattison, *The Balfour Lectures on Realism*, edited with a *Memoir of the Author* by G. F. Barbour (Edinburgh and London, Blackwood, 1933), 164.

[93]Jones, *PL*, 4.

[94]There are powerful parallels with Rorty's project in *Philosophy and the Mirror of Nature*, although Jones, in rejecting epistemology, did not go down the path of radical reflexivity and hermeneutics and would not have been prepared to accept Rorty's thoroughgoing relativism nor his edifying philosophical world of conversation.

[95]Jones, 'Idealism and Epistemology', I, 298.

[96]Ibid., II, 459. Jones also discusses this point in TJN, vol. I, Lecture XXXII.

[97]Ibid., 461.

[98]Ibid.

[99]Ibid., 462.

[100]Ibid., 465. Although the epistemologist starts with subjective facts of experience, for Jones, he 'then slips the existential side of the idea up his sleeve and treats it *merely* as having meaning; then he looks up and asks, where can we find the reality which corresponds to this meaning', ibid., 466.

[101]Jones, *PL*, 273.

[102]He states: 'As we do not *create* the objective world in knowing it, so we do not *create* the moral world by our moral action. The process of morality is a process of intepretation, of obedience, and of the appropriation of that which is, and which is deemed right and good. As we wrong the world by assuming that it awaits the systematizing activity of our intelligence in order to escape from the condition of chaotic disconnectedness; so also we wrong the world of morality by assuming that it waits upon our activity to introduce into it a law of righteousness to which it is itself foreign', *IPC*, 271–2; see ibid., 127 and 269; and *PL*, 367.

[103]Jones, *PL*, 113 and 368.

[104]Ibid., 369.

[105]Ibid., 6–7 and 371.

[106]Jones, 'Balfour as Sophist', 458; *BPRT*, 174; *PL*, 371; 'Morality as Freedom', 7. Jones also makes similar points in his lectures on Kant delivered in University College, Bangor, in 1888, see notes taken by Edward Edwards, NLW, 9394C.

[107]Bernard Bosanquet, *The Principle of Individuality and Value* (London, Macmillan, 1912), 190–1.

[108]Ibid., Lecture X, xxxvii.

[109]F.H. Bradley, *Appearance and Reality* (Oxford, Clarendon Press, 1969), 217; Bosanquet, *The Value and Destiny of the Individual* (London, Macmillan, 1912), 69.

[110]Bernard Bosanquet, *Psychology of the Moral Self* (London, Macmillan, 1897), 95.

[111]Andrew Seth Pringle Pattison, *Hegelianism and Personality*, 2nd Series of Balfour Lectures (Edinburgh and London, Blackwood, 1887).

[112]Bosanquet, *Individuality and Value* and *Value and Destiny*; Andrew Seth Pringle Pattison, *The Idea of God in the Light of Recent Philosophy* (Oxford, Oxford University Press, 1920) and *The Idea of Immortality* (Oxford, Clarendon Press, 1922).

[113]Seth Pringle Pattison, *Idea of God*, 265.

[114]Ibid., 266.

[115]See, for example, C. C. J. Webb, *Divine Personality and Human Life* (London, George Allen & Unwin, 1920), especially Lectures IX and X; John McTaggart Ellis McTaggart, *Studies in Hegelian Cosmology* (Cambridge, Cambridge University Press, 1901), 5–6.

[116]Jones 'Aims of Philosophy', 165.

[117]Jones 'Divine Immanence', 764.

[118]Jones engaged, in his Glasgow lectures, in a long and complex analysis and criticism of Bradley's *Appearance and Reality* for his Honours students, see TJN (Hons) December lectures, 1899.

[119]Jones, *IPC*, 263. Caird, apart from his dissatisfaction with Bradley's notion of the self (see letter to Jones on 29 August 1893 in Jones and Muirhead, *LPEC*, 192) also commented critically upon Bradley's Absolute: 'This Absolute is to be "all the attributes" and yet none of them – like Spinozism', ibid., 193. In a later letter to Mary Talbot he noted 'there always seems to me to be two Bradleys, one an idealist and the other a sceptic who can never be satisfied', Jones and Muirhead, ibid., 13 April 1895, 206.

[120]Jones, *FE*, 187.

[121]Ibid., 357. In a letter to J. B. Baillie Jones stated: 'I have always felt and tried to express my dissatisfaction with the (partial at least) dissipation of the integrity of the individual by Bradley and Bosanquet. And I have insisted, too, on the at least relative independence of the ideals of the intellect, the will, and the emotions.' Letter, 8 March 1918, EUL.

[122]Ibid., 358.

[123]Jones, *The Philosophy of Martineau*, 33.

NOTES TO CHAPTER THREE (pp. 48–60)

[1]Jones, *BPRT*, 25

[2]Ibid., 6.

[3]Jones, *ELE*, 174

[4]Jones, 'Reflective Thought Towards Religion', 238.

[5]Jones, *BPRT*, 15.

[6]Jones, Introduction, *History of Philosophy*, vii.

[7]Charles Gore (ed.), *Lux Mundi: A Series of Studies of the Religion of the Incarnation* (London, John Murray, 1889). See also recent commemorative volume Robert Morgan (ed.), *The Religion of the Incarnation: Anglican Essays in Commemoration of Lux Mundi* (Bristol, Thoemmes, 1989). For Green's theological side see essays by Andrew Vincent and Bernard Reardon in Andrew Vincent (ed.), *The Philosophy of T.H. Green* (Aldershot, Gower, 1986). On the broader context of liberal theology in relation to Ritschl see B. M. G. Reardon (ed.), *Liberal Protestantism* (London, Adam & Charles Black, 1968); in Britain the context is superbly analysed by C. C. J. Webb, *A Study of Religious Thought in England from 1850* (Oxford, Clarendon Press, 1933) and by B. M. G. Reardon, *From Coleridge to Gore: A Century of Religious Thought* (London, Longmans, 1971).

[8]Jones, *FE*, 72.

[9]On Jones's unorthodox position in Wales see 'Yr Athro Syr Henry Jones', NLW 15631B, 8–9, also 'Traethawd Syr Henry Jones: y Dyn a'i Waith', NLW 18284C, 23.

[10]T. H. Green made a similar point in his 'Essay on Christian Dogma', in Green, *Collected Works*, vol. III (London, Longmans, 1888). For a discussion of this and Green's and Hegel's views on Catholicism see Andrew Vincent, 'T.H. Green and the Religion of Citizenship' in Vincent (ed.), *The Philosophy of T.H. Green*, 51ff. On Jones's view of Protestantism also see 'Yr Athro Syr Henry Jones', ibid., 14.

[11]Jones, *FE*, 107. On the changing role of the churches as Jones envisaged it see letter to William George, NLW 16350D, 4--5.

[12]Jones, 'Divine Immanence', 748.

[13]Ibid., 252. On the separation of reason and superstition see also Jones, 'Y Diwygiad: a'r hyn eill ddod ohono', 63–5.

[14]Jones, *FE*, 5. Faith was not contrasted to reason. On the contrary faith was the root to reason. As Jones put it 'Faith is not indeed against reason – no one openly holds that now', TJN, vol. i, 9.

[15]For Jones the Ritschl school wanted to 'take [the] whole thing out of the hands of philosophy', TJN (Hons), lecture two, 35. In lecture three he describes Lotze to the students as 'the metaphysical father of all Ritschlians'; and he goes on 'Lotze and Co. simply assert the two sides [concepts and percepts] without any . . . attempt of bringing them together', ibid., 67. Caird also noted to Mary Talbot that 'Ritschl and his school all seek to free theology from philosophy and not by means of it, which leads to a curious mixture of reason and unreason; but they have so much force and have had such great influence that it is well worth trying to understand them', Caird to Mary Talbot on 28 July 1903, in Jones and Muirhead, *LPEC*, 239.

[16]Jones *FE*, 13.

[17]Ibid., 116.

[18]Jones, 'Immanence of God', 23.

[19]Kantian theology has a strong element of immanentism, partly because of the stress laid on religion reduced to practical reason. However, such immanentism, which is premised upon a separation between reason and value, fact and value, and so forth, is markedly distinct from that promulgated by Jones.

[20]Jones, *IPC*, 11.

[21]Jones, *BPRT*, 57.

[22]Jones, 'Present Attitude', 249.

[23]Jones, *Philosophy of Martineau*, 15.

[24]Jones, *FE*, vii. Jones also says at another point 'Mankind has never civilised itself except by humanising its God', Jones, 'Idealism and Politics', II, 742. He also remarks that 'the return of man to God is his return to self, until that is done – and it is never quite done – human life is a contradiction. It is a continual death to the past, a continual dissatisfaction with [the] present', TJN, vol. i, lecture XVII, 49.

[25]Jones, *FE*, 42. Jones also discusses this in TJN, vol. ii, lecture on 6 January 1898.

[26]Jones, 'Divine Immanence', 18.

[27]Jones, 'Immanence of God', 37.

[28]Jones, *FE*, 43.

[29]Jones, 'Idealism of Jesus', 88.

[30]Ibid., 96. In a letter from 1909 Jones remarked 'it is this "Jesus only" that is irritating and untrue. I prefer him as the firstborn of many brethren', TJC, Class U, vol. ii, 169.

[31]Jones, 'Idealism of Jesus', 90.

[32]Jones, *BPRT*, 344. As Caird put it: 'Love is a loss of self in others or in God; but the self cannot be lost. It lives in losing itself, and therefore lives to die. This is the first answer to all theories that reduce the concrete whole to an abstraction', Caird to Mary Talbot, September 1893, in Jones and Muirhead, *LPEC*, 197.

[33]Jones, 'Idealism of Jesus', 83.

[34]Jones, *FE*, 215.

[35]Jones, *BPRT*, 251.

[36]Ibid., 256. Caird remarked 'Do we find those who have the deepest consciousness of such evil, and the most intense desire to overcome it, ever believe in it as ultimate?', Caird to Mary Talbot, 1 October 1891, Jones and Muirhead, *LPEC*, 173.

[37]Jones, *FE*, 58.

[38]Ibid., 245.

[39]Ibid., 248.

[40]Ibid., 216–17.

[41]Ibid., 233. This sounds rather like Mark Twain's comment that death is nature's way of telling one to slow down. Jones remarks though that 'Everything that involves the well-being of men in one another favours morality', ibid., 233. It is difficult to see though how Jones would have fitted the majority of diseases, cholera, typhoid, leprosy etc., into this view. How are these related to evil actions?

[42]Ibid., 253–4. In his Glasgow lectures Jones describes evil as 'perverted good', TJN, vol ii, 56.

[43]Kant, *Religion within the Limits of Reason Alone* (1793), tr. T. M. Greene and H. H. Hudson (Chicago, Open Court, 1934). For a discussion of Kant on radical evil see Lewis White Beck, *A Commentary on Kant's Critique of Practical Reason* (Chicago, Chicago University Press, 1963), 203ff.

[44]Jones, *FE*, 244.

[45]Bradley, *Essays on Truth and Reality* (Oxford, Clarendon Press, 1968), 428.

[46]Jones, *FE*, 320. Bernard Bosanquet took exception to Jones's criticism of himself and Bradley on this whole issue. He felt that Jones had not done justice to his and Bradley's view on the individual, see J. H. Muirhead (ed.), *Bernard Bosanquet and His Friends* (London, George Allen & Unwin, 1935), 233.

[47]Hastings Rashdall, 'Personality: Human and Divine', in Sturt (ed.), *Personal Idealism* (London, Oxford University Press, 1902), 390.

[48]Ibid., 379.

[49]Ibid. Bradley did actually recognize some of the potential implications of a limited God, in *Essays on Truth and Reality*, 432–6.

[50]Rashdall, *Personal Idealism*, 392–3.

[51]William James, *Pragmatism* (New York, Meridian, 1964: 1st publ. 1907), 167.

[52]Ibid., 169.

[53]William James, *Varieties of Religious Experience* (London, Fontana, 1971).

[54]Ibid., 429. See this whole lecture, XVIII, for complete discussion.

[55]Jones, 'Divine Immanence', 750.

[56]Jones, *FE*, 317. Caird reflects a similar point to Jones. In a letter he comments on F. C. S. Schiller: 'Mr S seems to me always to take his stand on the difference as his *fact*, and to look upon the attempt to reach unity as involving a *mauvais pas* which must necessarily end in an abstraction or a hypothesis; whereas to me differences always seems to presuppose and explicate unity . . . if I know the self and the not-self in the distinction and relation – and only so – I imply their unity as manifesting itself in their difference', Caird to Mary Talbot, 28 October 1891, Jones and Muirhead, *LPEC*, 172.

[57]Ibid., 318.

[58]Ibid., 323.

[59]'Religion cannot compromise its God', Jones, 'Divine Immanence', 758.

[60]Ibid., 759.

[61]Ibid., 761. He remarks on page 762 that 'the unity of the whole is immanent in all the parts'.

NOTES TO CHAPTER FOUR (pp. 61–86)

[1]Jones, *FE*, 229.

[2]Jones, 'Are Moral and Religious Beliefs Capable of Proof?', in *SP*, 109.

[3]Jones, *PL*, 372–5; Jones, 'The Present Attitude', 247; Jones, *WFSR*, 209; Jones, *FE*, 280.

[4]Jones, *BPRT*, 4.

[5]Jones, *IPC*, 23; *BPRT*, 69, 195, 198 and 199; Jones, 'Aims of Philosophy', 164; *WFSR*, 100, 206, 220, 231 and 255; *FE*, 98.

[6]Jones, *IPC*, 22.

[7]Ibid., 196.

[8]Jones, *WFSR*, 231.

[9]See, for example, W. G. Runciman, *A Treatise on Social Theory*, vol. II *Substantive Social Theory* (Cambridge, Cambridge University Press, 1989); Hiram Caton, *The Politics of Progress: The Origins and Development of the Commercial Republic, 1600–1835* (Gainesville, University of Florida Press, 1988); and, John A. Hall, *Powers and Liberties* (Oxford, Blackwell, 1985).

[10]Joseph le Conte, 'The Theory of Evolution and Social Progress', *The Monist*, v (1895), 481.

[11]Anonymous, 'Darwin on the Origin of Species', *Westminster Review*, NS XVII (1860), 541. 1860, of course, was the year in which Garibaldi and Cavour were making their triumphal strides towards Italian unification. The Volunteer movement was a response to fears of renewed French hostility and prospective aggression towards England, and aimed to strengthen home defence by strengthening the available forces.

[12]J. W. Burrow, *Evolution and Society: A Study in Victorian Social Theory* (Cambridge, Cambridge University Press, 1966), 20 and 100.

[13]David G. Ritchie, *Darwin and Hegel with other Philosophical Studies* (London, Swan Sonneschein, 1893), 42.

[14]Jones, *IPC*, 25.

[15]Henry Jones, reader's report on *Fitness of the Environment* by Professor Henderson of Harvard. MA, Readers Reports, 3rd series, vol. MCC 111, 1911–21, fol. 28. BM, 5598.

[16]Jones, *FE*, 52.

[17]Jones, *WFSR*, 44.

[18]Reported in the *Sydney Morning Herald*, 15 July 1908.

[19]Michael Freeden, 'Biological and Evolutionary Roots of the New Liberalism in England', *Political Theory*, 4 (1976), 472–3; Michael Freeden, *The New Liberalism: An Ideology of Social Reform* (Oxford, Clarendon Press, 1978), 77–9. For an account of Hobhouse's response to the Spencerian version of social evolution see Stefan Collini, *Liberalism and Sociology: L.T. Hobhouse and Political Argument in England 1880–1914* (Cambridge, Cambridge University Press, 1979), chs 5 and 6.

[20]Vincent and Plant, *Philosophy, Politics and Citizenship*, 7–8.

[21]Charles Darwin, *The Origin of Species by means of natural selection or the preservation of favoured races in the struggle for life* (New York, Avenel, 1979), 458.

[22]Geoffrey Thomas, *The Moral Philosophy of T.H. Green* (Oxford, Clarendon Press, 1987), 27.

[23]Le Conte, 'Theory of Evolution and Social Progress', 489.

[24]Emma Marie Caillard, 'Man in the Light of Evolution', *The Contemporary Review*, 64 (1893), 881.

[25]Emma Marie Caillard, 'Evolution a Note on Christianity', *The Contemporary Review*, 64 (1893), 440.

[26]Jones, *IPC*, 29.

[27]Jones, *IPC*, 24.

[28]Jones, *BPRT*, 69, 195, 198 and 199; Jones, 'Aims of Philosophy', 164; Jones, *WFSR*, 100, 206, 220, 231 and 255; Jones, *IPC*, 296; and Jones, *FE*, 131, 280 and 293.

[29]Henry Jones, 'The Obligations and Privileges of Citizenship – A Plea for the Study of Social Science', *Rice Institute Studies* VI (Houston, Rice Institute, 1919), 146.

[30]Jones, *WFSR*, 231. Cf. Jones, 'Aims of Philosophy', 164; Jones, *BPRT*, 195; and Jones, *IPC*, 195.

[31]Jones, *FE*, 25. Jones argues that: 'religion, in so far as it demands a perfect and absolute being as the object of worship, is vitally concerned in maintaining the unity of the world. It must assume that matter, in its degree, reveals the same principle as that which, in a higher form, manifests itself in spirit.' Jones, *BPRT*, 183.

[32]Jones, *BPRT*, 210–11.

[33]Jones quoted verbatim by R. V. Lennard, notes on the Dunkin lectures, MS TOP OXON e 417, fol.3, BLO.

[34]TJN, vol. i, Lecture XXXVI, 8 December 1897, p. 226.

[35]Jones, *FE*, 98.

[36]Jones, *BPRT*, 177–92.

[37]Jones, *IPC*, 25

[38]Ritchie, *Darwin and Hegel*, 44–5.

[39]Edward Caird, *A Critical Account of the Philosophy of Kant* (Glasgow, Maclehose, 1877), vol. I, 35.

[40]David G. Ritchie, *The Principles of State Interference* (London, Swan Sonnenschein, 1896: 2nd edn.), 44.

[41]His most famous critique being, *The Metaphysical Theory of the State* (London, Allen & Unwin, 1951: 1st publ. 1918). Also see L.T. Hobhouse, *Democracy and Reaction* (London, Fisher Unwin, 1904) which Jones criticizes in *WFSR*, 179–225.

[42]Jones, *WFSR*, 195.

[43]Cited by Collini, *Liberalism and Sociology*, 181.

[44]Jones, *WFSR*, 220.

[45]Reported in *Sydney Daily Telegraph*, 11 July 1908.

[46]TJN, 227.

[47]Reported in *The Brisbane Courier*, 1 August 1908.

[48]Jones, *FE*, 98.

[49]Jones, 'Obligations and Privileges', 150. Cf. *WFSR*, 78.

[50]Bosanquet, *Principles of Individuality and Value*, 340.

[51]Jones, *WFSR*, 206.

[52]Jones frequently invokes Burke. See, for example, *BPRT*, 52; *WFSR*, 23, 24 and 129; 'Is the Order of Nature Opposed to the Moral Life?', 10; *SP*, 82; 'The University of Wales', 14; 'Present Attitude of Reflective Thought Towards Religion', 242, *IPC*, 62 and 216–17.

[53]Jones, *FE*, 98. Cf. 'For all is one scheme. Evolution tolerates no break, brings forth nothing altogether new, permits nothing to become altogether old. It builds the living present from the dying past, forgetting nothing, abandoning nothing in its course, least of all the dormant promise of the merging ideal.' *IPC*, 146.

[54]Jones, *WFSR*, 23.

[55]David Wiltshire, *The Social and Political Thought of Herbert Spencer* (Oxford, Oxford University Press, 1978), 225.

[56]Herbert Spencer, 'The Social Organism', *Westminster Review*, NS XVII (1860), 90–121.

[57]See, for example, T. H. Huxley, 'Administrative Nihilism', *Fortnightly Review*, NS 10 (1871), 525–43.

[58]Herbert Spencer, *Principles of Sociology*, vol. I (London, Williams & Norgate, 1876). Volumes II and III were published in 1893 and 1896 respectively.

[59]Spencer, 'Social Organism', 91.

[60]Ibid., 95.

[61]Ibid., 98–9.

[62]Herbert Spencer, *The Data of Ethics* (New York, Collier, 1911: 1st publ. 1879), 220. Interference, for Spencer, constitutes 'any arrangements which in considerable degree prevent superiority from profiting by the rewards of superiority, or shield inferiority from the evils it entails'. Cited in Wiltshire, *Social and Political Thought of Herbert Spencer*, 138. We will see in relation to the dispute

over inherited character that Spencer thought natural selection, or the principle of the survival of the fittest, as insufficient in itself to account for the evolution of morals and character.

[63]This is persuasively argued by T. S. Gray in 'Herbert Spencer's Theory of Social Justice – Desert or Entitlement?', *History of Political Thought*, 11 (1981), 161–86.

[64]Spencer, 'Social Organism', 111.

[65]Ibid, 120.

[66]Huxley, 'Administrative Nihilism', 535.

[67]Ibid., 536.

[68]Ibid., 537.

[69]James Paradis and George C. Williams (eds.), *Evolution and Ethics: T. H. Huxley's Evolution and Ethics With New Essays on Its Victorian and Sociobiological Context* (Princeton, Princeton University Press, 1989), p.138. The 'Prolegomena' and 'Evolution and Ethics' were published by Macmillan in 1893.

[70]Ibid., 132.

[71]Ibid., 88.

[72]Ibid., 139.

[73]Ibid., 93–4. As well as delivering a severe blow to Herbert Spencer in denying the ethical efficacy of the principle of the survival of the fittest, which was in any case insufficient in Spencer's view to account for social evolution, Huxley's essay also argued strongly against Francis Galton and his followers who advocated social progress engineered by eugenics. Because of the complexity of society and the uncertainties about what constitutes the fittest individuals, Huxley argues, the 'horticultural process' which circumvents nature in the garden is inappropriate for advancing social progress; 'apart from other reasons, because I do not see how such selection could be practised without a serious weakening, it may be destruction, of the bonds which hold society together'. Ibid., 94.

[74]Herbert Spencer, 'Evolutionary Ethics', *The Atheneum*, No. 3432 (1893), 193–4; and, Leslie Stephen, 'Ethics and the Struggle for Existence', *The Contemporary Review*, 64 (1893), 157–70. Stephen put forward a number of objections to Huxley's argument on eugenic grounds.

[75]Spencer, 'Evolutionary Ethics', 193.

[76]Stephen, 'Ethics and the Struggle for Existence', 170.

[77]Andrew Seth, *Man's Place in the Cosmos* (Edinburgh and London, Blackwood, 1897), 13.

[78]Ibid., 15.

[79]Henry Jones, 'Is the Order of Nature Opposed to the Moral Life', an inaugural address delivered in the University of Glasgow on 23 October 1894 (Glasgow, Maclehose, 1894), 27.

[80]Ibid., 28.

[81]Ibid., 29. Cf. Jones, 'Obligations and Privileges', 143 and 181; and, Henry Jones, 'Modern Scientific and Philosophical Thought Regarding Human Society', *Christ and Civilization*, eds. J. B. Paton, P. W. Bunting, and A. E. Garvie (London,

National Council of Evangelical Free Churches, 1910), 514: 'Little by little philosophy, aided by the poets, is teaching the implication of man in mankind, of mankind in man, and of nature in both.'

[82]John McTaggart Ellis McTaggart, *Studies in Hegelian Cosmology* (Cambridge, Cambridge University Press, 1901), 178.

[83]Ibid., 178. McTaggart directs a good deal of his argument to the conception of a social organism articulated by J. S. MacKenzie in his *An Introduction to Social Philosophy* (Glasgow, Maclehose, 1890).

[84]Bernard Bosanquet, 'Hegel's Theory of the Political Organism', *Mind*, NS VII (1898), 6.

[85]Ibid., 8.

[86]Bosanquet specifically mentions section 270 of *The Philosophy of Right*. 'Hegel's Theory of the Political Organism', 14.

[87]Jones, 'Social Organism'. See the letters from Jones to Andrew Seth and Edward Caird regarding the composition of this essay, TJC, Class U, vol. ii, fols. 9–25.

[88]Jones, *WFSR*, 39. This was the theme of a lecture which Jones gave in Melbourne during his tour of Australia in 1908. He complained that the problem of ordinary thinking was not that it used too many metaphors, but that, on the contrary, metaphors used it. See 'Metaphors that Mislead', *The Melbourne Argus*, 11 August 1908. Cf. *The Melbourne Age*, 11 August 1908. Herbert Spencer also warned of the propensity for metaphors to mislead: 'Figures of speech in general, valuable as they are in poetry and rhetoric, cannot be used without danger in science and philosophy.' Herbert Spencer, 'The Inadequacy of Natural Selection', I, *The Contemporary Review*, 63 (1893), 159.

[89]Jones, *WFSR*, 40.

[90]Jones, 'Social Organism', 194.

[91]Henry Jones, 'Function of the University', 6. Cf. *WFSR*, 41.

[92]Jones, 'Modern Scientific and Philosophical Thought', 493.

[93]Jones, 'Social Organism', 208. Cf *FE*, 39.

[94]Jones, 'Obligations and Privileges', 143.

[95]Jones, *FE*, 97.

[96]Henry Jones, letter to Andrew Seth, 1 June 1882, TJC, Class U, vol. ii, fol.9.

[97]Jones, 'Social Organism', 193.

[98]Ibid., 208–9.

[99]See the debate between Spencer and Weismann in the pages of *The Contemporary Review*. Herbert Spencer, 'The Inadequacy of "Natural Selection" ', I and II, vol. 63 (1893), 153–66 and 439–56; Herbert Spencer, 'Professor Weismann's Theories', vol. 63 (1893), 743–60; August Weismann, 'The All-Sufficiency of Natural Selection: a reply to Herbert Spencer', I and II, vol. 64 (1893), pp.309–38 and 596–610; Herbert Spencer, 'A Rejoinder to Professor Weismann', vol. 64 (1893), 893–912; Herbert Spencer, 'Weismannism Once More', vol. 66 (1894), 592–608; and August Weismann, 'Heredity Once More', vol. 68 (1895), 420–56. In gaining an understanding of the terms of reference of the

controversies consequent upon the evolution debate in the nineteenth century we have benefited enormously from reading Derek Freeman, 'The Evolutionary Theories of Charles Darwin and Herbert Spencer', *Current Anthropology*, 15 (1974); and Robert J. Richards, *Darwin and the Emergence of Evolutionary Theories of Mind and Behaviour* (Chicago, University of Chicago Press, 1987).

[100]Weismann, 'All-Sufficiency of Natural Selection I', 309–10.

[101]Theodore Gilman, 'Heredity versus Evolution', *The Monist*, IV-V (1893–4), 90.

[102]Spencer, 'Inadequacy of "Natural Selection" II', 454.

[103]Spencer, 'Weismannism Once More', 592. The question is still not entirely resolved. Dr E. J. Steele in his foreword to a collection of essays, recently published by a nineteenth-century anti-Darwinian, suggests that the issue of whether our genes are affected by the environment, and whether acquired characters are inherited, are questions the answers to which have implications for us all. Dorothy Green (ed.), *Descent of Spirit: Writings of E. L. Grant Watson* (Sydney, Primavera, 1990).

[104]Spencer, 'Inadequacy of 'Natural Selection' II', 456; and 'Weismannism Once More', 608. Also see, Herbert Spencer, *The Factors of Organic Evolution* (London, Williams & Norgate, 1887), iv.

[105]August Weismann, *The Germ-Plasm: A Theory of Heredity* (New York, AMS Press, 1974).

[106]See Stefan Collini, 'Sociology and Idealism in Britain 1880–1920', *Archives Européennes de Sociologie*, 19 (1978), 12. For the popular acceptance of the view see Marcus Hartog, 'The Spencer-Weismann Controversy', *The Contemporary Review*, 64 (1893), 54.

[107]See Gertrude Himmelfarb, 'Varieties of Social Darwinism', in *Victorian Minds* (New York, Knopf, 1968), 314–32; R. J. Halliday, 'Social Darwinism: A Definition', *Victorian Studies*, 15 (1971), 389–405; and J. A. Rogers, 'Darwinism and Social Darwinism', *Journal of the History of Ideas*, 33 (1972), 265–80.

[108]H. I. Jensen, *The Rising Tide* (Sydney, Worker Trustees, 1909), 20. First published as newspaper articles between October 1908 and March 1909 in *The Worker* (Sydney, Australia).

[109]Ritchie, *Darwinism and Politics*, 53 and 55.

[110]See MA, 2nd Series and 3rd Series, Reader Reports. Reels 6 and 7 of the Chadwyk-Healy microfilm edition.

[111]Jones, *WFSR*, 154.

[112]Ibid., 56–7.

[113]Ibid., 162–3.

[114]Ibid., 58; and, Martin Hollis, *Models of Man* (Cambridge, Cambridge University Press, 1977), chs 2 and 3. Plastic Man, Hollis argues, is conditioned, or shaped, by an enduring human nature, or alternatively, moulded by social conditions.

[115]For a discussion of character and the independence of the individual see Vincent and Plant, *Philosophy, Politics and Citizenship*, 101–12; and Freeden, *New Liberalism*, 170–7.

[116]Stefan Collini, 'Political Theory and the "Science of Society" in Victorian Britain', *The Historical Journal*, 23 (1980), 217.

[117]Ritchie, *Principles of State Interference*, 11. Cf. F. H. Bradley, *Ethical Studies* (Indianapolis, Bobbs-Merril, 1951), 110–11.

[118]Jones, *DB*, 30.

[119]Jones, *WFSR*, 50.

[120]Jones, *FE*, 140.

[121]Jones, *SP*, 27 and 32; Jones, 'Obligations and Privileges of Citizenship', 178; and Jones, *PC*, 94.

[122]Jones, *WFSR*, 175–6.

[123]Jones, 'Social Organism', 198; Jones, *BPRT*, 199; and Jones, *WFSR*, 39 and 41.

[124]Henry Jones, *WP*, 5.

[125]Jones, 'Social Organism', 199.

[126]Jones, *WFSR*, 169, Cf. ibid., 48.

[127]Jones, *SP*, 32; and, Jones, *PC*, 102–3.

[128]Jones, 'Social Organism', 197.

[129]Jones, *SP*, 31.

[130]Jones, *WFSR*. 52 and 56.

[131]Jones, *SP*, 32.

[132]Jones, 'Immanence of God', 33.

[133]Jones, *WFSR*, 174.

[134]Ibid., 176. Cf. 'No child is born vicious or virtuous', ibid., 175.

[135]Jones, 'Obligations and Privileges', 146–7.

[136]Jones, 'The Moral Life', 10.

[137]Jones, *WFSR*, 34.

[138]Jones, *FE*, 97. Cf. 'a cross section of any social world would show that its cells and fibres are the rational activities of its component individuals'. Jones, *WFSR*, 52.

[139]Jones, 'Function of the University', 6.

[140]Jones, *WFSR*, 233.

[141]Hegel, *Philosophy of Right*, section 27.

[142]Reported in *Sydney Morning Herald*, 29 July 1908. Cf. Jones, *IPC*, 80.

[143]Bosanquet, 'Hegel's Theory of the Political Organism', 7.

[144]Jones, 'Social Organism', 200 and 207 respectively.

[145]Ibid., 209.

[146]D. G. Ritchie, *Philosophical Studies* (London, Macmillan, 1905), 252–3.

[147]Quoted by A. Seth Pringle Pattison, 'The Life and Philosophy of Herbert Spencer', *Quarterly Review*, 200 (1904), 256.

[148]Henry Jones, 'Morality as Freedom', *Time* (London), March 1888; 320–6.

[149]Jones, *FE*, 283.

[150]Ibid., 144–5, 283, and 290–1; Jones, *IPC*, 37–9, 57, and 80; and Jones, *PC*, 60 and 85.

[151]Jones, 'Morality as Freedom', p.321.

[152]Jones, *FE*, 356–9.

[153]Jones, *IPC*, 29.

[154]See McTaggart, *Hegelian Cosmology*, 194; and, Jones, *IPC*, 1 33–138.

[155]Jones used these terms in his lectures at Sydney University in 1908, but they are not employed in the book, *IPC*, which grew out of them. See, 'The Renewal of Ideals', and 'Idealism Vindicated', *Sydney Morning Herald*, 29 July and 8 August, respectively.

[156]TJN, vol. ii, fol.96.

[157]Jones, *IPC*, 41.

[158]Ibid., 56; Jones, *PC*, 94–5; and Jones, 'Obligations and Privileges of Citizenship', 78.

[159]Jones, *WFSR*, 34.

[160]Jones, *IPC*, 54.

[161]Ibid., 56.

[162]Ibid., 62.

[163]Jones, *WFSR*, 34. Cf. Jones, *IPC*, 63–4.

[164]Jones, 'Obligations and Privileges of Citizenship', 179.

[165]Jones, *WFSR*, 81–2; Jones, *IPC*; and Jones, *PC*, 141.

[166]Jones, 'Social Organism', 201.

[167]Jones, *PC*, 141.

[168]Jones, *IPC*, 81.

[169]Jones, *WFSR*, 291.

[170]Jones, *PC*, 148. Cf. Jones *IPC*, 108 and 116.

NOTES TO CHAPTER FIVE (pp. 87–109)

[1]R. G. Mulgan, *Aristotle's Political Theory* (Oxford, Clarendon Press, 1977), 53–5.

[2]Some of the most significant scholarship on this topic has been done by J. G. A. Pocock. See Pocock's *Virtue, Commerce and History: Essays on Political Thought and History, chiefly in the Eighteenth Century* (Cambridge, Cambridge University Press, 1985). There has, however, been an enormous growth in the body of literature in this area in the last few years. The general direction of such work has tended recently to shift away from historical to more prescriptive or normative concerns. Although Pocock is a little more elusive on this point, some recent theorists like Quentin Skinner and Michael Sandel have been quite explicit on the virtues of a republican form of theory for the present era as an alternative to liberalism. Skinner, for example, has commented that 'the Roman stoic way of thinking about political liberty is indeed the tradition we need above all to recapture if we wish to provide a corrective to the dogmatism about the topic of social freedom that marks both Hobbes' *Leviathan* and the writings of more recent theorists of natural

or human rights', Skinner, 'The Idea of Negative Liberty', in Richard Rorty, J. B. Schneewind, and Quentin Skinner (eds.), *Philosophy in History* (Cambridge, Cambridge University Press, 1984), 204. For a very recent discussion and critique of this movement see J. C. Isaac, 'Republicanism vs Liberalism? A Reconsideration', *History of Political Thought*, vol. IX, 2, 1988, 349–78.

[3]See previous note, specifically the article by Isaacs, 'Republicanism vs Liberalism?'.

[4]For the Hegelian theory in more detail see Andrew Vincent, *Theories of the State* (Oxford, Blackwell 1987), ch. 4.

[5]On Idealist notions of citizenship see Vincent and Plant, *Philosophy Politics and Citizenship*.

[6]Such an idea is also related to the extension of economic freedoms. The two ideas were linked in the minds of many campaigners like Bright and Cobden and the Anti-Corn Law League.

[7]T. H. Marshall, *Citizenship and Social Class* (Cambridge, Cambridge University Press, 1980).

[8]This point was discussed in chapter two. Jones spent a lot of philosophical energy attacking dualism. As Jones comments 'just as practice implies the theoretic activity of the intellect, so, on the other hand, the theoretic use of intelligence implies the operation of powers deemed practical', *FE*, 110–11.

[9]Notes of an address in Merthyr, January 1918, TJC, Class U, vol. iv, fol. 143. See chapter four for Jones's view on the relation of man to his environment.

[10]Jones to Hadow, 22 July 1918, TJC, Class U, vol. iv, fol. 66.

[11]See Jones's comment on Hadow's view to Hetherington. Jones wrote: 'I think that he is *wrong*, for if the book is worth anything, it will *stimulate*, and teaching is just that and a little beyond', 17 November 1918, TJC, Class U, vol. iv, fol. 78.

[12]Jones, 'Idealism and Epistemology', 1, 292.

[13]Jones, *IPC*, 57. Jones contends that 'society lends to [the individual] her wisdom, imparts to him the rational elements of her own life, in order that by means of them he may scrutinize her opinions, challenge her faith, and reform her ways. Otherwise, her customs would become stale and her faith a lifeless creed', *IPC*, 56.

[14]See ibid. Jones is thinking here of the universal premised in the state, however, the universal as such transcended the state; religion, for example, and philosophy moved beyond the confines of the state.

[15]He is in fact far closer here to Burke and the conservative position than to liberalism, to which he was overtly politically committed. The main difference from Burke, and Oakeshott for that matter, is the way he deploys the concept tradition in the argument. Tradition certainly does not denote unreason or practical knowledge. Jones was conscious of his relation to Burke: see, *IPC*, 61ff. Tradition is viewed by Jones as 'wiser' and 'wider' than any particular individual, *IPC*, 50.

[16]Jones, 'Modern Science and Philosophical Thought', 493.

[17]Jones, *IPC*, 54.

[18]Jones, 'Obligations and Privileges', 128.

[19]Ibid., 144.

[20]Jones, *IPC*, 53.

[21]Ibid., 48. It followed for Jones that given that the self was characterized by reason and purposes, derived from tradition, the greater and more comprehensive the purposes the greater and more comprehensive the self. Thus, for Jones, 'It is the morally great man who takes upon himself the burdens of the world', *FE*, 167.

[22]Jones, 'Obligation and Privileges', 150.

[23]Ibid., 133.

[24]Jones, *IPC*, 31.

[25]As he commented: 'Undoubtedly ideas rule the world, and the makers of good books are its true kings', *ELE*, 222; in another work he maintained: 'There is no practice which is not the carrying out of some conception, and no theory which is otiose and inert. Ideas have hands and feet. We live to carry them out. A wrong theory of the State and of its relations to its citizens . . . is bound in the long run to tell upon its practice', Jones, *PC*, 35.

[26]Jones, 'Obligations and Privileges', 176.

[27]Ibid., 165.

[28]Jones, 'Morality as Freedom', 317. He refers to the good on the next page as an 'eternal law'. There is a problem here in Jones's argument between his insistence on a changing historical process, evolving over time, and an underlying unchanging unity of substance. It is something he never quite resolved in his whole metaphysical enterprise. This is discussed in David Phillips, *Athroniaeth Syr Henry Jones*, 18–19.

[29]Jones, *BPRT*, 59.

[30]Jones, 'Social Organism', 192.

[31]Jones, 'Obligations and Privileges', 178–9.

[32]Jones, 'Reflective Thought Towards Religion', 229.

[33]This particular difficulty can be clearly seen in his address 'Corporate and Individual Charity' given to the Sixth Annual Conference of the Charity Organization and Relief Societies of the United Kingdom in May 1897. The gist of Jones's paper is that there is no hard and fast distinction to be made between individual and corporate charity. Corporate power 'is nothing more nor less than an expression, more or less inadequate, of the wills of the individuals who have created it', 35. Corporate methods are 'instruments for the realisation of individual, or private ends, and nothing more', 36. Each municipal and state function, for Jones, is ultimately traceable back to private desires and will. The public/private distinction or corporate and individual distinction is another phantom or false dualism. Such an idea did not go down well with the COS president, C. S. Loch, who complained in his reply that private charity was needed and could never be adequately performed by a corporate body like the state, 43. For Jones, however, 'the municipality, or the State, or . . . the Charity Organisations, were only an instrument to carry out the desires of individuals', 46.

[34]Jones, 'Obligations and Privileges', 180.

[35]Ibid., 180.

[36]Jones, *WFSR*, 253–4.

[37]Jones, *PC*, 50.

[38]Jones, 'The Function of a University', 5; see also *IPC*, 100.

[39]Jones, 'Social Organism', 190–1.

[40]Jones, *IPC*, 218.

[41]Many of these themes are discussed in more detail in chapter six.

[42]Jones, 'Obligations and Privileges', 170–1.

[43]Ibid., 172. See also *PC*, 173, where a more complete discussion and critique of natural rights is given.

[44]See Jones, *WFSR*, 291.

[45]See 'The Education of the Citizen' in *ELE*.

[46]Aristotle, *The Politics*, ed. Stephen Everson (Cambridge, Cambridge University Press, 1988), 1337a, p. 185.

[47]Jones, *PC*, 123.

[48]J. G. Fitch, 'Education and the State', *Contemporary Review*, LXVIII (1895), 144.

[49]Green, *Principles of Political Obligation*, 209.

[50]Peter Gordon and John White, *Philosophers as Educational Reformers: The Influence of Idealism on British Educational Thought and Practice* (London, Routledge & Kegan Paul, 1979).

[51]Ibid., 156; H. A. L. Fisher, 'The Place of the University in National Life', Barnett House Papers, No. 4 (London, Oxford University Press, 1919), 3–5; and letter from Henry Jones to Sir Ronald Munro Ferguson, 29 December 1916. TJC, Class U, vol iii, fol. 46/2.

[52]H. A. L. Fisher, *Educational Reform Speeches* (Oxford, Clarendon Press, 1918), 48.

[53]Jones, 'North Wales Heroes Memorial Speeches', 6.

[54]Jones, *ELE*, 234.

[55]Jones, 'Function of the University in the State', 13.

[56]Jones, *PC*, 129.

[57]Ibid., 130.

[58]See J. S. MacKenzie, *Outlines of Social Philosophy* (London, Allen & Unwin, 1918), 94; and R. B. Haldane, 'The Nature of the State', *Contemporary Review*, CXVII (1920), 770.

[59]Hegel, *Philosophy of Right*, par. 315, p. 294. For a discussion of Hegel's theory of education see A. W. Vincent and Michael George, 'Development and Self-Identity: Hegel's Concept of Education', *Educational Theory*, 32 (1982), 131–41.

[60]Plato, *The Republic*, tr. Desmond Lee (Harmondsworth, Penguin, 1987), 191.

[61]Jones, *WFSR*, 176.

[62]Jones, 'Obligations and Privileges', 122.

[63]Jones, 'Higher Learning', 10.

[64]Jones, 'League of Learning', 297; Jones, *ELE*, 239; and Jones, 'North Wales Heroes Memorial Speeches', 12.

[65]Jones, *PC,* 123–4, 137 and 144.

[66]Jones, *WFSR,* 177. Jones quotes Pythagoras in answering the question what education is best for the child: 'by making him the citizen of a people with good institutions'. Hegel also cites this passage, *Philosophy of Right,* par. 153, 109.

[67]Jones, *WFSR,* 176–8, and 304–5.

[68]Ibid., 114.

[69]Jones, *ELE,* 243.

[70]Jones, *WFSR,* 305.

[71]MS Fisher, 61, fol. 215. BLO.

[72]Green, *Works,* vol. III, 403; and, R. B. Haldane, *Education and Empire: Addresses on Certain Topics of the Day* (London, Murray, 1902), 26–38.

[73]Gordon and White, *Philosophers as Educational Reformers,* 98–108; and W. S. Fowler, 'The Influence of Idealism upon State Provision of Education', *Victorian Studies,* IV (1961), 343–4.

[74]Jones, 'Function of the University of the State', 11.

[75]Jones calls this a 'cardinal moral' maxim. 'Ethics and Politics', 402.

[76]Jones, *PC,* 135.

[77]Jones, *ELE,* 230.

[78]Jones, 'Higher Learning', 20; Jones, *PC,* 133; and, Jones, *ELE,* 247.

[79]Fisher, *Educational Reform Speeches* (Oxford, Clarendon Press, 1918), 43.

[80]Jones, *PC,* 122, and 135.

[81]Jones, 'North Wales Heroes Memorial Speeches', 7.

[82]Jones, *ELE,* 261. Jones also suggests that motives ulterior to those of education for the sake of the individual 'should have no more place in our schemes than they have in the mind of the mother when she suckles her infant at her breast'. Ibid., 246.

[83]Green, *Works,* vol. III, 460.

[84]He argued: 'Educate your people, and you have reduced to comparatively insignificant dimensions the problems of temperance, of housing, and of raising the condition of your masses.' *Education and Empire,* 39.

[85]Fisher, *Educational Reform Speeches,* 75.

[86]Printed letter to William George, 15 August 1919 (in Welsh). NLW 1635OD, p. 4.

[87]Jones, 'League of Learning', 301.

[88]Letter to H. A. L. Fisher, 16 July 1916. MS Fisher, 61, fol. 215. BLO.

[89]The Commissioners were Lord Haldane (Chairman), Hon. W. N. Bruce, Sir William Osler, Sir Daniel Hall, Sir O. M. Edwards, Sir Henry Hadow, and Miss Emily Penrose. Jones successfully persuaded the Commission to include the penny rate in its report, and not to recommend the greater centralization of the University of Wales.

[90]Cited by Hetherington, *Life and Letters,* 130. Also see Jones *ELE,* 280, and letters to Hetherington dated 27 April 1921. TJC, Class U, vol. iii, fol. 152, and Fisher, dated 16 July1916. MS Fisher, 61, fol. 215. BLO.

[91]Green, *Works,* III, 409.

[92]Letter to William George, 3.

[93]See the open letter from Percy E. Watkins, Honorary Secretary *pro tem,* dated 14 August 1919. NLW 16350D. Newspaper articles in Welsh, the printed scheme itself, and correspondence regarding it between Jones and Lloyd George accompany this letter.

[94]Letter to William George.

[95]Newspaper cutting, undated, but certainly August 1919, held in NLW 16350D.

NOTES TO CHAPTER SIX (pp. 110–33)

[1]There is some evidence to the effect that by 1920 his belief in and friendship with Lloyd George was becoming strained, see letter Henry Jones to J. H. Muirhead, 3 September 1920, TJC, Class U, vol. iii. They were at the turn of the century on opposite sides of the imperialism question in the Liberal Party, see chapter seven.

[2]J. W. Scott, who, as a tutor at Glasgow took Jones's classes while he was giving his lectures in Wales, later wrote a more systematic critique of syndicalism, *Syndicalism and Philosophical Realism.*

[3]Jones, 'Idealism and Politics', 1, 615. Jones's comment on the state is also revealing; he says 'to call the State "the kingdom of heaven upon Earth", as Hegel did, seems to be vain babbling', Jones, 'Function of the University', 5.

[4]Jones to Fisher, 16 December 1918, Fisher MS, BLO, fol 62, 259–60.

[5]See Jones, 'Fiscal Question'.

[6]Jones, 'Function of the University', 9. In one of his essays there is a fairly detailed discussion of German and British education, where he expands some of these points, although tempered at the time by the anti-German feeling of the First World War, *ELE*, 229–66.

[7]Ibid., 11. In another essay Jones speaks of the need to rescue education 'from the clutches of industrialism', *ELE*, 245. In Britain, he says, education is 'narrow in range and wrong in kind', ibid., 244. The commercial mentality has nothing whatsoever to do with living in a community, developing culturally or feeling any sense of loyalty. As Jones comments later in the essay, presumably during the war period, 'the customary economic world has little place in the field of France', ibid., 263.

[8]Ibid., 16.

[9]Jones, *WFSR*, 18.

[10]Jones, 'Scientific and Philosophical Thought', 494. Jones was particularly irritated by Bosanquet's and Bradley's insistence on the distinction between theory and practice in moral thought. He dismissed it as 'bad philosophy'. Every human being functions with some notion of what is 'good'. 'What', asks Jones, 'buckles his bag on the back of a German private I wonder? and keeps him mucking in the trenches, except false notions of *the* good?', letter Henry Jones to Sir Henry Hadow, 14 July 1918, TJC, Class U, vol. iii.

[11]Ibid., 495.

[12]Jones, 'Ethics and Politics', 495; see also 'Ethical Demand', 272.

[13]' "Masses" is a word which no one who has learnt to respect his fellow citizens is willing or tempted to use', ibid., footnote, 403.

[14]Jones, 'Ethical Demand', 527. Jones's view was that politics must be concerned with the most ethical minds – 'the whole aim of the practical politician must be directed towards calling forth *that mind*', 'Ethics and Politics', 402.

[15]Jones, 'Ethics and Politics', 411.

[16]Ibid., 402. In another essay he commented 'The State is not safe unless public opinion is enlightened opinion', *WFSR*, 291.

[17]Jones, 'Ethics and Politics', 408.

[18]Jones, for example, commented in a letter, after reading one of R. H. Tawney's works: 'I have just read Tawney's "Sickness of Acquisitive Society" with very great pleasure and very great pain. I'd put it in the hands of *every capitalist*, big or little and into the hands of *not one workman*', Henry Jones to Hetherington, 31 March 1920, TJC, Class U, vol. iii.

[19]See Martin Pugh, *The Making of Modern British Politics 1867–1939* (Oxford, Blackwell, 1983), 3.

[20]A very rigorous élitism was present in the Webbs, combined with eugenic theories and labour colonies for the workshy. As one writer has put it, for the Fabians, 'Socialism represented an organization of society capable of inducing the most efficient performance from its resources; as long as society was run by people with the requisite expertise collectivism was the answer', J. Callaghan, *Socialism in Britain* (Oxford, Blackwell, 1990), 34–5. Beatrice Webb, in a famous quotation, remarked that 'we have little faith in the "average sensual man", we do not believe that he can do much more than describe his grievances, we do not think that he can prescribe the remedies . . . We wish to introduce the professional expert', Beatrice Webb, *Our Partnership* (London, Longmans, 1948), 120. Both the Webbs and Shaw had little but contempt for average rank and file socialist and labour leaders, whom Beatrice Webb described as 'feather-headed failures'. Their approach to democracy might legitimately be compared to Schumpeter. It was élitist, seeking to return, in as cost-efficient a manner as possible, an efficient élite group, not to consult or encourage citizens to participate. The Webbs would have valued, like certain political scientists in the 1950s, apathy in politics from the average citizen.

[21]Jones wanted universities to be set up in all the major industrial centres of Britain as 'spiritual centres', see letter Henry Jones to Sir Henry Hadow, 20 June 1918, TJC, Class U, vol. iii; also Jones to Hetherington, 10 September 1919, TJC, Class U, vol. iii. His views parallel closely those of R. B. Haldane, see Vincent and Plant, *Philosophy, Politics and Citizenship*, chapter eight, and E. Ashby and M. Anderson, *Portrait of Haldane at Work on Education* (London, Macmillan, 1974).

[22]See Jones, 'Ethical Demand', 527. Graham Wallas, *Human Nature in Politics* (1st edn. 1908, 3rd edn. New York, Alfred Knopf, 1921). Jones's repudiation of this

psychologistic thesis is also rooted in his rejection of both William James's and Bergson's philosophies, discussed in chapter two.

[23]Jones, *WFSR*, 20.

[24]Ibid., 9.

[25]Jones, 'Ethical Demand', 539. In another letter to Sidney Webb he wrote: 'I should find it difficult to name any better way of spending what remnant of my life that may stand over to me than that of working for the working class: I belong to it', Jones to Sidney Webb, 29 March 1918, TJC, Class U, vol. iii. See also *IPC*, 218.

[26]Jones remarks 'Individualism and Socialism, Nationalism and Internationalism, Egotism and Altruism, in all forms, must be recognised as false and futile when apart. They become true only when they are found to be not merely inextricably intertwined but as impossible when sundered', 'Obligations and Privileges', 165. This point will be taken up in the final section of this chapter.

[27]Some would of course trace socialism back much farther to the radical natural law tradition, Thomas More, the Levellers and Diggers of the English Civil War, religious Nonconformity, William Cobbett and so forth. However, the first explicit uses of the word socialism, to denote a political persuasion and collection of beliefs, quite clearly date from the 1820s in France and Britain.

[28]See R. Pearson and G. Williams, *Political Thought and Public Policy in the Nineteenth Century* (London, Longmans, 1984), 136.

[29]The most recently deeply researched work on this period is G. Claeys, *Citizens and Saints: Politics and Anti-Politics in Early British Socialism* (Cambridge, Cambridge University Press, 1989). See also the useful discussion on the history of socialism in Britain by Collini in *Liberalism and Sociology*, 32ff.

[30]See Pearson and Williams, *Political Thought and Public Policy*, 109–10.

[31]Keir Hardie, Bruce Glasier, Robert Blatchford, Ramsay MacDonald, Philip Snowden, R. H. Tawney, Sidney and Beatrice Webb, Sidney Ball, to name but a few, remained unimpressed by or uninterested in Marx.

[32]A. W. Wright, *Socialisms* (Oxford, Oxford University Press, 1987), 1; see also Greenleaf's recognition of the same point, W. H. Greenleaf, *The British Political Tradition: The Ideological Heritage*, vol. ii (London, Methuen, 1983), 349–50.

[33]On the socialist revival in the 1880s see opening chapters of Willard Wolfe, *From Radicalism to Socialism: Men and Ideas in the Formation of Fabian Socialist Doctrines 1881–1889* (New Haven, Conn., Yale University Press, 1975).

[34]Jones, 'Ethical Demand', 538.

[35]As a recent book has stated: 'The history of socialism is marked with the simplistic identification of the concept with, for example, collectivism or statism or common ownership of property. In reality divisions within socialism have been as bitter and crucial as conflict between socialism and its competing ideologies', N. Dennis and A. H. Halsey, *English Ethical Socialism* (Oxford, Clarendon Press, 1988), 4. Even writers like Sidney Webb in the 1890s were 'to be found trying to disabuse people of the "misapprehension" that socialism implied "a rigidly centralised national administration" ', A. W. Wright, *British Socialism* (London, Longmans, 1983), 60. It is also clear that collectivism should be kept distinct from

socialism. Socialism denotes a body of beliefs and values, whereas collectivism is a method of social, economic and political organization which has been used by other ideological movements, like conservatism. This point is made with some force in M. Freeden, *The New Liberalism*, 31; and Collini, *Liberalism and Sociology*, 33ff.

[36]Edward Caird, *Individualism and Socialism: Inaugural Lecture to the Civic Society of Glasgow* (Glasgow, James Maclehose, 1897), 9.

[37]William Wallace has two interesting essays on socialism – 'The Ethics of Socialism' and 'The Relation of Fichte and Hegel to Socialism' in E. Caird (ed.), *Lectures and Essays on Natural Theology and Ethics* (Oxford, Clarendon Press, 1898), 399–447. The first of the essays is particularly acute and well-informed about Marx. A. Schäffle, *The Quintessence of Socialism* (London, Swan Sonnenschein, 1889). The translation of the latter work was supervised by Bernard Bosanquet.

[38]J. S. MacKenzie, *An Introduction to Social Philosophy* (Glasgow, Maclehose, 1895), 323. There were other writers at the time who adopted a moderate ethical socialism. See Revd and Mrs Barnett, *Practicable Socialism* (London, Isbister, 1894) and John Rae, *Contemporary Socialism* (London, Swan Sonnenschein, 1901).

[39]Bernard Bosanquet, 'The Antithesis between Individualism and Socialism Philosophically Considered' in *Civilization of Christendom*, 304–57. Bosanquet in another work did express some sympathy with the Guild Socialist movement for obvious reasons concerned with their belief in self-government, see Bernard Bosanquet, *Social and International Ideals: Being Studies in Patriotism* (London, Macmillan, 1917).

[40]Fabianism, for example, included the instrumental, positivist and Benthamite, administrative vision of the Webbs and the ethical vision of S. Ball, S. Olivier and for that matter D. G. Ritchie, see Willard Wolfe, *From Radicalism to Socialism*; A. M. McBriar, *Fabian Socialism and English Politics 1884–1918* (Cambridge, Cambridge University Press, 1966). For Fabian essays see G. B. Shaw (ed.), *Fabian Essays in Socialism* (original edn. 1889; 6th edition London, George Allen & Unwin, 1962); Sidney Ball, 'The Moral Aspects of Socialism', *International Journal of Ethics*, VI, 1896, or 'The Socialist Ideal', *Economic Review*, IX, 1899.

[41]Jones, Report on lecture in Australia 'True and False Socialism', *Newcastle Morning Herald*, 6 August 1908, 6. In another work he writes 'It is not seen that a socialised State brought upon a people morally unprepared would be the deepest calamity any nation could be called upon to meet . . . A genuine democracy demands the highest civic virtues', Jones, *IPC*, 219.

[42]The masses to Sidney Webb were 'apathetic, dense [and] unreceptive to any unfamiliar ideas' . . . 'you have got to work your governmental machine in some way that will enable you to get on notwithstanding their denseness', S. Webb, 'A Stratified Democracy', *The New Commonwealth*, 28 November 1919, suppl., 5. This point also links up with Webb's élitism.

[43]See Jones, *IPC*, 219. Jones notes with disquiet: 'The view seems to be gaining ground that the State is really a charitable institution, on whose resources each class, and each townlet, must draw as much as it can, putting as many of its causes

on the local rates as cannot be put on Imperial taxes and asking the Government to protect its industry; while the Chancellor of the Exchequer stands alone . . . like *Athanasius contra mundum*', 'Scientific and Philosophical Thought', 519.

[44]This particular point was the occasion of a fierce dispute in the *International Journal of Ethics*, see Sidney Ball, 'The Moral Aspects of Socialism', VI, 1896; a reply by Bernard Bosanquet in the same 503–6. The issue of character was a central social category of Charity Organization Society (COS), see Andrew Vincent, 'The Poor Law Reports of 1909 and the Social Theory of the Charity Organization Society', *Victorian Studies*, vol. 27, 1984. Sidney Webb joined the dispute in a later volume of the journal, VII. It is worth noting though that Jones, despite an overt sympathy with the COS (see his address, 'Individual and Corporate Charity'), was none the less not at home with their particular views on character as is evidenced by C. S. Loch's (the leading light of the COS) hostile response to Jones, reported at the end of the above address by Jones.

[45]Jones, *WFSR*, 271. The strength of belief in the role of character can even be found in Beatrice Webb; speaking of the nature of poverty, she maintained 'character is the key factor in destitution', Sidney and Beatrice Webb, *The Prevention of Destitution* (London, Longmans, 1911), 293.

[46]Jones, 'Corporate and Individual Charity', 35.

[47]This is not to say that he did not realize the significance of class. He remarked in one work 'Society is stratified into classes, and the impact of their collision shakes the State', *WFSR*, 22. He rather deeply regretted that people should think of themselves and others as class members rather than as citizens.

[48]Jones, 'Ethical Demand', 539–40. Jones also attacks Keir Hardie on the same ground: 'I don't like the banner under which Labour fights. Some members of it, and especially Mr Keir Hardie, are bitter and harmful, and they are corrupting the working men . . . Liberals and Conservatives stand for ideals that are not in themselves class ideals', Jones to Lloyd Thomas, 9 April 1910, TJC, Class U, vol. ii.

[49]Jones, 'Corruption of Citizenship'. The same view was taken by Helen Bosanquet, *Rich and Poor* (London, Macmillan, 1898), 90.

[50]Jones to Sidney Webb, 29 March 1918, TJC, Class U, vol. iii.

[51]For Shaw see S. Ingle, 'Socialist Man: William Morris and Bernard Shaw', in B. Parekh (ed.), *The Concept of Socialism* (London, Croom Helm, 1975). MacDonald argued that the class war is 'nothing but a grandiloquent and aggressive figure of speech', in B. Barker (ed.), *Ramsay MacDonald's Political Writings* (London, Allen Lane, 1972), 84; also see Wright, *British Socialism*, 203.

[52]See Jones, *DB*, 23 and 26; *WFSR*, 298; 'The University of Wales', 10,11 and 14. He told Australian audiences that 'The attempt to get things done for one class is the aggregated selfishness of individuals', *Argus* (Melbourne, 12 August 1908); see also 'True and False Socialism' in *The Newcastle Morning Herald* and *Miner's Advocate*, 6 August 1908 (New South Wales) and *The South Coast Times*, 25 July 1908 (New South Wales).

[53]For the individualist principle objection to public ownership see H. Spencer, *The Man Versus the State*; Lord Bramwell, *Laissez-Faire* (1884); Bruce Smith, *Liberty*

and Liberalism (1887); E. Playdell-Bouverie, *The Province of Government* (1884). Many Spencerians associated socialism with evolutionary regression, a moving back from industrial society to militant society, or to use the categories of Henry Maine (which had equal resonance at the time) from contract back to status.

[54]Jones, *WFSR*, 95.

[55]Jones comments 'This was the truth which, in trying times, Edmund Burke enforced with many strong arguments . . . It is a truth generally urged in the interests of social and political conservatism. I press it, rather, in the interests of reform', ibid., 23–4. For Jones revolutionary socialism was not really a form of collectivism but was 'deeply tainted with the selfishness of Individualism', *IPC*, 87.

[56]Ibid.

[57]See Jones, *FE*, 281–3; or *IPC*, 54. In one of his earliest essays Jones contended 'that an individual has no life except that which is social and that he cannot realise his own purposes except in realising the larger purpose of society', 'Social Organism', 193.

[58]Jones, *IPC*, 100. He comments in another work 'the State while limiting caprice has enlarged freedom; that in appropriating industrial enterprises it has liberated the economic power of its citizens', *WFSR*, 105.

[59]Jones, 'Function of the University', 16.

[60]Jones to Fisher, 1916, Fisher MS, BLO, fol 259–60, 7. In another work Jones writes 'It is quite true that common ownership and common enterprise turn us into limited proprietors; but they make us limited proprietors of indefinitely large utilities', *WFSR*, 110.

[61]Jones, 'Ethical Demand', 537.

[62]Ibid.

[63]Ibid.

[64]Jones states that, for example, nationalization of the Post Office means that we are 'all shareholders in a vast enterprise whose services and utilities are greater to each because they are open to all', *WFSR*, 105.

[65]See H. Sidgwick, *Elements of Politics* (London, Macmillan, 1897), ch. 10; Sidney Webb, *Socialism in England* (London, Swan Sonneschein, 1890).

[66]Jones to Fisher, 16 December1918, Fisher MS, BLO, fol. 62, 7–8. In one of his essays Jones comments: 'Does London repent of the change in its method of supplying itself with water? Or Glasgow of many of its civic enterprises? Taxation is growing apace, it is true, but so are the social services', Jones, 'Ethical Demand', 538.

[67]Jones, *WFSR*, 58.

[68]There are arguments to the effect that there were regional differences in the effects of the new liberalism. London is one area discussed in Paul Thompson's *Socialists, Liberals and Labour: The Struggle for London 1885–1914* (London, Routledge & Kegan Paul, 1967). More significant in terms of Henry Jones, Wales is another area singled out by K. O. Morgan in 'The New Liberalism and the Challenge of Labour: The Welsh Experience', *Welsh History Review*, vol. 6 (1973), 282–312. In relation, for example, to Henry Jones's admired friend and the tribune

of the English new liberalism, David Lloyd George, Morgan comments 'For Lloyd George Welsh and English Liberalism represented different worlds . . . After 1908, he was a New Liberal in England, an Old Liberal in Wales', 303. This is not, however, an uncontested thesis. For rejoinders to the Morgan and Thompson arguments, see P. F. Clarke, *Lancashire and the New Liberalism* (Cambridge, Cambridge University Press, 1971) and Neal Blewett, *The Peers, The Parties and the People: The General Election of 1910* (Toronto, University of Toronto Press, 1972). If we accepted Morgan's point, it would be truer to say that Jones's liberalism reflected more the maincurrents of the English new liberalism.

[69]In fact socialists like Hardie, Glasier and Blatchford and later Tawney, had far more (if simpler) moralistic religiousity about them than anything Jones produced, even in his most purple moments, for examples of such socialist religiousity see Callaghan, *Socialism in Britain*, 55, 57–8. Tawney also believed that moral evolution preceded political evolution, see Wright, *British Socialism*, 13. Tawney maintained that 'in order to believe in human equality [which was crucial for socialists] it is necessary to believe in God', see J. M. Winter and D. M. Joslin (eds.) *R. H. Tawney's Commonplace Book* (Cambridge, Cambridge University Press, 1972), 6 March 1913, 53. L. T. Hobhouse also exhibited the same tendency comparing the development of collectivism with the morality of the Sermon on the Mount, see Hobhouse, 'The Ethical Basis of Collectivism', *International Journal of Ethics*, vol. VIII, 1898. Collini makes the point that Sidney Ball utilized many of Hobhouse's ideas for constructing his own conception of ethical socialism, see Collini, *Liberalism and Sociology*, 74.

[70]See P. Weiler, *The New Liberalism: Liberal Social Theory in Great Britain 1889–1914* (New York, Garland Publishing, 1982); H. V. Emy, *Liberals, Radicals and Social Politics 1892–1914* (Cambridge, Cambridge University Press, 1973); Freeden, *The New Liberalism*; Collini, *Liberalism and Sociology*; Peter Clarke, *Liberals and Social Democrats* (Cambridge, Cambridge University Press, 1978); John Allett, *New Liberalism, The Political Economy of J. A. Hobson* (Toronto: Toronto University Press, 1981); Vincent and Plant, *Philosophy, Politics and Citizenship*.

[71]This section draws upon material in Andrew Vincent, 'Classical Liberalism and its Crisis of Identity', *History of Political Thought*, vol. XI, (1990).

[72]See J. N. Gray, *Liberalism* (Milton Keynes, Open University Press, 1986), 92, and by the same author *Hayek on Liberty*, 2nd edn. (Oxford, Blackwell, 1986), x. The source of Gray's judgement is most likely Hayek, for example, see Hayek's *New Studies in Philosophy, Economics and the History of Ideas* (London, Routledge & Kegan Paul, 1978), 130.

[73]Probably the most traditional account of this was E. Halevy's *Imperialism and the Rise of Labour 1895–1905* (London, Ernest Benn, 1961) and *The Rule of Democracy 1905–14* (London, Ernest Benn, 1961).

[74]See D. A. Hamer, *Liberal Politics in the Age of Gladstone and Rosebery: A Study in Leadership and Policy* (Oxford, Clarendon Press, 1972).

[75]G. L. Bernstein, *Liberalism and Liberal Politics in Edwardian England* (London, Allen & Unwin, 1986).

[76]Bosanquet remarked on such groups as the LPDL 'The Economic Individualist . . . who thinks the State to be unconcerned with morality, and to be unjustified in any interference on moral grounds, is a fanatic doctrinaire, and is the precise counterpart of the Economic Socialist [*vis-à-vis* Marxist]': Bosanquet, 'The Antithesis between Individualism and Socialism', 318.

[77]See A. V. Dicey in *Lectures on the Relation between Law and Public Opinion During the Nineteenth Century* (London, Macmillan, 1905); Herbert Spencer, *The Man Versus the State*; Sidgwick in *The Elements of Politics*. Their anxious and critical views on the crisis in liberal thought and practice were shared with more traditional Whigs like Henry Maine and William Lecky. Both Maine's *Popular Government* (1886) and Lecky's *Democracy and Liberty* (1896) were mordant reflections on the dangers of popular democracy and the effect it was having on the British political system and the liberal tradition. Both books were written in the context of the fears over the effects of what Maine called 'unmodified democracy' and also the growth of collectivist ideas within the Liberal Party. Whereas Maine saw government passing from the hands of wise men, skilled in debate, to crude caucus politics appealing to the majority whims; Lecky saw a new type of working-class leadership demanding more state restriction (as in the 1880s administrations) and returning society to a new form of feudalism. It is interesting that Maine, at the same time as writing his *Popular Government*, was also contributing a series of articles to the *St James Gazette*, over the 1880/1 period, on the dangers of the policy changes within the Liberal Party. Other writers and practicing liberals like Wordsworth Donisthorpe, Auberon Herbert, Thomas Mackay, and W. C. Crofts, conscious of the same liberal anxieties on betrayal and crisis, were involved in setting up societies like the State Resistance Union (1880), which had mutated from the Political Evolution Society; the Non Interference Union (1881); the Liberty and Property Defence League (1882). The latter was the most noted society and formed alliances with other interested groups, like the Middle Class Defence League, for propaganda against *any* increase in state intervention or growth. It also attracted a large amount of support from conservatives, like Lord Wemyss, conservatives who saw Tory democracy as potentially dangerous and collectivist as any liberal radicalism. For a detailed discussion of the Liberty and Property League and the context of its arguments, see E. J. Bristow 'The Liberty and Property Defence League and Individualism', *Historical Journal*, xviii (1975). For a very brief discussion of some of the worries of the more classical British liberalism, see Vincent and Plant, *Philosophy, Politics and Citizenship*, ch. 4.

[78]Arnold Toynbee, *Industrial Revolution* (London, Rivington, 1884), 203. Toynbee was in fact commenting on a fairly widely held view in liberal circles. There had been a gradual movement of figures like Arnold, Fitzjames Stephen and Froude away from the Liberal Party after the Second Reform Act. However, during the 1880s Liberal Administration, this exodus increased and the charge brought by figures like Maine, Dicey, Spencer and Lecky, amongst others, was that a form of socialism was coming into practice, and betraying the purity of

liberal doctrine. Liberal radicalism (or 'constructivism' as Gladstone himself uneasily referred to it) was being associated with socialism, thus the title of Toynbee's essay. Part of the problem here was that the term socialism was being used without much precision. Sidney Webb caught this ambiguity in his book *Socialism in England*. Webb virtually identifies socialism with every collective or municipal action taken in the nineteenth century. Beatrice Webb also referred to the liberal legislation of the 1880s as 'empirical socialism', see B. Webb, *My Apprenticeship* (London, Longmans, 1926), 184.

[79]See Jones, *IPC*, 92; for Caird, *Individualism and Socialism*, 12–13.

[80]Jones, *IPC*, 90. The metaphysical equivalent for this argument is some form of philosophical logical atomism. Jones's reading of individualism here bears directly upon Hegel's interpretation in *The Phenomenology of Spirit*; see chapter two for some discussion of this point. Bosanquet also develops the same point in his article 'The Antithesis between Individualism and Socialism', 307.

[81]This discussion links up to the notions of thin and thick individualism in chapter 5.

[82]Jones, *WFSR*, 107–8. When J. S. MacKenzie discussed this point he noted intelligently 'I have purposely abstained from any reference to the common argument that Socialism would tend to crush out individuality, and would thus lead to a monotonous uniformity. It does not seem to me obvious that it would do so, any more than it is obvious that a system of individual liberty tends to produce excessive variety', MacKenzie, *Introduction to Social Philosophy*, 321, n. 2. MacKenzie, taking Bryce's *American Commonwealth* as his authority, argues that American life and liberty have not, in fact, led to the vaunted distinctive variety of life. There was as much uniformity as anywhere.

[83]Jones, *WFSR*, 107–8.

[84]Ibid., 110.

[85]Ibid., 113–14. Jones comments earlier that 'even if the danger of State interference were considerable, I should still say, after Plato and Aristotle, that the first, the paramount care of the State, is to educate its citizens, and that the State itself is, in the last resort an educational institution', ibid., 50.

[86]'The educative power of a community towards its own children is thus measured by the amount of virtue and wisdom which it shows in its customary conduct', Jones, *WFSR*, 177–8.

[87]Jones, 'League of Peace', 10; see also Jones, *FE*, 19, 182–3; or *ELE*, 227.

[88]Jones to Sir Henry Hadow, 14 July 1918, TJC, Class U, vol. iii, also in Hetherington, *Life and Letters*, 251.

[89]Jones, *FE*, 182–5.

[90]Jones, ibid., 182.

[91]Ibid., 183.

[92]Jones, 'The Moral Aspect', 121.

[93]Jones, *ELE*, 179.

[94]For Jones we should not 'call a man wealthy because he has much property; for property may be lumber and worse, and is so in the hands of many. And assuredly

we cannot measure a country's wealth by its imports and exports . . . The world is suffering from Abstract Economics as from a great falsehood; and we are very slow to lay our Ruskin to heart', Jones, 'The Huge Machinery', 60. For similar arguments which bring Burke into the same equation, see 'The Moral Aspect', 130.

[95]Ibid., 186–7. See chapters two and three for the metaphysical critique of the Absolute.

[96]In Wales general accounts of the unrest can be found in D. Evans, *Labour Strife in the South Wales Coalfield 1910–11* (Cardiff, Educational Publishing, 1911) and E. W. Evans, *The Miners of South Wales* (Cardiff, University of Wales Press, 1961), R. Arnot Page, *South Wales Miners: A History of the S.W.M.F. 1898–1914* (London, Cymric Federation Press, 1967).

[97]The most recent and most complete scholarly assessment of the syndicalists in France is Jeremy Jennings, *Syndicalism in France* (London, Macmillan, 1990).

[98]The more traditional views on the important role of syndicalism can be found in George Dangerfield, *The Strange Death of Liberal England* (London, MacGibbon and Kee, 1936) and Halevy, *The Rule of Democracy*. A more recent defence of this view is Martin Barclay, 'The Slaves of the Lamp – The Aberdare Miners' Strike 1910', *Llafur* II, 3, 1978. A much more sceptical reading of the role of syndicalism can be found in Pugh, *The Making of Modern British Politics, 108–9*, H. Pelling, *The History of British Trade Unionism* (Harmondsworth, Penguin Books, 1969), 136–8, and Peter Stead, 'Working-Class Leadership in South Wales 1900–1920' *Welsh History Review*, vol. 6, 1973. A completely negative account can be found in Anthony Mor-O'Brien, who argues 'Industrial unrest and syndicalism were thought to go hand in hand, whereas in reality syndicalists merely hung on the coat tails of the non-political, non-ideological discontent and initiated nothing', in 'Patriotism on Trial: The Strike of the South Wales Miners July 1915', *Welsh History Review*, vol. 12, 1984, 81.

[99]Bob Holton, *British Syndicalism 1900–1914: Myths and Realities* (London, Pluto Press, 1976), 17.

[100]In Wales see K. O. Morgan, 'Socialism and Syndicalism: The Welsh Miners Debate 1912', *Bulletin of the Society for the Study of Labour History*, n. 30, 1975.

[101]Holton, *British Syndicalism*, 35.

[102]See *The Industrial Syndicalist: Documents in Social History*, No. 3, introduced by G. Best (Nottingham, Spokesman Books, 1974), 65. On the *Bourse du Travail* see J. Joll, *The Anarchists* (Boston, Little Brown and Co., 1964), 197–200.

[103]See Holton, *British Syndicalism*, 79ff, Greenleaf, *British Political Tradition*, 500ff.

[104]Holton comments, 'although the impact of syndicalism as a systematic social theory was generally seen as limited, many prominent and well-informed observers were convinced that a syndicalist mood of revolt and dissaffection was widespread. The proceedings of the Employers Parliamentary Council and the Association of Chambers of Commerce indicate that many employers took this view as did Askwith, the leading government advisor on labour affairs', Holton, *British Syndicalism*, 76.

[105]K. O. Morgan, *Rebirth of a Nation: Wales 1880–1980* (Oxford, Clarendon Press and University of Wales Press, 1981), 175.

[106]Ibid., 176.

[107]See letter to J.W. James on his early lectures in Wales in Hetherington, *Life and Letters,* 231–2.

[108]Tom Jones to Principal Sir David Maccalister, 25 August 1917, TJC, Class U vol. i.

[109]Writing to Tom Jones in October 1917 he says 'May I not give a series of addresses on different aspects of Citizenship all bearing on the war and its aims, of course, and out of range of wrangling', he goes on, 'Could not the addresses be such as to contribute to our educational and spiritual aims for Wales, and even the book', Henry Jones to Tom Jones, 3 October 1917, TJC, Class U vol. i. His pamphlet *DB* contained lectures on 'Pure Citizenship' delivered to the North Wales Quarrymen's Union. These essentially contain the same body of arguments as are explored in more depth in his later book *PC*.

[110]Henry Jones to Tom Jones, 3 October 1917, TJC, Class U, vol. i.

[111]As he wrote: 'I cannot and do not intend trying to speak to a ready made programme: I *must* have freedom. Secondly I am going to devote my summer to working out some new issues concerned with Citizenship and I know that things will develop under my fingers', Henry Jones to Tom Jones, 16 May 1919, TJC, Class U, vol. i.

[112]Hadow who had asked Jones to write the book and lectures was disappointed, finding it too hard, see Henry Jones to Hetherington, 17 November 1918, TJC, Class U, vol. iii.

[113]Hetherington, *Life and Letters,* 137.

[114]Jones, *BPRT,* 62.

[115]Jones, 'Obligations and Privileges', 180.

[116]Jones, *IPC,* 100. As he states in another work: 'The expansion of the activities of communal units has proceeded *pari passu* with the awakening of the powers and extension of the liberties of the individuals that constitute them. An effective State always implies free and effective citizens. In a word, in the teaching of history it is obvious that communal and private functions . . . grow together', Jones, 'Corporate and Individual Charity', 35.

[117]Jones, 'Function of the University', 14.

[118]L. T. Hobhouse, *Democracy and Reaction,* 217. Hobhouse later comments: 'I venture to conclude that the differences between a true, consistent, public-spirited Liberalism and a rational Collectivism ought, with genuine effort at mutual understanding to disappear', ibid., 237. Interestingly, Hobhouse quotes extensively from the German SPD programme and argues that it is very close to liberal beliefs, 234ff.

[119]For Jones true political awareness is 'content neither with public order nor private freedom; it will neither make the State subordinate to the individual, nor the individual to the State; it is neither Socialism nor Individualism. Yet it will

curtail none of the *rights* of either. It will even make the evolution of the one depend upon the evolution of the other', 'Idealism and Politics', II, 742.

[120]Jones says that 'the State while limiting caprice has enlarged freedom; that in appropriating industrial enterprises it has liberated the economic power of its citizens', *WFSR*, 105. Jones is obviously reading socialism as collectivism or state socialism. It is a shame, in this context, that we do not have any detailed response to guild socialism. For similar views to Jones see Caird, 'Individualism and Socialism', 3–4; J. S. MacKenzie, *A Manual of Ethics* (London, W. B. Clive, 1897), 308; Hobhouse, *Democracy and Reaction*, 237; H. Haldar, *Neo-Hegelianism*, 357; Guido de Ruggiero, tr. R. G. Collingwood, *The History of European Liberalism* (Oxford, Oxford University Press, 1927), 393.

[121]Jones, 'Function of the University', 14.

[122]See Freeden, *The New Liberalism*, 145–9 for more on this argument. Freeden comments earlier in the text that 'no meaningful contrast is evident between individualism and socialism or individualism and collectivism', 32.

[123]The French socialist Jaurès, for example, saw socialism coming to fulfil the traditional liberal 'rights of man', see Wright, *Socialisms*, 26.

[124]As Jones says: 'whenever it becomes a right, [it] is due not alone nor primarily to his having said Mine, but to the State having said Thine', *WFSR*, 97.

[125]Ibid., 98.

NOTES TO CHAPTER SEVEN (pp. 134–54)

[1]See Elie Kedourie, *Nationalism* (London, Hutchinson, 1974: 3rd edn.)

[2]This was the view which Muirhead took and, as we shall see, it was to a certain extent shared by Hobhouse.

[3]A. C. Bradley, 'International Morality: The United States of Europe' in *The International Crisis in its Ethical and Psychological Aspects* by Eleanor M. Sidgwick, Gilbert Murray, A. C. Bradley, L. P. Jacks, G. F. Stout, and B. Bosanquet (London, Oxford University Press, 1915), 72–3.

[4]T. H. Green, *Lectures on the Principles of Political Obligation* (London, Longmans, 1917), 166.

[5]H. J. W. Hetherington and J. H. Muirhead, *Social Purpose: A Contribution to a Philosophy of Civic Society* (London, Allen & Unwin, 1918), 262–3.

[6]Bernard Bosanquet, 'The Teaching of Patriotism' (1911) in *Social and International Ideals: Being Studies in Patriotism* by Bernard Bosanquet (London, Macmillan, 1917), 3.

[7]Ibid., 3.

[8]Ibid., 16.

[9]David G. Ritchie, 'War and Peace' in David G. Ritchie, *Studies in Political and Social Ethics* (London, Sonnenschein, 1902), 147 and 161.

[10]David G. Ritchie, 'The Moral Problems of the War: In Reply to Mr J. M. Robertson', *International Journal of Ethics*, 11 (1900–1), 494.

[11]Ritchie, 'War and Peace', 147–8.

[12]Ritchie, 'The Moral Problems of the War', 494.

[13]Edmund Burke, *Works*, vol. VI, 85 and 163.

[14]Jones, 'The Obligations and Privileges of Citizenship', 127.

[15]Jones, *WP*, 5.

[16]Ibid., 1 and 20.

[17]Ibid., 12. Cf. Jones, 'On Some of the Social and Economical Aspects of The Land Question in Wales', *Philosophical Society of Glasgow*, 1888, 3.

[18]Jones, 'Land Question in Wales', 5.

[19]Letter to Munro-Ferguson, 5 May 1893. TJC, Class U, vol. ii, fols. 66–61/2.

[20]Jones, *OM*, 132.

[21]Evidence to the Cross Royal Commission on the Working of the Elementary Education Acts, England and Wales, Third Report, London, Her Majesty's Stationery Office, 1887, 327.

[22]Ibid., 321 and 327. Also see John Hughes, 'Sir Henry Jones and the Cross Commission', *Aberystwyth Studies*, 5 (1923).

[23]Jones, 'The Land Question in Wales', 3, and, Jones, *WP*, 16.

[24]Henry Jones, contribution to the discussion, 'Home Rule for Wales', *Westminster Review*, 133 (1890), 401; *WP*, 22 and 39; and, letter from Jones to Monro Ferguson, 4 February, 1911, TJC, Class U, vol. ii, fols. 191–191/2. In a letter to Thomas E. Ellis, a Welsh Liberal MP from 1886, who became chief whip, Jones says: 'Bye the bye, I have met some of your leaders at Munro Ferguson's. They did not seem to me to take our Welsh Disestablishment question to heart as they should. They think all of us Welshmen a little wild on the matter.' Letter dated 7 January 1894. Thomas Edward Ellis Papers, NLW, Ellis 1069. For an account of Ellis's career see Neville Masterman, *The Forerunner:The Dilemmas of Tom Ellis 1859–1899* (Swansea, Christopher Davies, 1972).

[25]Jones, *WP*, 5.

[26]Gwyn A. Williams, *When Was Wales?* (Harmondsworth, Penguin, 1985), 226–7.

[27]Jones, 'The Function of a University', 6. Cf. 'For the British Empire is not the English Empire: it is English, Scotch, Welsh and Irish'. Henry Jones, 'The Ethical Demand of the Present Political Situation', *Hibbert Journal*, VIII (1909–10), 534.

[28]Jones, *WP*, 20.

[29]Jones, 'Home Rule for Wales', 403.

[30]J. H. Muirhead, 'What Imperialism Means', *The Fortnightly Review*, CCCCIV, NS 1 August 1900, p. 178.

[31]John Gallagher and Ronald Robinson, 'The Imperialism of Free Trade', *The Economic History Review*, 2nd series, VI (1953), 1–15. Also see Richard Koebner, 'The Concept of Economic Imperialism', *The Economic Review*, second series, II (1949), 1–29.

[32]E. J. Hobsbawm, *The Age of Empire: 1875–1914* (London, Weidenfeld and Nicolson, 1987), 69.

[33]The account of social imperialism given here is drawn from Bernard Semmel, *Imperialism and Social Reform: English Social-Imperial Thought 1895–1914* (London, Allen & Unwin, 1960).

[34]For a summary of Hobson's views see Peter Clarke, *Liberals and Social Democrats* (Cambridge, Cambridge University Press, 1978), 90–9.

[35]L. T. Hobhouse, 'The Foreign Policy of Collectivism', *Economic Review* (Christian Social Union), 9 (1899), 198.

[36]L. T. Hobhouse, *Democracy and Reaction* (London, Fisher Unwin, 1904), 5.

[37]Ibid., 12.

[38]Ibid., 45 and 31 respectively.

[39]Ibid., 47–8 and 147.

[40]Ibid., 157.

[41]See L. T. Hobhouse, *The Metaphysical Theory of the State: A Criticism* (London, Allen &Unwin, 1951: 1st publ. 1918).

[42]Hobhouse, *Democracy and Reaction*, 77–84.

[43]Ritchie, 'The Moral Problems of War', 497.

[44]Ritchie, 'War and Peace', 164.

[45]Jones, *WFSR*, 184–5.

[46]Henry Jones's reader's report on L. T. Hobhouse, *Progress and Reaction*, MA, 3rd series, vol. MCCI, fols. 120–5.

[47]Jones, *WFSR*, 193.

[48]Ibid., 192.

[49]Ibid., 193.

[50]Herbert Samuel, *Liberalism: An Attempt to State the Principles of Contemporary Liberalism* (London, Grant Richards, 1902), 345. Cf. Vincent and Plant, *Philosophy, Politics and Citizenship*, 89. Both Eric Stokes, who cites Bosanquet and Caird, and Peter Clarke, who cites Bosanquet, Caird and Muirhead, imply that avowed opposition to the Boer War entailed opposition to imperialism. See Eric Stokes, *The Political Ideas of English Imperialism: An Inaugural Lecture* (London, Oxford University Press, 1960), 16; and Clarke, *Liberals and Social Democrats*, 73. Caird opposed the Boer War and strongly protested against Oxford University conferring a doctorate on Cecil Rhodes in 1899. He had been offered the degree in 1892, before the Jameson Raid, but only decided to attend in 1899 when he heard that the Royals were to be present. For recollections of this incident by Caird's acquaintances see Jones (Sir Henry) and Muirhead (J. H.), 'Materials for *Life* of Edward Caird', Glasgow University Library, MS Gen. 1475. This is insufficient evidence to suggest he was anti-imperialist. Muirhead, as we shall see, certainly favoured a certain type of imperialism, whereas Bosanquet who was pro-Boer could accommodate Empire when nothing was allowed to interfere with the possibility of self-government. Because he believed that a genuine community, or general will, must be a condition of any unity of nations, any arrangement whereby the members were of unequal standing were united only by the imposition of an external law and could be justified only in terms of the potential end, that is, when members had been trained to attain freedom and equality and

either 'go their own way in peace, or choose to form an effective unity with the other members, which shall be a true state'. See 'The Function of the State in Promoting the Unity of Mankind' in Bosanquet, *Social and International Ideals*, 294. For Bosanquet's pro-Boer stance see J. H. Muirhead (ed.), *Bernard Bosanquet and His Friends* (London, Allen & Unwin, 1915), 95.

[51]Henry Jones, 'The Moral Aspect of the Fiscal Question' (1903–4) reprinted in *WFSR*, 121–2.

[52]Ibid., 129.

[53]Ibid., 132.

[54]Ibid., 131.

[55]For the similarities between Green and Bosanquet in this respect see Peter Nicholson, *The Political Philosophy of the British Idealists* (Cambridge, Cambridge University Press, 1990), 80.

[56]Jones, *WFSR*, 135–6.

[57]Ibid., 150.

[58]Ibid., 184.

[59]Henry Jones, 'A League of Learning', *Rice University Studies* (Houston, Texas, 1919), 291.

[60]Henry Jones, 'The Ethical Demand of the Present Political Situation', *Hibbert Journal*, VII (1909–10).

[61]Jones, 'Why We are Fighting', 56.

[62]Ibid., 56–7.

[63]Muirhead, *Reflections by a Journeyman*, 112 and 114.

[64]Muirhead, 'What Imperialism Means', 177.

[65]Ibid., 183.

[66]Burke, Works, II, 272. Cf. *Works*, V, 44.

[67]Jones, 'A League of Learning', 292; and Jones, PC, 26.

[68]Jones, 'The Ethical Demand', 530.

[69]Jones, 'Extracts From Addresses', *Rice University Studies*, vol. IV, 339–40. Despite many inconveniences Britain had, Jones thought, tried many new experiments in government and in establishing a united South Africa in which people of British and Dutch Boer descent were of equal status, she had been generous to a fault, Jones, 'The Ethical Demand', 530.

[70]Henry Jones, letter to Munro-Ferguson, 27 February 1916. TJC, Class U, vol. iii, fols. 26/2.

[71]Jones, 'The Ethical Demand', 533.

[72]Depending upon how the evidence was read different conclusions could be drawn. Edward Pulsford in his article 'An Australian Lesson', *The Nineteenth Century*, XXIV (1888) argues that in every respect free trade proves to be superior to protectionism. On the other hand G. H. D. Gossip, in his article 'Protection versus Free Trade in Australia', *Fortnightly Review*, 47 (1890), argues the exact opposite.

[73]See W. Pember Reeves, *State Experiments in Australia and New Zealand*, introduced by John Child (Melbourne, 1968: 1st publ. 1902) 2 vols.

[74]W. Pember Reeves, 'The Nation's Duties to the Empire', in J. E. Hand and Charles Gore (eds.), *Good Citizenship* (London, George Allen, 1899), 260. Cf. John Watson, *The State in Peace and War* (Glasgow, Maclehose, 1919), 273.

[75]Ibid., 263.

[76]Report of Jones's lecture 'The Making of Character', *Adelaide Register*, 15 August 1908.

[77]Edmund Burke, *Speeches on the Impeachment of Warren Hastings* (Delhi, Discovery, 1987), vol. I, 23.

[78]Ibid., 21.

[79]Burke, *Works*, II, 149–50 and 199.

[80]This, of course, is the thrust of Burke's case against Warren Hastings.

[81]Burke, *Works*, II 184.

[82]Jones, 'A League of Learning', 291.

[83]Jones, 'The Making of Character', *Adelaide Advertiser*.

[84]Watson, *State in Peace and War*, 273.

[85]Hetherington and Muirhead, *Social Purpose: A Contribution to a Philosophy of Civic Society*, 278–9. Even Ritchie was of the opinion that any conquest of another people could only be justified if it was 'followed by the introduction of better government and a higher type of civilization than the conquered people enjoyed before', Ritchie, 'Moral Problems of the War', 501.

[86]Jones, 'A League of Learning', 291.

[87]Jones, 'The Ethical Demand', 530.

[88]Jones, *PC*, 26, and 'A League of Learning', 292.

[89]Jones, *WP*, 19–20. Cf. Bosanquet, *Philosophical Theory of the State*, lvi-lvii.

[90]Jones, *IPC*, 70. Jones may have come to hold this view as a result of visiting his son Harry in Burma.

[91]Jones, *Wales and Its Prospects*, 20

[92]Muirhead, 'What Imperialism Means', 186. Cf. Muirhead, *The Service of the State*, 106.

[93]Watson, *State in Peace and War*, 274.

[94]Hobhouse, 'Foreign Policy of Collectivism', 215.

[95]Hobhouse, *Democracy and Reaction*, 45.

[96]Ibid., 47.

[97]Ibid., 154.

[98]L. T. Hobhouse, *Liberalism* (London, Oxford University Press, 1942: 1st publ. 1911) 239.

NOTES TO CHAPTER EIGHT (pp. 155–77)

[1]Jones, *PC*, 50.

[2]G. W. F. Hegel, *Philosophy of Right*, tr. T. M. Knox (Oxford, Oxford University Press, 1967), pars. 322 and 331. Individuality is a technical term within philosophical idealism, and need not imply a person or an organism. Andrew Vincent defines it in these terms: 'Individuality was a logical concept which implied a comprehensive unity, completeness, wholeness and coherence. The

more perfect individuality was the more self-consistent and self-complete', Andrew Vincent, 'Can Groups be Persons?' *Review of Metaphysics*, 42 (1989), 695.

[3]Johann Kaspar Bluntschli, *The Theory of the State*, translated from the sixth German edition by D. G. Ritchie, P. E. Matheson and R. Lodge (Oxford, Clarendon Press, 1893: 3rd edn.), 22.

[4]Ibid., 23.

[5]Henrich von Treitschke, *Politics*, tr. by Blanche Dugdale and Torben de Bille with an introduction by Arthur James Balfour (London, Constable, 1916), 16.

[6]Ibid., 64 and 97.

[7]Ibid., 64–5.

[8]Ibid., 105.

[9]Ibid., vol.II, 591.

[10]Hegel, *Philosophy of Right*, par. 324(A). Bernhardi approvingly quotes Treitschke in the following condemnation of the desire for peace: 'This desire for peace has rendered most civilized nations anaemic, and marks a decay of spirit and political courage such as has often been shown by a race of Epigoni. "It has always been", H. von Treitschke tells us, "the weary, spiritless, and exhausted ages which have played with the dream of perpetual peace."' Friedrich von Bernhardi, *Germany and the Next War*, tr. by Allen H. Powles (London, Arnold, 1914), 17.

[11]Ibid., 18 and 21.

[12]Ibid., 34.

[13]A. C. Bradley, for example, argues that: 'It is true that in Hegel's *Rechtsphilosophie* there are a few expressions which, taken in isolation and exaggerated as a philosopher's ideas are apt to be, might do harm; but in all its pages, while there is much about will and the will for good, there is little enough about force'. A. C. Bradley, 'International Morality: The United States of Europe', *The International Crisis in its Ethical and Psychological Aspects* by Eleanor M. S. Sidgwick, Gilbert Murray, A. C. Bradley, L. P. Jacks, G. F. Stout and Bernard Bosanquet (London, Oxford University Press, 1915), 76: Cf. John Watson, 'German Philosophy and the War', *Queen's Quarterly*, XXIII (1916), 366; John Watson, 'German Philosophy and Politics', *Queen's Quarterly*, XXII (1915), 330; J. H. Muirhead, *German Philosophy and the War*, Oxford Pamphlets 1914–15 (Oxford, Clarendon Press, 1915), 3, 21 and 25–6; J. H. Muirhead, *German Philosophy in Relation to the War* (London, Murray, 1917), 3, 36, 39, 85 and 102. Also see John Morrow, 'British Idealism, "German Philosophy" and the First World War', *Australian Journal of Politics and History*. 28 (1982), 380–90.

[14]W. R. Sorley, 'The State and Morality', *The International Crisis: The Theory of the State* by Louise Creighton, W. R. Sorley, J. S. MacKenzie, A. D. Lindsay, H. Rashdall and Hilda Oakeley (Oxford, Oxford University Press, 1916), 38–9. Sorley was one of the contributors to the Idealist testament, *Essays in Philosophical Criticism*.

[15]J. S. MacKenzie, 'Might and Right', *International Crisis: The Theory of the State*, 60.

[16]Ernest Barker, *Nietzsche and Treitschke: The Worship of Power in Modern Germany*, Oxford Pamphlets 1914 (London, Oxford University Press, 1914), 4.

[17]George Santayana, *Egotism in German Philosophy* (London, Dent, 1940: 1st edn. publ. 1916), 82–3. Cf. ibid., 6–7, and 169.

[18]Commenting upon the self-confessed selective and impressionistic account which Santayana gives, F. C. S. Schiller makes the amusing observation that 'he has not merely cut up German philosophy but has put it together again with an anatomical skill exceeding Wells's "Dr. Moreau".' See review of *Egotism in German Philosophy*, in *Mind*, NS XXVI (1917), 224.

[19]John Dewey, *German Philosophy and Politics* (New York, Books for Libraries, 1970, repr. of 2nd edn. 1942: 1st edn. 1915), 63 and 69.

[20]Ibid., 84 and 87.

[21]Ibid., 98.

[22]Ibid., 126.

[23]Ibid., 135.

[24]Letter from Henry Jones to Harry Reichel, 12 May 1915, TJC, Class U, vol. iii, fol. 3. He thought it right that Haldane should not make public his concerns because of the danger of exacerbating a delicate situation, and thought it preposterous that Haldane should be unpopular during the war because of his known liking for German philosophy. Ibid., and 5 March, 1916, fol. 27/2.

[25]Hetherington, *Life and Letters*, 121.

[26]Jones, 'Obligations and Privileges', 165.

[27]Jones, 'Philosophical Landmarks', 216.

[28]Jones, 'North Wales Heroes Memorial Speech', 11.

[29]Jones, 'Why We Are Fighting', 61.

[30]Jones, 'Obligations and Privileges', 137.

[31]Jones, 'Why We Are Fighting', 61.

[32]Jones, 'North Wales Heroes Memorial Speech', 11

[33]Jones, 'Why We Are Fighting', 62. Also see Jones, 'Ethical and Religious Problems', 36.

[34]Morrow, 'British Idealism, "German Philosophy" and the First World War', 381.

[35]Dewey, *German Philosophy and Politics*, 139.

[36]F. C. S. Schiller, review of *German Philosophy and Politics* by John Dewey, *Mind*, NS XXV (1916), 254.

[37]Hobhouse, *Questions of War and Peace*, 19; and Hobhouse, *Metaphysical Theory of the State*, 23.

[38]Hobhouse, *Democracy and Reaction*, 81; William Clark, 'Bismarck', *The Contemporary Review*, 75 (1899), 1–2; Hobhouse, *Questions of War and Peace*, 19; Hobhouse, *Metaphysical Theory of the State*, 6.

[39]See D. Boucher, *The Social and Political Thought of R. G. Collingwood* (Cambridge, Cambridge University Press, 1989), 187.

[40]Hobhouse, *Democracy and Reaction*, 80.

[41]Hobhouse, *Metaphysical Theory of the State*, 6.

[42]Ibid., 24.

[43]J. A. Hobson, 'The War and British Liberties', *The Nation*, 10 June 1916, p.307. We would like to thank David Blaazer of the Australian National University for bringing this item to our attention.

[44]Ibid., 308.

[45]Hobhouse, *Metaphysical Theory of the State*, especially lecture IV; and G. D. H. Cole, 'Conflicting Social Obligations', *Proceedings of the Aristotelian Society*, 15 (1914–15), 150, 153–4, 157 and 159; and G. D. H. Cole, 'Symposium: The Nature of the State in View of its External Relations', *Proceedings of the Aristotelian Society*, XVI (1915–16), 313–4, and 323–5. Bosanquet is also the target of Ralph Barton Perry's criticism of the Absolute Idealist conception of the state. *The Present Conflict of Ideas* (London, Longmans Green, 1918), chapters XVIII-XIX.

[46]Hobson, 'War and British Liberties', 308.

[47]Jones, reader's report on Hobhouse, *Metaphysical Theory of the State*, 117. For Bosanquet's own defence see 'Note on Mr Cole's Paper', *Proceedings of the Aristotelian Society*, 15 (1914–15), 161–2; and Bosanquet, *Philosophical Theory of the State*, (3rd edn. 1920), xii-xvi, and liv-lix.

[48]Jones, *PC*, 158.

[49]Jones, 'Ethical and Religious Problems', 26.

[50]Jones, *PC*, 157.

[51]Ibid., 158, Pacificists, in Jones's view, fall outside this category, because 'an ignorant will is a bad will'. Letter to Henry Hadow, 16 April 1919. TJC, Class U, vol.iii, 94/2.

[52]Jones, *PC*, 63.

[53]Jones, 'Ethical and Religious Problems', 33–4; and Jones, *PC*, 169–77; Haldar, *Neo-Hegelianism*, 362–3; and Jones, *WFSR*, 215–16.

[54]Jones, *PC*, 149.

[55]Cole, 'The Nature of the State in view of its External Relations', 323–4.

[56]Hobhouse, *Metaphysical Theory of the State*, 25.

[57]Ibid., 79.

[58]Hobhouse, *Democracy and Reaction*, 87.

[59]Hobhouse, 'Foreign Policy of Collectivism', 216.

[60]Hobhouse, *Democracy and Reaction*, 196.

[61]Ibid., 199–200.

[62]Ibid., 207.

[63]Hobhouse, 'Foreign Policy of Collectivism', 215.

[64]J. A. Hobson, 'Is International Government Possible', *Hibbert Journal*, 15 (1916–17), 203.

[65]Hobhouse, *Questions of War and Peace*, 220–21.

[66]Hobhouse, *Metaphysical Theory of the State*, 24.

[67]Hegel, *Philosophy of Right*, 11; and Bosanquet, *Philosophical Theory of the State*, 232. Bosanquet argues elsewhere: 'you should remember that philosophy can tell you no new facts and can make no discoveries. All that it can tell you is the significance of what you already know. And if you know little or nothing,

philosophy can tell you little or nothing'. Bernard Bosanquet, *The Essentials of Logic* (London, Macmillan, 1903), 166.

[68]Bradley, *Ethical Studies*, 193; and Watson, 'German Philosophy and Politics', 330.

[69]Metz, *Hundred Years of Philosophy*, 302.

[70]Jones, 'Francis Hutcheson', 20.

[71]Jones, *PC*, 35.

[72]Letter from Jones to Henry Hadow, 14 July 1918. TJC, Class U, vol. iii, 65/2.

[73]Hegel, *Philosophy of Right*, 213–14 and 297.

[74]Bradley, *Ethical Studies*, 342; Bosanquet, 'Patriotism in the Perfect State', 150; and Bosanquet, *Social and International Ideals*, 291.

[75]*Bosanquet and His Friends*, Muirhead (ed.), 164. Cf. Bosanquet, 'Patriotism in the Perfect State', 136.

[76]Ritchie, 'The Moral Problem of the War', 495; and Bosanquet, 'Patriotism in a Perfect State', 149.

[77]Ritchie, 'War and Peace', 156.

[78]Ibid., 136. He also argues that: 'The evils of war may have to be endured for the sake of a more lasting and more widespread peace than could be obtained without them'. Ritchie, 'The Moral Problems of War', 505.

[79]Green, *Principles of Political Obligations*, 167.

[80]D. A. Routh, 'The Philosophy of International Relations: T. H. Green versus Hegel', *Politica*, III (1938), 230.

[81]T. H. Green, *Lectures on the Principles of Political Obligation*, 166, 170 and 173. Watson, *State in Peace and War*, 248–450; Bosanquet, *Social and International Ideals*, 277–8. For the similarities between Green and Bosanquet see Peter Nicholson, *The Political Philosophy of the British Idealists*, 221–9. Cf Muirhead and Hetherington, *Social Purpose*, 275–6.

[82]Bosanquet, *Some Suggestions in Ethics*, 141 and 243.

[83]Bosanquet, *Social and International Ideals*, 277.

[84]Bosanquet, 'Patriotism and the Perfect State', 134; and Bosanquet, *Social and International Ideals*, 16.

[85]Bosanquet, *Philosophical Theory of the State*, l.

[86]Jones, 'Ethical and Religious Problems', 31; Jones, *WFSR*, 121, and 125; Jones, Obligations and Privileges', 140.

[87]Jones, 'Ethical and Religious Problems', 37.

[88]Ibid., 35. Cf. Sorley, 'State and Morality', 52.

[89]Ibid., 37; and Jones, 'Why We are Fighting', 56–7 and 58; and *PC*, 65 and 73.

[90]Jones, 'Obligations and Privileges', 143 and 156; Jones, 'Why We are Fighting', 56; Jones *PC*, 95–6; and Jones, 'Ethical and Religious Problems', 22.

[91]Jones says: 'The true good of the state is at the same time the true good of humanity and of the individual', *PC*, 70.

[92]Jones, *PC*, 111.

[93]Jones, 'Why We are Fighting', 63.

[94]Jones, *ELE*, 257–8. Cf. A.C. Bradley, 'International Morality', 60.

[95]Jones, 'Why We are Fighting', 64.

[96]Jones, *WFSR*, 216.

[97]Jones, 'Why We are Fighting', 59.

[98]Hetherington, *Life and Letters*, 124.

[99]Jones, 'Why We are Fighting', 56.

[100]Hegel, *Philosophy of Right*, 215 and 297.

[101]See Vincent, *Theories of the State*, 134.

[102]Viscount Haldane, *Selected Addresses and Essays* (London, Murray, 1928), 68.

[103]Ibid., 82; Ritchie, 'Moral Problems of the War', 495; and, Bosanquet, *Philosophical Theory of the State*, lix; and, Muirhead (ed.), *Bosanquet and His Friends*, 164.

[104]Bosanquet, 'Patriotism in the Perfect State', 137 and 149.

[105]Bosanquet, *Philosophical Theory of the State*, l; and Muirhead (ed.), *Bosanquet and His Friends*, 162–3.

[106]Ritchie, 'War and Peace', 170. Cf. ibid., 160; and Ritchie, 'Moral Problems of the War', 504; Also see Sorley, 'State and Morality', 49 and 52; Hetherington and Muirhead, *Social Purpose*, 286–90; Green, *Lectures on the Principles of Political Obligation*, 179.

[107]Jones, 'Obligations and Privileges', 136–8.

[108]Jones, *IPC*, 212.

[109]Henry Jones, *Form the League of Peace Now: An Appeal to my Fellow Citizens* (London, League of Nations Union, 1918), 6.

[110]Ibid., 10; and Jones, 'Privileges and Obligation', 136–40.

[111]Jones, *ELE*, 249.

[112]Jones, 'League of Learning', 299.

[113]Jones, 'Form the League of Peace Now', 14–15. He says in a letter dated September 1918: 'I want the churches to fling *all* their power into securing "a lasting peace".' TJC, Class U, vol.iii, 72/2.

[114]Jones, *SP*, 64–5.

[115]Jones, 'Form the League of Peace Now', 15–16.

[116]Jones, 'Ethical and Religious Problems', 41. Bosanquet says, 'I do not believe that any moral being can divest itself of moral responsibility or limit that responsibility's *ultima ratio*'. Bosanquet, *Philosophical Theory of the State*, l.

NOTES TO CONCLUSION (pp. 178–83)

[1]Richard Norman, *Hegel's Phenomenology: A Philosophical Introduction* (London, Chatto & Windus, 1976), chapter one. Our summary of Jones's principles here draws freely on David Boucher, 'Practical Hegelianism: Henry Jones's Lecture Tour of Australia', *Journal of the History of Ideas*, 51 (1990).

[2]Michael Oakeshott, *On Human Conduct* (Oxford, Clarendon Press, 1975); Michael Oakeshott, 'The Rule of Law' in *On History and Other Essays* (Oxford, Blackwell, 1983); Paul Franco, *The Political Philosophy of Michael Oakeshott* (New Haven and London, Yale University Press, 1990)

[3]See D. Boucher, 'Reconciling Ethics and Interests in the Person of the State: The International Dimension', in *Ethics and Foreign Policy*, Paul Keele (ed.) (Sydney, Allen & Unwin, 1992).

BIBLIOGRAPHY

PUBLISHED WRITINGS OF SIR HENRY JONES[1]

'The Social Organism' in A. Seth and R. B. Haldane (eds.), *Essays in Philosophical Criticism* (London, Longmans, 1881).

'On Some of the Social and Economic Aspects of the Land Question in Wales' (Philosophical Society of Glasgow, 1888).

Morality as Freedom (London, Swan Sonnenschein, 1888). Also published in *Time*, NS, 7 (1888).

Wales and Its Prospects (Wrexham, North Wales Liberal Federation, no date. Preface dated 1889). Simultaneous Welsh edition.

'Home Rule For Wales', *Westminster Review*, CXXXIII (1890).

Browning as a Philosophical and Religious Teacher (Glasgow, Maclehose, 1891).

'The Nature and Aims of Philosophy', *Mind* NS II (1893).

'Idealism and Epistemology', *Mind*, NS II (1893), in two parts.

Browning as a Dramatic Poet (Boston, Poet-Lore, 1894).

'Is the Order of Nature Opposed to the Moral Life?' An Inaugural Lecture delivered in the University of Glasgow on 23 October 1894–5 (Glasgow, Maclehose, 1894).

'The Higher Learning in its Bearing Upon the National Life of Wales', An Address delivered at the closing ceremony of the session 1894–5, 28 June 1895 (Bangor, Jarvis and Foster, 1895).

A Critical Account of the Philosophy of Lotze: The Doctrine of Thought (Glasgow, Maclehose, 1895).

'Browning as a Dramatic Poet', read before the Boston Browning Society, 24 October 1893 (New York and London, Boston Browning Society Papers, 1886–97).

'Corporate and Individual Charity', Sixth Annual Conference of the Charity and Relief Societies of the United Kingdom held in Glasgow, 11 to 13 May, 1897 (Glasgow, Glasgow Charity Organization Society, 1897).

'Principal Caird', an Address delivered to the Moral Philosophy class on the opening day of the Session 1898–99 (Glasgow, Maclehose, 1898).

'How to Attain Liberal Unity', *New Liberal Review*, No. 21 (1902).

'The Late Professor Adamson', *Mind*, NS XI (1902).

'The Present Attitude of Reflective thought Towards Religion', in two parts, *Hibbert Journal*, I and II (1902–3 and 1903–4).

Scottish Education Reform: A Scheme of District School Boards and a National Council, with Charles M. Douglas (Glasgow, Maclehose, 1903).

'The Moral Aspect of the Fiscal Problem', *Hibbert Journal*, II (1903–4). Reprinted in *WFSR*, 1910.

'Mr Balfour as a Sophist', *Hibbert Journal*, III (1904–5).

'The Philosophy of Martineau in Relation to the Idealism of the Present Day'. Being an Address delivered in Manchester College, Oxford at the celebration of the Centenary of Dr Martineau (London, Macmillan, 1905).

'The Child and Heredity' in Thomas Stephens (ed.), *The Child and Religion* (London, Williams and Norgate, 1905).

'The Immortality of the Soul in the Poems of Tennyson and Browning'. A lecture delivered at Essex Hall (London, Philip Green, 1905).

'The Library as a Maker of Character'. An Address given to the Annual Meeting of the Subscribers to Stirling and Glasgow's Public Library, April 1905 (Glasgow, Aird and Coghill, 1905). Reprinted in *ELE* 1924.

'The Function of the University in the State'. An Inaugural Lecture delivered for the Session, 1905–6, at the University College of Wales, Aberystwyth, Wednesday, 4 October 1905 (Aberystwyth, *Welsh Gazette*, 1905).

'The University of Wales: The Line of Its Growth'. An Address delivered at Cardiff, 3 October 1905 (Bangor, Jarvis and Foster, 1905).

Social Responsibilities: Lectures to Businessman (Glasgow, Maclehose, 1905).

'Y Diwygiad: a'r hyn eill ddod ohono' (Caernarfon, Cwmni Cyhoeddwyr Cymraeg, 1905).

'The Working Faith of the Social Reformer' in four parts, *Hibbert Journal*, IV (1905–6).

'Francis Hutcheson'. A Discourse delivered in the University of Glasgow on Commemoration Day 18 April 1906 (Glasgow, Maclehose, 1906).

'Divine Immanence', *Hibbert Journal*, V (1906–7).

'Divine Transcendence'. An Address given at Manchester College, Oxford, on the occasion of the opening of the 122nd Session, 14 October 1907.

'Idealism and Politics', in two parts, *Contemporary Review*, 42 (1907). Reprinted in *WFSR*.

'Will Jones: 1889–1906. A Memoir' [1907] printed in Hetherington, *Life and Letters of Sir Henry Jones*.

'The Idealism of Jesus', *Hibbert Journal*, Supplement for 1909.

Idealism As A Practical Creed (Glasgow, Maclehose, 1909).

'Tennyson', *Proceedings of the British Academy*, iv (1909–10) and *Hibbert Journal*, VIII (1909–10). Reprinted in *ELE*.

'The Ethical Demand of the Present Political Situation', *Hibbert Journal*, (1909–10).

'Ethics and Politics'. Lecture to the Friend's Social Union, London. *Quarterly Examiner*, XLIV (1910).

The Working Faith of the Social Reformer and other Essays (London, Macmillan, 1910).

'Modern Science and Philosophical Thought Regarding Human Society' in J. B. Paton, P. W. Bunting and A. E. Garvie (eds.), *Christ and Civilization* (London, 1910).

Dinasyddiaeth Bur ac Areithiau Ereill (Caernarfon, Undeb Chwarelwyr Gogledd Cymru, no date: preface dated 16 September 1911).

'The Corruption of the Citizenship of the Working Man', *Hibbert Journal*, X (1911–12).

'The Immanence of God and the Individuality of Man', Provincial Assembly Lecture, Manchester (Manchester, Rawson, 1912).

Social Powers: Three Popular Lectures on the Environment, the Press and the Pulpit (Glasgow, Maclehose, 1913).

'Why We Are Fighting', *Hibbert Journal* , XIII (1914–15).

'Philosophical Landmarks. Being a Survey of the Recent Gains and the Present Problems of Reflective Thought', *Rice Institute Studies*, I (1915).

'Morality and Its Relation to the War' in J. E. Carpenter (ed.), *Ethical and Religious Problems of the War* (London, Lindsey, 1916).

'Robert Browning and Elizabeth Barret Browning', in *Cambridge History of English Literature*, XIII (Cambridge, Cambridge University Press, 1916). Reprinted in *ELE* 1924.

'The Huge Machinery of Sin and Sorrow', *The Free Catholic*, I (1916).

'The Education of the Citizen', *The Round Table*, VII (1916–17).

Speeches Delivered by the Right Hon. Lord Kenyon and Prof. Sir Henry Jones in the Town Hall, Holyhead, 24 April 1917. North Wales Heroes Memorial (Bangor, North Wales Chronicle Co., Ltd., Caxton Press, 1917).

'Form A League of Peace Now: An Appeal to My Fellow-Citizens' (London, League of Nations Union, 1918). Series 2, pamphlet no. 5.

'A League of Learning', *Rice Institute Studies*, VI (1919).

'The Obligations and Privileges of Citizenship – A Plea for the Study of Social Science', *Rice Institute Studies*, VI (1919).

Extract from remarks made on various public occasions during the Rice Institute visit of the British Educational Mission, *Rice Institute Studies*, VI (1919).

The Principles of Citizenship (London, Macmillan, 1919).

The Life and Philosophy of Edward Caird (Glasgow, Maclehose, 1921), with J. H. Muirhead.

A Faith That Enquires. The Gifford Lectures delivered in the University of Glasgow in the years 1920 and 1921 (London, Macmillan, 1922).

Old Memories. Autobiography of Sir Henry Jones, C. H., Late Professor of Moral Philosophy in the University of Glasgow, edited by Thomas Jones (London, Hodder and Stoughton, 1922).

Essays on Literature and Education, ed. H. J. W. Hetherington (London, Hodder & Stoughton, 1924).

EDITED WORKS

A History of the Problems of Philosophy by Paul Janet and Gabrielle Seailles, tr. Ada Monahan (London, Macmillan, 1902).

Encyclopaedia of Philosophical Sciences, ed. W. Windelland and A. Ruge. Vol. I, *Logic*, tr. B. E. Meyer (London, Macmillan, 1913).

A Study of Calvin and Other Papers, A. Menzies (London, Macmillan, 1918).

The Schools of Philosophy: A History of the Evolution of Philosophical Thought:

1. *The Evolution of Educational Theory* by John Adams (London, Macmillan, 1912).
2. *Greek Philosophy. Part I Thales to Plato* by John Burnett (London, Macmillan, 1914).

CRITICAL NOTICES AND REVIEWS

H. Gallwitz, *Das Problem der Ethik in der Genenwart*, in *Critical Review*, II (1892).

J. H. Muirhead, *Elements of Ethics*, in *International Journal of Ethics*, 3 (1892–3).

J. Friedlander and M. Berendt, *Der Pessimismus*, in *Critical Review*, IV (1894).

E. Dreher, *Der Materialismus*, in *Critical Review*, IV (1894).

Josiah Royce, *The World and the Individual*, two vols. in *Hibbert Journal*, (1902–3).

S. Dill, *Roman Society from Nero to Marcus Aurelius*, in *Hibbert Journal*, IV (1905–6).

A. C. Bradley, *Shakespearean Tragedy* , in *International Journal of Ethics*, XVI (1905–6).

Sociological Papers. Published by the Sociological Society in *Review of Theology and Philosophy*, I (1905–6).

A. Fouillée, *Le Moralisme de Kant et l'Amoralisme Contemporain*, in *Review of Theology and Philosophy*, 2 (1906–7).

Bernard Bosanquet, *The Meaning of Teleology*, in *Review of Theology and Philosophy*, 2 (1906–7).

H. Munsterberg, *The Eternal Life*, in *Review of Theology and Philosophy*, 2 (1906–7).

John Watson, *The Philosophical Basis of Religion: A Series of Lectures*, in *Hibbert Journal*, VI (1907–8).

Bernard Bosanquet, *The Principle of Individuality and Value* , in *Hibbert Journal*, X (1911–12).

Bernard Bosanquet, *Value and Destiny of the Individual*, in *Hibbert Journal*, XI (1912–13).

MANUSCRIPTS BY, OR RELATING TO, HENRY JONES

THE NATIONAL LIBRARY OF WALES, ABERYSTWYTH, DYFED[2]

The vast majority of manuscript material relating to Henry Jones is to be found in the Thomas Jones C. H. Collection. Many, but not all, of the letters Hector Hetherington used for *Life and Letters of Sir Henry Jones* are to be found in this collection. For the most part they are typed copies, the originals of which appear to have been destroyed. There are hundreds of other items which are not related to Hetherington's project.

Class U, vol. i: Correspondence between HJ and Thomas Jones, 1907–22 (136 items).

Class U, vol. ii: Correspondence between HJ and various correspondents 1878–1914.

Class U, vol. iii: Correspondence between HJ and various correspondents, 1915–22.

Class U, vol. iv: Papers mainly relating to HJ and to the publication of *Old Memories*, but includes 2 letters to HJ, and correspondence with Thomas Jones about HJ's death and autobiography. Includes a draft of the chapter which was excluded from *Old Memories* on Jones's work as a 'teacher and citizen of Glasgow'. Nothing remains of the account which Thomas Jones says Henry Jones dictated just before his death regarding his lecturing tours of USA and Australia, and of his visit to his eldest son in Burma. *Old Memories*, vii.

Class D, vol. iii, no. 24: letter from HJ to William George, 1919, printed in Welsh.

Class D, vol. xi, no. 15: copy letter, A. A. Bowman to HJ, 1917.

Class H, vol. xiii, nos. 1–4: Letters from HJ to Lloyd George and to Thomas Jones, 1915.

Class J. vol. i, No. 33: copy letter from Thomas Jones to HJ., 1915.

Class J, vol. 14 Nos. 18, 15, 34: copy letters from Thomas Jones to HJ, 1915.

General

NWL MS 5930B; No. 17: letter from HJ to Evan Davies, Trefriw, n.d.

NLW MS 9493B, includes 17 letters from HJ to the Revd H. Cernyw Williams, Corwen, 1897–1921, 10 of which are in Welsh.

NLW MS 10440C, Nos. 14–15: 2 letters from HJ to the Revd H. Cernyw Williams, Corwen, 1905 and 1919.

NLW MS 10572B, includes 1 letter from HJ to Howell Elvet Lewis, 1892, in Welsh.

NLW MS 10852C, includes 8 letters from HJ to E. W. Evans, 1883-1921, in Welsh, together with two copy replies, 1921 in Welsh.

NLW MS 12135C, includes 1 letter to Eleazar Roberts, Holylake, 1891.

NLW MS 16350D, comprises correspondence and papers relating to HJ's scheme to bring university culture closer to the Welsh people via the churches, and includes 1 copy letter from HJ to John Griffith with a copy of the reply, 1919.
NLW MS 194552D, No. 324: 1 letter from HJ to Stuart Rendel, 1891.
NLW MS 20471C, No. 2980: 1 letter from HJ to Lloyd George, 1905.
NLW MS 21482D, includes 2 letters from HJ to J. Nield, 1903.
NLW MS 21787E, ff. 19–20, 56, 77–8: 2 letters to Lloyd George and one in Welsh to his secretary, John Rowland, all 1906.
NLW MS 21788E, ff. 116–17, 140, 153–4, 159–60, 194, letters from HJ to Lloyd George, all 1907.

Sir Samuel T. Evans Papers:

No. 78: draft letter from Sir John Williams, probably to HJ, 1906.
Nos. 103-4: 2 copy letters from Lloyd George to HJ, 1907.

Thomas Edward Ellis Papers:

No.1069: 1 letter from HJ to TEE, 1894.

Mrs Yale, Llanbedrog Papers:

Nos. 126–31: 6 letters from HJ to Ellis Edwards, all 1884.

R. Vaughan Jones Papers:

Includes 1 postcard and 1 letter from HJ to RVJ, 1911.

Dr Griffith Evans:

No. 422: copy letter (15 pages) from GE to HJ, 1905.
No. 433: 1 letter from HJ to GE, 1904.
No. 443: letter from HJ to GE, 1905.
No. 446: transcripts by Dr Erie Evans of a letter from HJ to herself and her reply.

Edward Hall Purchase March 1971:

Includes 1 letter from HJ to William A. Bayley, 1914.

NLW MS 7817A, Notes by Sir Henry Lewis on HJ, 1910s. (7ff).
NLW MS 9394C, Notes taken by Edward Edwards at HJ's lectures on Kant in Bangor, n.d.
NLW MS 9409C, includes testimonial to Edward Edwards by HJ, 1892.
NLW 9848B, draft address, 1887, by HJ, in presenting a portrait of Edward Caird to the University of Glasgow. 8ff. in manuscript, followed by a printed brochure which includes the text of HJ's speech.
NLW MS 15631B, lecture on HJ in Welsh, n.d. (21pp.).
NLW MS 18284C, an essay entitled 'Syr Henry Jones, y dyn a'i waith' (Sir Henry Jones, the man and his work), in Welsh, by 'Menlli', typescript. This appears to

have been entered for an eisteddfod competition. The author is unidentified, but the volume is from the library of E. E. Jones, Borth-y-gest.

T. Gwynn Jones Papers:

Includes a testimonial for TGJ by HJ, 1919.

Revd J. Dyfnallt Owen MSS and Papers:

Includes a lecture on HJ by an unidentified author, in Welsh, n. d. (20c)

Papurau W. J. Gruffydd:

No. 126 includes a typescript article 'The Late Sir Henry Jones and the University College of Wales, Aberystwyth', which was published in *Dragon*, xlv (1922–3), pp. 178–80, where it is signed by the editor, apparently Iorwerth C. Peate.
No. 885, a letter from T. H. Williams, in Welsh, 1929, includes a reference to HJ.

J. L. Williams Papers:

No. 3/8 contains the text of a lecture in Welsh, 'Y Diwygiad a'r hyn eill ddod ohono' delivered by HJ to the Quarrymen's Annual Labour Festival at Caernarfon, 1 May 1905. Subsequently published in Welsh.

THE TRUSTEES OF 'Y CWM'.

Moral Philosophy Lectures (Pass), vols. 1 and II 1897–8.
Moral Philosophy Lectures (Honours), vol. 1 1899–1900.

BALLIOL COLLEGE LIBRARY, OXFORD UNIVERSITY.

Caird Papers:

7. Letters of John Watson to Caird and Sir Henry Jones, 1880–1911; includes 1 letter from Watson to Jones dated 3 October 1911.

EDINBURGH UNIVERSITY LIBRARY, SCOTLAND.

MS Gen 1416, ff. 63–69. Letters from Henry Jones to Norman Kemp Smith.

NATIONAL LIBRARY OF SCOTLAND, EDINBURGH.

MS 10527, ff. 36, 40, 270. Letters to Sir Patrick Geddes, 1895.
MS 9987, f. 63. Letter to Sir William Craigie, 1897.
MS 6019, ff. 135, 146. Letters to Lord Haldane, 1906.
MS 5915, f. 36. Letter to Lord Haldane, 1921.

BODLEIAN LIBRARY, OXFORD UNIVERSITY.

H. A. L. Fisher Papers:

MSS Fisher 61, ff.. 214–15, 218–19. Letters from HJ.

MSS Fisher 62, ff.. 70–1, 259–260. Letters from HJ.
MS AUTOG e 12, ff.. 119–126. Letters to Mrs Thompson.
MS TOP OXON e 417, ff. 1–9. R. V. Lennard's notes on the Dunkin Lectures on Sociology, Nov. 1904. Delivered by Henry Jones at Manchester College.

Gilbert Murray Papers:

MS 3, ff. 193–5. Letter from HJ.
MS 7, ff. 144–5. Letter from HJ.
MS 9, fol. 179–180. Letter from HJ.
MS 17, ff. 40, and 151. Letters from HJ.
MS 19, ff.. 101–2. Letter from HJ.
MS 37, ff. 169–70 and 203–4. Letters from HJ.
MS 403, ff. 110, and 121. Letters from HJ.
MS 536, ff. 85–6 and 192–3. Letters from HJ.

BRITISH MUSEUM LIBRARY, LONDON

Macmillan Archives:

MSS Add. No. 55161–12. 1st series vols. MCLXIX – MCLXXV, 1895–1899. 8201. [Chadwyck-Healy microfilm reel 3].
MSS Add No. 55988. 3rd series, vols MCCI – MCCXI, 1895–1924. [Chadwyck-Healy microfilm reel 7].
Includes hundreds of reports and letters among which are to be found comments on all the leading thinkers of the time. For example, Douglas Ainslie, J. B. Baillie, H. Bergson, J. B. Bury, B. Croce, R. G. Collingwood, H. Fielding, G. Gentile, W. R. Boyce Gibson, L. T. Hobhouse, J. A. Hobson, B. Kidd, H. Lotze, W. Mitchell, John Laird, D. G. Ritchie, Guido de Ruggiero and Henry Sturt.

READING UNIVERSITY LIBRARY

Macmillan Archives:

MSS 1089, Letters from HJ to Frederick and William Edward Frank Macmillan.

GLASGOW UNIVERSITY LIBRARY

MS Gen. 1475. Henry Jones and J. H. Muirhead, 'Materials for Life of Caird'. Includes drafts of sections of chapters and material by friends of Caird for the purpose of writing the volume which Jones co-authored with Muirhead.
MS Gen 50512. Includes a letter to J. B. Baillie.

UNIVERSITY OF NEWCASTLE LIBRARY

Bosanquet Papers:

Includes 6 letters from HJ to Bernard Bosanquet.
1 A (1) i. One letter to HJ.
1 A (7). Five letters to HJ.

UNIVERSITY COLLEGE OF NORTH WALES, BANGOR
Letters to various correspondents mainly in Welsh.
MS 3248.76–93.
MS 3590. 55 and 56.
MS 5466. 135.
MS 20673. lxvi.
MS 385.
MS 32966.
MS 480. 77, 167–172.

MISCELLANEOUS WRITINGS CONCERNING SIR HENRY JONES

[Conventional books and articles are cited in the main bibliography of contemporary and secondary sources]

Report of the British Educational Mission (Manchester, Morris and Yeaman, 1919), written by J. Joly, Henry Jones, Henry Miers (Chairman), A. E. Shipley, Caroline F. E. Spurgeon, E. M. Walker.

Items by Henry Jones appeared in *Goleuad*, the official organ of the Welsh Calvinist Methodists.

Welsh Outlook had the serial rights to Henry Jones's *Old Memories*.

Evidence to the Royal Commission appointed to inquire into the working of the Elementary Education Acts. *Third Report* (London, Eyre and Spottiswoode, 1887), 320–30.

'Sir Henry Jones Dead: Romantic Career of Famous Welshman: From Cobbler's Bench to University Chair' by Thomas Jones, *Western Mail*, 6 February, 1922.

'Sir Henry Jones C. H.', by Thomas Jones, *Y Cymmrodor*, xxxii, 1922.

Revd Puleston Jones on Henry Jones's moral and social philosophy, in *Y Cymmrodor*, vol. xxxii, 1922.

'Sir Henry Jones Memorial Fund' appeal leaflet. Officers include J. Ramsay MacDonald and D. Lloyd George.

Henry Jones article in *The Welsh Leader*, 3 March 1904.

Peter Ellis Jones, thesis 'Bangor' held in Bangor City Library.

Megan Lloyd Ellis, *Hyfryd Lais Leila* (Llandysul, Gwasg Gomer, 1979). Includes a chapter on Henry Jones.

Jean Ware, 'Life With Taid Jones', *Y Gymdogaeth*, 1953, 1–9. (Reprinted from *The Liverpool Post*. 'Life With Father's Father' and 'Farewell Rewards and Fairies!').

Manchester Guardian, 4 December 1912, reported on 'Are Religious Truths Capable of Proof'. Lecture delivered on 3 December 1912 in Milton Hall (Congregation Church House), Manchester.

Fortuna Domus; A series of lectures delivered in University of Glasgow 1950–51 to commemorate the fifth century of its foundation (Glasgow, University of Glasgow, 1952),

'Sir Henry Jones Memorial', *North Wales Times*, 21 July 1934.

Henry Jones's lecture tour of Australia, July–August 1908 is well documented in the Australian press. Extensive reports on his life and lectures appear in *The Sydney Morning Herald, The Sydney Daily Telegraph, The Newcastle Morning Herald, The South Coast Mercury, The Illawara Mercury, The Melbourne Age, The Melbourne Argus, The Brisbane Courier, The Adelaide Advertiser*, and *The Adelaide Register*.

For related items see minutes of the University of Adelaide, Education Committee, Friday, 8 May 1908, and Letter book vol. 28, 912 (letter to Mungo MacCallum concerning arrangements for Jones's visit to Adelaide).

J. A. La Nauze and Elizabeth Nurser (eds.), *Walter Murdoch and Alfred Deakin on Books and Men* (Melbourne, Melbourne University Press, 1974). Contains letters concerning Henry Jones's visit to Australia.

Walter Murdoch, *Loose Leaves* (Melbourne, George Robertson, 1910). Contains reviews which refer to Jones. Reprinted from *The Melbourne Argus*.

John Docker, 'Can the Centre Hold? Conceptions of the State 1890-1925', Sydney Labour History Group, *What Rough Beast? the State and Social Order in Australian History* (Sydney, Allen & Unwin, 1982). Includes reference to Jones's tour. Also see item under Boucher in main bibliography.

BIBLIOGRAPHY OF CONTEMPORARY AND SECONDARY SOURCES

Addison, W. G., 'Academic Reform at Balliol 1854-1882, T. H. Green and Benjamin Jowett', *Church Quarterly Review* (January 1952).

Allett, John, *New Liberalism: The Political Economy of J. A. Hobson* (Toronto, Toronto University Press, 1981).

Angell, Norman, *The Peace Treaty and the Economic Chaos of Europe* (London, Swarthmore, 1919).

Anonymous, 'Darwin on the Origin of Species', *Westminster Review*, NS XVII (1860).

——, 'The Apocalypse of War', *Hibbert Journal*, 14 (1915-16).

Archer, W., *Fighting A Philosophy*, Oxford Pamphlets 1914-15 (London, Oxford University Press, 1915).

Aristotle, *The Politics*, edited by Stephen Everson (Cambridge, Cambridge University Press, 1988).

Ashby, E., and Anderson, M., *Portrait of Haldane at Work on Education* (London, Macmillan, 1974).

Band, D. C., 'The Critical Reception of English Neo-Hegelianism in Britain and America, 1914–1960', *Australian Journal of Politics and History*, 26 (1980).

Barker, Ernest, *et al.*, *Why We Are at War: Great Britain's Case* (Oxford, Clarendon Press, 1914).

——, *Nietzsche and Treitschke: The Worship of Power in Modern Germany*, Oxford Pamphlets 1914 (London, Oxford University Press, 1914).

Barnett, Canon and H. O., *Practicable Socialism* (London, Longmans, 1888).

Beck, Lewis White, *A Commentary on Kant's Critique of Practical Reason* (Chicago, Chicago University Press, 1963).

Bernhardi, General Friedrich von, *Germany and the Next War* (London, Arnold, 1914).

Bernstein, G. L., *Liberalism and Liberal Politics in Edwardian England* (London, Allen & Unwin, 1986).

Best, G. (ed.), *The Industrial Syndicalist: Documents in Social History* (Nottingham, Spokesman, 1974).

Blewett, Neal, *The Peers, the Parties and the People: The General Election of 1910* (Toronto, University of Toronto Press, 1972).

Bluntschli, J. K., *The Theory of the State*, tr. from the sixth German edn. by D. G. Ritchie, P. E. Matheson, and R. Lodge (Oxford, Clarendon Press, 1898).

Bosanquet, Bernard, *Essays and Addresses* (London, Swan Sonnenschein, 1891).

——, (ed.), *Aspects of the Social Problem* (London, Macmillan, 1895).

——, *Psychology of the Moral Self* (London, Macmillan, 1897).

——, 'Hegel's Theory of the Political Organism', *Mind*, 7 (1898).

——, *The Civilization of Christendom* (London, Sonnenschein, 1899).

——, *The Essentials of Logic; Being Ten Lectures on Judgment and Inference* (London, Macmillan, 1903).

——, *The Value and Destiny of the Individual* (London, Macmillan, 1912).

——, *The Principle of Individuality and Value* (London, Macmillan, 1912).

——, 'Note on Mr Cole's Paper', *Proceedings of the Aristotelian Society*, NS XV (1914–15).

——, *Social and International Ideals; Being Studies in Patriotism* (London, Macmillan, 1917).

——, *Some Suggestions in Ethics* (London, Macmillan, 1918).

——, *The Philosophical Theory of the State* (London, Macmillan, 1965: 4th edn., 1st publ. 1923).

——, *The Meeting of Extremes in Contemporary Philosophy* (London, Macmillan, 1924).

Boucher, D., *Texts in Context: Revisionist Methods For Studying the History of Ideas* (Dordrecht, Martinus Nijhoff, 1985).

——, *The Social and Political Thought of R. G. Collingwood* (Cambridge, Cambridge University Press, 1989).

——, (ed.), *Essays in Political Philosophy by R. G. Collingwood* (Oxford, Clarendon Press, 1989).

——, 'Practical Hegelianism; Henry Jones's Lecture Tour of Australia', *Journal of the History of Ideas*, 51 (1990).

——, 'Michael Oakeshott 1901-1990: Politics in a Different Mode', *History of Political Thought* 12 (1991).

——, 'Evolution and Politics: The Naturalistic, Ethical and Spiritual Bases of Evolutionary Arguments', *The Australian Journal of Political Science*, 27 (1992).

——, 'Reconciling Ethics and Interests in the Person of the State' in *Ethics and Foreign Policy*, ed. Paul Keal (Sydney, Allen & Unwin, 1992).

Boucher, D. (ed.), *The New Leviathan*, revised edn. by R. G. Collingwood (Oxford, Clarendon Press, 1992)

Bradley, A. C., 'International Morality' in *The International Crisis and its Ethical and Psychological Aspects*, edited by Louise Creighton *et al.* (London, Oxford University Press, 1916).

Bradley, F. H., *Ethical Studies* (Oxford, Clarendon Press, 1927, 2nd edn: 1st edn. published 1876).

——, *Appearance and Reality* (Oxford, Clarendon Press, 1969; 1st publ. 1893).

——, *Essays On Truth and Reality* (Oxford, Clarendon Press, 1968: 1st publ. 1914).

Brailsford, H. N., *The War of Steel and Gold* (London, Bell, 1914).

——, *A League of Nations* (London, Headley, 1917).

——, *The Covenant of Peace: An Essay on the League of Nations* (London, Headley, 1918).

Bristow, E. J., 'The Liberty and Property Defence League and Individualism', *Historical Journal*, XVIII (1975).

Burke, Edmund, *Speeches on the Impeachment of Warren Hastings* (Delhi, Discovery, 1987).

Burns, C. D., 'The Idea of the State', *Mind*, NS XXVII (1918).

Burrow, J. W., *Evolution and Society: A Study in Victorian Social Theory* (Cambridge, Cambridge University Press, 1966).

Butlin, N. G., 'Colonial Socialism in Australia 1860–1900' in *The State and Economic Growth*, edited by H. G. J. Aitken (New York, Social Science Research Council, 1959).

Caillard, Emma Marie, 'Man in the Light of Evolution', *The Contemporary Review*, 64 (1893).

——, 'Evolution a Note of Christianity', *The Contemporary Review*, 64 (1893).

Caird, Edward, *A Critical Account of the Philosophy of Kant* (Glasgow, Maclehose, 1877).

——, 'The Problem of Philosophy at the Present Time', *Journal of Speculative Philosophy*, January 1882.

——, *Essays on Literature and Philosophy* (Glasgow, Maclehose, 1892), two vols.

——, *The Critical Philosophy of Immanuel Kant* (Glasgow, Maclehose, 1889), two vols.

——, *Individualism and Socialism: Inaugural Lecture to the Civic Society of Glasgow* (Glasgow, Maclehose, 1897).

——, *The Evolution of Religion* (Glasgow, Maclehose, 1899), two vols.

Callaghan, J., *Socialism in Britain* (Oxford, Blackwell, 1990).

Campbell, C. A., 'Philosophy', in *Fortuna Domus* (Glasgow, Maclehose, 1952).

Carpenter, J. Estlin (ed.), *Ethical and Religious Problems of the War: Fourteen Addresses* (London, Lindsay, 1916).

Carritt, E. F., 'An Ambiguity of the Word "Good"', *Proceedings of the British Academy*, 23 (1937).

Caton, H., *The Politics of Progress: The Origins and Development of the Commercial Republic, 1600–1835* (Gainesville, University of Florida Press, 1988).

Claeys, Gregory, *Citizens and Saints: Politics and Anti-Politics in Early British Socialism* (Cambridge, Cambridge University Press, 1989).

Clark, William, 'Bismarck', *The Contemporary Review*, 75 (1899).

Clarke, Peter, *Liberals and Social Democrats* (Cambridge, Cambridge University Press, 1978).

Clarke, P. F., *Lancashire and the New Liberalism* (Cambridge, Cambridge University Press, 1971).

Coker, Francis, W., *Organismic Theories of the State: Nineteenth Century Interpretations of the State as Organism or as Person* (New York, Columbia University Press, 1910).

Cole, G. D. H., 'Conflicting Social Obligations', *Proceedings of the Aristotelian Society*, 15 (1914–15).

——, 'Symposium: The Nature of the State in View of its External Relations', *Proceedings of the Aristotelian Society*, XVI (1915–16).

Collingwood, R. G., *Speculum Mentis* (Oxford, Clarendon Press, 1924).

——, *An Essay on Philosophical Method* (Oxford, Clarendon Press, 1977: 1st publ. 1932).

——, *An Essay on Metaphysics* (Oxford, Clarendon Press, 1940).

——, *Essays in Political Philosophy*, edited by D. Boucher (Oxford, Clarendon Press, 1989).

——, *The New Leviathan*, revised edn., edited by D. Boucher (Oxford, Clarendon Press, 1992)

Collini, Stefan, 'Hobhouse, Bosanquet and the State: Philosophical Idealism and Political Argument in England, 1888–1914', *Past and Present*, 72 (1976).

——, 'Sociology and Idealism in Britiain 1880–1920', *Archives Européennes de Sociologie*, 19 (1978).

——, *Liberalism and Sociology: L. T. Hobhouse and Political Argument in England 1880–1914* (Cambridge, Cambridge University Press, 1979).

——, 'Political Theory and the "Science of Society" in Victorian Britain', *Historical Journal*, XXIII (1980).

Conte Joseph le, 'The Theory of Evolution and Social Progress', *The Monist*, V (1895).

Croce, B., *Logic as the Science of the Pure Concept*, tr. Douglas Ainslie (London, Macmillan, 1917).

———, *Philosophy of the Practical: Economic and Ethic*, tr. Douglas Ainslie (London, Harrap, 1921).

Dangerfield, George, *The Strange Death of Liberal England* (London, MacGibbon & Kee, 1936).

Darwin, Charles, *The Origin of Species by Means of Natural Selection or the Preservation of Favoured Races in the Struggle for Life* (New York, Avenel, 1979).

Dennis, N. and Halsey, A. H., *English Ethical Socialism* (Oxford, Clarendon Press, 1988).

Dewey, John, *German Philosophy and Politics* (New York, Putman, 1942, 2nd edn: 1st edn. publ. 1915).

Dicey, A. V., *Lecture on the Relation Between Law and Public Opinion During the Nineteenth Century* (London, Macmillan, 1905)

Dickey, B., *No Charity There: A Short History of Social Welfare in Australia* (Melbourne, Nelson, 1980).

Dickinson, G. Lowes *The Choice Before Us* (London, Allen & Unwin, 1917).

Epstein, M. A., 'Some Recent German War Literature', *Hibbert Journal*, 14 (1915-16).

Evans, D., *Labour Strife in the South Wales Coalfield 1910–11* (Cardiff, Educational Publishing Company, 1911).

Evans, E. W., *The Miners of South Wales* (Cardiff, University of Wales Press, 1961).

Farrel, F., 'Australia: A Laboratory of Social Reform' in Australian Labor Party (New South Wales Branch), *Traditions of Reform in New South Wales* (Sydney, Pluto, 1987).

Fisher, H. A. L., *The War, Its Causes and Issues* (London, Longmans, 1914).

——, *The Value of Small States*, Oxford Pamphlets 1914 (London, Oxford University Press, 1914).

——, *The British Share in the War* (London and Edinburgh, Nelson, 1915).

——, *Two Speeches in Support of the Education Bill* (London, Stationery Office, 1917).

——, *Educational Reform Speeches* (Oxford, Clarendon Press, 1918).

——, *The Place of the University in National Life*, Barnett House Papers. No. 4 (London, Oxford University Press, 1919).

——, *An Unfinished Autobiography* (Oxford, Oxford University Press, 1940).

——, *Studies in History and Politics* (Oxford, Clarendon Press, 1920).

Flint, Robert, *Socialism* (London, Isbister, 1894).

Fitch, J. G., 'Education and the State', *Contemporary Review*, LXVIII (1895).

Fowler, W. S., 'The Influence of Idealism Upon State Provision of Education', *Victorian Studies*, IV (1961).

Franco, Paul, *The Political Philosophy of Michael Oakeshott* (New Haven and London, Yale University Press, 1990)

Freeden, M., 'Biological and Evolutionary Roots of the New Liberalism in England', *Political Theory*, 4(1976).

——, *The New Liberalism: An Ideology of Social Reform* (Oxford, Oxford University Press, 1978).

Gadamer, Hans-Georg, *Truth and Method*, tr. W. Glen-Doepel (London, Sheed and Ward, 1979).

Gallagher, John, and Robinson, Ronald, 'The Imperialism of Free Trade', *The Economic History Review*, VI (1953).

Gardner, Percy, 'Two Studies of German "Kultur" ', *Hibbert Journal*, 13 (1914–15).

Gascoyne-Cecil, The Revd Lord William, 'German Patriotism', *Hibbert Journal*, 14 (1915-16).

Gordon, P., and White, J., *Philosophers as Educational Reformers: The Influence of Idealism on British Educational Thought and Practice* (London, Routledge and Kegan Paul, 1979).

Gore, Charles (ed.), *Lux Mundi: A Series of Studies of Religion of the Incarnation* (London, Murray, 1889).

Gossip, G. H. D., 'Protection versus Free Trade in Australia', *Fortnightly Review*, 47 (1890).

Gray, J. N., *Hayek on Liberty* (Oxford, Blackwell, 1986).

——, *Liberalism* (Milton Keynes, Open University Press, 1986).

Gray, T. S., 'Herbert Spencer's Theory of Social Justice – Desert or Entitlement?', *History of Political Thought*, II (1981).

Green, Dorothy (ed.), *Descent of the Spirit: Writings of E. L. Grant Watson* (Sydney, Primavera, 1990).

Green, T. H., *The Works*, edited by L. Nettleship (London, Longmans Green, 1885–88).

——, *Lectures on the Principles of Political Obligation*, with a Preface by Bernard Bosanquet (London, Longmans Green, 1917).

Greenleaf, W.H., *The British Political Tradition*, vol. II, *The Ideological Heritage* (London, Methuen, 1983).

Haldane, R. B., *Education and Empire: Addresses on Certain Topics of the Day* (London, Murray, 1902).

——, *The Conduct of Life and Other Addresses* (London, Murray, 1914).

——, 'The Nature of the State', *Contemporary Review*, 117 (1920).

——, *Before the War* (London, Murray, 1920).

——, *The Reign of Relativity* (London, Murray, 1921).

——, *The Philosophy of Humanism and Other Subjects* (London, Murray, 1926).

——, *Selected Addresses and Essays* (London, Murray, 1929).

——, *An Autobiography* (London, Murray, 1929).

Haldar, Hiral, *Neo-Hegelianism* (London, Heath Cranton, 1927).

Halevy, E., *Imperialism and the Rise of Labour* 1895–1905 (London, Benn, 1961).

——, *The Rule of Democracy 1905–14* (London, Benn, 1961).

Hall, J. A., *Powers and Liberties* (Oxford, Blackwell, 1985).

Halliday, R. J., 'Social Darwinism: A Definition', *Victorian Studies*, 15 (1971).

Hamer, D. A., *Liberal Politics in the Age of Gladstone and Rosebery: A Study in Leadership and Policy* (Oxford, Clarendon Press, 1972).

Harris, F. P., *The Neo-Idealist Political Theory: Its Continuity with the British Tradition* (New York, King's Crown, 1944).

Hartog M., 'The Spencer-Weismann Controversy', *The Contemporary Review*, 64 (1893).

Hayek, F., *New Studies in Philosophy, Economics and the History of Ideas* (London, Routledge and Kegan Paul, 1978).

Hegel, G. W. F., *Philosophy of Right*, tr. T. M. Knox (Oxford, Oxford University Press, 1967).
——, *Lectures on the Philosophy of World History: Introduction: Reason in History*, tr. H. B. Nisbet (Cambridge, Cambridge University Press, 1975).
——, *The Phenomenology of Spirit*, tr. A. V. Miller (Oxford, Oxford University Press, 1977).
Hetherington, H. J. W., *The Life and Letters of Sir Henry Jones* (London, Hodder & Stoughton, 1924)
——, 'Jones, Sir Henry (1852–1922)', *Dictionary of National Biography 1922–1930* (Oxford, Oxford University Press, 1937).
Hetherington, H. J. W. and Muirhead, J. H., *Social Purpose: A Contribution to a Philosophy of Civic Society* (London, Allen & Unwin, 1918).
Hicks, G. Dawes, 'German Philosophy and the Present Crisis', *Hibbert Journal*, 13 (1914–15).
Himmelfarb, G., *Victorian Minds* (New York, Harper Torchbooks, 1970).
Hobhouse, L. T., 'The Ethical Basis of Collectivism', *International Journal of Ethics*, VIII (1898).
——, 'The Foreign Policy of Collectivism', *Economic Review* (*Christian Social Union*), 9 (1899).
——, 'The Diversions of a Psychologist', *Pilot*, V (Jan.-April 1902)
——, *Democracy and Reaction* (London, T. Fischer Unwin, 1904).
——, *Liberalism* (London, Oxford University Press, 1942: 1st publ. 1911).
——, *Social Evolution and Political Theory* (New York, Columbia University Press, 1928: 1st publ.1911).
——, *Questions of War and Peace* (London, T. Fischer Unwin, 1916).
——, *The Metaphysical Theory of the State* (London, Allen & Unwin, 1951: 1st publ. 1918).
Hobsbawm, E. J., *The Age of Empire 1875–1914* (London, Weidenfield & Nicholson, 1987).
Hobson, J. A., *Towards International Government* (London, Allen & Unwin, 1915).
——, 'Is International Goverment Possible', *Hibbert Journal*, 15 (1916–17).
——, 'The War and British Liberties', *The Nation*, 10 June 1916.
Hollis, Martin, *Models of Man* (Cambridge, Cambridge University Press, 1977).
Holton, Bob, *British Syndicalism 1900–1914: Myths and Realities* (London, Pluto Press, 1976).
Hughes, John, 'Sir Henry Jones and the Cross Commission', *Aberystwyth Studies*, 5 (1923).
Huxley, T. H., *Evolution and Ethics and Other Essays* (New York, 1898).
——, 'Administrative Nihilism', *Fortnightly Review*, 10 (1871).
——, 'Evolution and Ethics' in *Collected Essays* (London, 1894).
Isaac, J. C., 'Republicanism versus Liberalism? A Reconsideration', *History of Political Thought*, IX (1988).
James, William, *Pragmatism* (New York, Meridian, 1964: 1st publ. 1907).
Jennings, Jeremy, *Syndicalism in France* (London, Macmillan, 1990).

Joll, J., *The Anarchists* (Boston, Little Brown, 1964).

Jones, Thomas, 'Shoemaker's Son to University Professor', *John O'London's Weekly*, 11 March, 1922.

——, *A Theme With Variations* (Newtown, Gregynog, 1933).

——, *Welsh Broth* (London, Griffiths, 1950).

Kant, I., *Religion Within the Limits of Reason Alone*, tr. T. M. Greene and H. H. Hudson (Chicago, Open Court, 1934).

Kelly, G. A., *Idealism, Politics and History* (Cambridge, Cambridge University Press, 1969).

Keyserling, Hermann, 'On the Meaning of the War', *Hibbert Journal*, 13 (1914-15).

Koebner, R., 'The Concept of Economic Imperialism', *Economic History Review*, II (1949).

Kuhn, T. S., *The Structure of Scientific Revolutions* (Chicago, University of Chicago Press, 1970).

Ladd, George, T., 'The Human Mind versus the German Mind', *Hibbert Journal*, 14 (1915-16).

Lewis, H. D., 'Y Ffydd Sy'n Ymofyn', *Henry Jones 1852–1922* (Cardiff, University of Wales Press, 1953).

Lilly, W. S., 'The Burden of Empire', *Fortnightly Review*, LXVIII, (1900).

Lindsay, A. D., *War Against War*, Oxford Pamphlets 1914 (London, Oxford University Press, 1914).

Lindsay, A. D., 'Idealism of Caird and Jones', *Journal of Philosophical Studies*, 1 (1926).

Lotze, Hermann, *Microcosmus: An Essay Concerning Man and His Relation to the World*, tr. E. Hamilton and E. E. Constance Jones (New York, Books for Libraries Press, 1971: 1st publ. 1885).

Macbriar, A. M., *Fabian Socialism and English Politics 1884–1914* (Cambridge, Cambridge University Press, 1966).

MacKenzie, J. S., *An Introduction to Social Philosophy* (Glasgow, Maclehose, 1890).

——, *An Introduction to Social Philosophy* (Glasgow, Maclehose, 1895: second edition).

——, *A Manual of Ethics* (London, Clive, 1897).

——, 'Might and Right', in *International Crisis: The Theory of the State*, Louise Creighton *et al.* (London, Oxford University Press, 1916).

——, *Outlines of Social Philosophy* (London, Allen and Unwin, 1918).

Marriot, J. A. R., 'The War and the Theory of the State', *The Hibbert Journal*, 13 (1914–15).

Marshall, T. H., *Citizenship and Social Class* (Cambridge, Cambridge University Press, 1980).

Masterman, N., *The Forerunner: The Dilemmas of Tom Ellis 1859–1899* (Swansea, Christopher Davies, 1972).

McTaggart, J. M. E., *Studies in Hegelian Cosmology* (Cambridge, Cambridge University Press, 1901).

Metz, Rudolf, *A Hundred Years of British Philosophy* (London, Allen & Unwin, 1938).

M'Gilvary, E. B., 'The Warfare of Moral Ideals', *Hibbert Journal*, 14 (1915–16).

Mitchell, P. C., 'The Spencer-Weismann Controversy', *Nature*, 49 (1894).

Monson, C. H. Jnr., 'Prichard, Green and Moral Obligation', *Philosophical Review*, 63 (1954).

Morgan, K. O., 'New Liberalism and the Challenge of Labour: The Welsh Experience', *Welsh History Review*, 6 (1973).

——, *Rebirth of a Nation: Wales 1880–1980* (Oxford, Clarendon Press and University of Wales Press, 1981).

——, 'Socialism and Syndicalism: The Welsh Miners Debate 1912', *Bulletin of the Society for the Study of Labour History*, no. 30 (1975).

Morgan, Robert (ed.), *The Religion of the Incarnation: Anglican Essays in Commemoration of 'Lux Mundi'* (Bristol, Thoemmes, 1989).

Morgan, J. V., *Welsh Political and Educational Leaders in the Victorian Era* (London, James Nisbet, 1908).

Mor-O'Brien, Anthony, 'Patriotism on Trial: The Strike of the South Wales Miners July 1915', *Welsh History Review*, 12 (1984).

Morris-Jones, H. W., 'The Life and Philosophy of Sir Henry Jones', *Henry Jones 1852–1922* (Cardiff, University of Wales Press, 1953).

Morris-Jones, H. W., 'Syniadau Gwleidyddol Syr Henry Jones', *Efrydiau Athronyddol*, XVI (1953).

Morrow, John, 'British Idealism, "German Philosophy" and the First World War', *Australian Journal of Politics and History*, 28 (1982).

Muirhead, J. H., 'What Imperialism Means', *The Fortnightly Review*, CCCCIV NS, 1 August 1900.

——, Critical notice of H. Jones, *Idealism as a Practical Creed* in *Mind*, XIX (1910).

——, *German Philosophy and the War*, Oxford Pamphlets 1914 (London, Oxford University Press, 1914).

——, *German Philosophy in Relation to the War* (London, Murray, 1917).

——, 'Sir Henry Jones 1852–1922' *Proceedings of the British Academy*, X (1921–23).

——, 'Recent Criticisms of the Idealist Theory of the General Will, parts I, II, and III', *Mind*, XXXIII (1924).

——, (ed.), *Bernard Bosanquet and His Friends* (London, Allen & Unwin, 1935).

——, *Reflections by a Journeyman in Philosophy: On the Movements of Thought and Practice in his Time* (London, Allen & Unwin, 1942).

Mulgan, R. G., *Aristotle's Political Theory* (Oxford, Clarendon Press, 1977).

Murray, Gilbert, *How Can War Ever Be Right*, Oxford Pamphlets, 1914 (London, Oxford University Press, 1914).

——, *Ethical Problems of the War* (Edinburgh, T. Nelson, 1915).

——, *The Foreign Policy of Sir Edward Grey 1906–1915* (London, Oxford University Press, 1915).

——, 'Herd Instinct and the War', in *Faith, War and Policy* (Boston and New York, Houghton Mifflin, 1918).
——, *Satanism and the World Order* (London, Allen & Unwin, 1920).
——, *The League of Nations and the Democratic Idea* (Oxford, Oxford University Press, 1920).
——, *The Guarantees of the League* (London, League of Nations Union, 1922).
——, *Herd Instinct: For Good and Evil* (London, Allen & Unwin, 1940).
——, *An Unfinished Autobiography* (London, Allen & Unwin, 1960).
Nicholson, J. A., *Some Aspects of the Philosophy of L. T. Hobhouse* (Urbana, University of Illinois, 1926).
Nicholson, Peter P., 'Philosophical Idealism and International Politics: A Reply to Savigear', *British Journal of International Studies*, 2 (1976).
——, *The Political Philosophy of the British Idealists: Selected Studies* (Cambridge, Cambridge University Press, 1990).
Norman, R., *Hegel's Phenomenology* (London, Chatto & Windus for Sussex University Press, 1976).
Oakely, Hilda D., Review of Henry Jones, *The Principles of Citizenship*, in *Hibbert Journal*, 17 (1918–19).
Oakeshott, M., *On Human Conduct* (Oxford, Clarendon Press, 1975).
——, *On History and Other Essays* (Oxford, Blackwell, 1983)
Page, R. Arnot, *South Wales Miners: A History of the S.W.M.F., 1898–1914* (Cardiff, Cymric Federation Press, 1967).
Paradis, James G., *Evolution and Ethics: Essays on T. H. Huxley's Evolution and Ethics* (Princeton, Princeton University Press, 1989)
Pearson, R. and Williams, G., *Political Thought and Public Policy in the Nineteenth Century* (London, Longmans, 1984).
Pelling, H., *The History of British Trade Unionism* (Middlesex, Penguin Books, 1969).
Perry, Ralph Barton, *The Present Conflict of Ideals: A Study of the Philosophical Background of the World War* (New York, Longmans Green, 1918).
Phillips, David, *Athroniaeth Syr Henry Jones* (Dolgellau, Evans, 1922).
Plato, *The Republic*, tr. Desmond Lee (Harmondsworth, Penguin, 1987).
P. H. W., 'Philosophers of the Spirit', *The Inquirer*, November 25, 1905.
Pocock, J. G. A., *Virtue, Commerce and History: Essays on Political Thought and History, Chiefly in the Eighteenth Century* (Cambridge, Cambridge University Press, 1985).
Pollock, Frederick, 'The "Fight for Right" Movement', *Hibbert Journal*, 14 (1915–16).
Pugh, Martin, *The Making of Modern British Politics* (Oxford, Blackwell, 1983).
Pulsford, Edward, 'An Australian Lesson', *The Nineteenth Century*, XXIV (1888).
Quinton, A. M., 'Absolute Idealism', in *Thoughts and Thinkers* (Oxford, Oxford University Press,1972).
Rae, J., *Contemporary Socialism* (London, Swan Sonneschein, 1901).
Reardon, B. M. G. (ed.), *Liberal Protestantism* (London, Black, 1968).

——, *From Coleridge to Gore: A Century of Religious Thought* (London, Longmans, 1971).

Reeves, W. Pember, *State Experiments in Australia and New Zealand* (London, Allen & Unwin, 1902).

——, 'The Nation's Duties to the Empire', *Good Citizenship*, edited by J. E. Hand and Charles Gore (London, Allen, 1899).

Richard, J., *Class and Politics 1890–1910* (Canberra, Australian National University, 1976).

Richards, Robert J., *Darwin and the Emergence of Evolutionary Theories of Mind and Behaviour* (Chicago, Chicago University Press, 1087).

Ritchie, D. G., *The Principles of State Interference* (London, Swan Sonnenschein, 1896, 2nd edn: 1st edn. publ. 1891).

——, 'What are Economic Laws?', *Economic Review*, II (1892).

——, *Darwin and Hegel, with Other Philosophical Studies* (London, Swan Sonnenschein, 1893).

——, 'The Moral Problems of War – In Reply to Mr J. M. Robertson', *International Journal of Ethics*, 11 and 12 (1900–1902).

——, *Studies in Political and Social Ethics* (London, Swan Sonnenschein, 1902).

——, *Philosophical Studies* (London, Macmillan, 1905).

Robbins, Peter, *The British Hegelians 1875–1925* (New York and London, Garland, 1982).

Robinson, R., 'The Imperialism of Free Trade', *Economic History Review*, VI (1953).

Rockow, Lewis, *Contemporary Political Thought in England* (London, Leonard Parsons, 1925).

Rogers, J. A., 'Darwinism and Social Darwinism', *Journal of the History of Ideas*, 32 (1972).

Rolleston, T. W., 'Literature and Politics in Modern Germany', *Hibbert Journal*, 13 (1914–15).

Rorty, Richard, *Philosophy as the Mirror of Nature* (Oxford, Blackwell, 1980).

Rorty, R., Schneewind, J. B., and Skinner, Q. (ed.), *Philosophy in History* (Cambridge, Cambridge University Press, 1984).

Routh, D. A., 'The Philosophy of International Relations: T. H. Green *versus* Hegel', *Politica*, III (1938).

Royce, J., 'An American Thinker on the War', *Hibbert Journal*, 14 (1915–16).

Riggiero, Guido de, *The History of European Liberalism*, tr. R. G. Collingwood (Oxford, Oxford University Press, 1927).

Runciman, W. G., *A Treatise on Social Theory*, vol. II *Substantive Social Theory* (Cambridge, Cambridge University Press, 1989).

Sabine, G. H., 'The Social Origin of Absolute Idealism', *Journal of Philosophy, Psychology and Scientific Methods*, 12 (1915).

Salter, William Mackintire, 'The Philosopher of "the Will to Power": Nietzsche on Love and Pity', *Hibbert Journal*, 13 (1914–15).

Samuel, Herbert, *Liberalism: An Attempt to State the Principles of Contemporary Liberalism* (London, Grant Richards, 1902).

Santayana, George, *Egotism in German Philosophy* (London, Dent, 1940: 1st edn. publ. 1916).
Savigear, P., 'Philosophical Idealism and International Politics: Bosanquet, Treitschke and War', *British Journal of International Studies*, 1 (1975).
Saville, Agnes, 'The Late Sir Henry Jones', *John O'London's Weekly*, 8 April 1922.
Schiller, F. C. S., Review of John Dewey, *German Philosophy and Politics* in *Mind*, XXV (1916).
——, Review of G. Santayana, *Egotism in German Philosophy* in *Mind*, XXVI (1917).
Schwartz, Sanford, *The Matrix of Modernism; Pound, Eliot and Early Twentieth Century Thought* (New Jersey, Princeton University Press, 1985).
Scott, J. W., *Syndicalism and Philosophical Realism* (London, Black, 1919).
Semmel, Bernard, *Imperialism and Social Reform* (London, Allen & Unwin, 1960).
Seth, A. (Pringle Pattison), Haldane, R. B., *Essays in Philosophical Criticism*, with a preface by Edward Caird (London, Longmans Green, 1883).
Seth, A., (Pringle Pattison), *Hegelianism and Personality* (Edinburgh, Blackwood, 1887).
——, *Man's Place in the Cosmos* (Edinburgh, Blackwood, 1897).
——, 'The Life of Herbert Spencer', *Quarterly Review*, CC (1904).
——, *The Idea of God in the Light of Recent Philosophy* (Oxford, Oxford University Press, 1920.
——, *The Idea of Immortality* (Oxford, Clarendon Press, 1922).
——, *The Philosophical Radicals and Other Essays* (Edinburgh, Blackwood, 1907).
——, *Balfour Lectures on Realism: With a Memoir by G. F. Barbour* (Edinburgh, Blackwood, 1933).
Shelton, H. S., 'The Hegelian Concept of the State and Modern Individualism', *International Journal of Ethics*, 24 (1913).
Sloan, J. M., 'Carlyle's Germans', *Hibbert Journal*, 13 (1914–15).
Smith, J. A., 'Progress in Philosophy', *Progress and History*, edited by F. S. Marvin (Oxford, Oxford University Press, 1921).
——, 'The Influence of Hegel on the Philosophy of Great Britain', *Verhandlungen des ersten Hegelkongresses von 22 bis 25 April 1930 im Hang*, ed B. Wigersma (Tubingen and Haarlen, 1931).
Sorley, W. R., 'The State and Morality', *The International Crisis: The Theory of the State*, edited by Louise Creighton *et al.* (London, Oxford University Press, 1916).
Spencer, Herbert, 'The Social Organism', *Westminster Review*, NS XVII (1860).
——, *Principles of Sociology*, 3 vols. (London, Williams and Norgate, 1876, 1893 and 1896).
——, *The Data of Ethics* (New York, Collier, 1911: first published 1879).
——, 'Evolutionary Ethics', *The Atheneum*, No. 3432 (1893).
——, 'The Inadequacy of "Natural Selection" ', *Contemporary Review*, 63 (1893).
——, 'Professor Weismann's Theories', *Contemporary Review*, 64 (1893).
——, 'Weismannism Once More', *Contemporary Review*, 66 (1894).

——, 'Heredity Once More', *Contemporary Review*, 68 (1895).

Stead, Peter, 'Working-Class Leadership in South Wales 1900–1920', *Welsh History Review*, 6 (1973).

Stephen, Leslie, 'Ethics and the Struggle for Existence', *Contemporary Review*, 64 (1893).

Stokes, Eric, *The Political Ideas of British Imperialism: An Inaugural Lecture* (London, Oxford University Press, 1960).

Sturt, H., *Personal Idealism: Philosophical Essays by Eight Members of the University of Oxford* (London, Oxford University Press, 1902).

Thilly, Frank, Review of John Dewey, *German Philosophy and Politics* in *The Philosophical Review*, XXIV (1915).

Thomas, Geoffrey, *The Moral Philosophy of T. H. Green* (Oxford, Clarendon Press, 1987).

Thompson, Paul, *Socialists, Liberals and Labour 1885–1914* (London, Routledge & Kegan Paul, 1967).

Toynbee, Arnold, *Industrial Revolution* (London, Rivington, 1884).

Treitschke, Heinrich von, *Politics*, tr. Blanche Dugdale and Torben de Bille with an introduction by Arthur Balfour (London, Constable, 1916).

Vincent, Andrew, and George, Michael, 'Development and Self-Identity: Hegel's Concept of Education', *Educational Theory*, 32 (1982).

Vincent, Andrew, 'The Hegelian State and International Relations', *Review of International Studies*, 9 (1983).

——, 'The Poor Law Reports of 1909 and the Social Theory of the Charity Organization Society', *Victorian Studies*, 27 (1984).

——, and Plant, R., *Philosophy, Politics and Citizenship: The Life and Thought of the British Idealists* (Oxford, Blackwell, 1984).

——, (ed.), *The Philosophy of T. H. Green* (Aldershot, Gower, 1986).

——, *Theories of the State* (Oxford, Blackwell, 1987).

——, 'Can Groups Be Persons?', *Review of Metaphysics*, 42 (1989).

——, 'Classical Liberalism and its Crisis of Identity', *History of Political Thought*, XI (1990).

——, *Modern Political Ideologies* (Oxford, Blackwell, 1992).

——, 'Divine Immanence and Transcendence: Henry Jones and the Philosophy of Religion', *Idealistic Studies* (forthcoming, 1993).

Wallas, Graham, *Human Nature in Politics* (New York, Alfred Knopf, 1921: 1st publ.1908).

Wallace, William, 'The Relation of Fichte and Hegel to Socialism' and 'The Ethics of Socialism', in *Lectures and Essays on Natural Theology and Ethics* (Oxford, Clarendon Press, 1898).

Walsh W. H., 'Colligatory Concepts in History', in *The Philosophy of History*, edited by P. Gardiner (Oxford, Oxford University Press, 1974).

Walt, S., 'Hegel on War: Another Look', *History of Political Thought*, X (1989).

Walton, J. Lawson, 'Imperialism', *Contemporary Review*, 75 (1899).

Watson, John, 'German Philosophy and Politics', *Queen's Quarterly*, 22 (1915).

——, 'German Philosophy and the War', *Queen's Quarterly*, 23 (1916).
——, *The State in Peace and War* (Glasgow, Maclehose, 1919).
Webb, Beatrice, *Our Partnership* (London, Longmans, 1948).
Webb, C. C. J., *Divine Personality and Human Life* (London, Allen and Unwin, 1920).
——, *A Study of Religious Thought in England from 1850* (Oxford, Clarendon Press, 1933).
——, 'German Militarism in the Twelfth Century', *Hibbert Journal*, 17 (1918–19).
Weismann, A., 'The All-sufficiency of Natural Selection: A Reply to Herbert Spencer', *Contemporary Review*, 64 (1893).
——, 'Heredity Once More', *Contemporary Review*, 68 (1895).
Wilkins, B. T., James, 'Dewey and Hegelian Idealism', *Journal of the History of Ideas*, XVII (1956).
Williams, Gwyn A., *When Was Wales?* (Harmondsworth, Penguin, 1985).
Williams, J. Gwynn, *The University College of North Wales: Foundations 1884–1927* (Cardiff, University of Wales Press, 1985).
Willmore, Edward, 'Why We Are Fighting: A Reply', *Hibbert Journal*, 13 (1914–15).
Wiltshire, David, *The Social and Political Thought of Herbert Spencer* (Oxford, Oxford University Press, 1978).
Winkler, H. R., *The League of Nations Movement in Great Britain 1914–19* (New Brunswick, Rutgers University Press, 1952).
Winter, J. M., and Joslin, D. M. (eds.), *R. H. Tawney's Commonplace Book* (Cambridge, Cambridge University Press, 1972).
Wolfe, Willard, *From Radicalism to Socialism: Men and Ideas in the Formation of Fabian Socialist Doctrines 1881–1889* (New Haven, Conn., Yale University Press, 1975).
Woolf, L. S., 'Suggestions for the Prevention of War', *The New Statesman*, V, Saturday 10 July 1915.
——, *International Government* (London, Allen & Unwin, 1916).
Wright, A. W., *British Socialism* (London, Longmans, 1983).
——, *Socialisms* (Oxford, Oxford University Press, 1987).
Wyatt, H. F., 'The Ethics of Empire', *Nineteenth Century*, XLI (1897).

NOTES TO BIBLIOGRAPHY

[1]This compilation of Jones's published work is based upon a bibliography produced by Peter Nicholson in 1971. We are grateful for his generosity in allowing us to draw upon his efforts in this respect.

[2]The items listed for the National Library of Wales were compiled from the indices of collections by C. Lloyd Morgan, Assistant Archivist, Department of Manuscripts and Records. We greatly appreciate her assistance.

SUBJECT INDEX

INDEX OF NAMES